Loudoun County, Virginia

Deed Book Abstracts

1771–1773

Ruth and Sam Sparacio

Heritage Books
2025

HERITAGE BOOKS

AN IMPRINT OF HERITAGE BOOKS, INC.

Books, CDs, and more—Worldwide

For our listing of thousands of titles see our website
at
www.HeritageBooks.com

Published 2025 by
HERITAGE BOOKS, INC.
Publishing Division
5810 Ruatan Street
Berwyn Heights, MD 20740

International Standard Book Number
Paperbound: 978-1-68034-573-5

p.   May the 9th 1771
1   ARTICLES of AGREEMENT between THOMAS OWSLEY, Planter, and JAMES LEE, Schoolmaster, the said OWSLEY gives the said LEE his Freedom on the said LEE's paying him said OWSLEY Sixteen pounds ten shillings and teaching School untill the tenth day of December next where he now teaches and the said OWSLEY to receive the profit of the School to that time and said LEE is to teach there or somewhere else to the said OWSLEYs liking two years and teach two Children gratis, the said OWSLEY is to find said LEE untill December next in Accommodations, washing, making and mending, the said OWSLEY is to give said LEE one pair of Shoes, two Shirts and one pair of Trousers and said OWSLEY to give Twenty Shillings a year for each Schoolar he sends more than the two abovementioned and said OWSLEY is to find said LEE Accommodation in proportion to the Scholars he sends. To which agreement we both set our hands and seals the day and year above written

THOS.OWSLEY,
JAMS. LEE

  At a Court held for Loudoun County May 13th 1771
This Agreement between THOMAS OWSLEY and JAMES LEE was acknowledged by the parties and ordered to be recorded

pp.   TO ALL PEOPLE to whom these presents may Come, I ANNE POTTS of the Parish of
1-   Cameron in County of Loudoun in Colony of Virginia, Widow, send Greeting.
2   KNOW YE that I the said ANNE POTTS in consideration of the natural love and affection which I have and bear unto SAMUEL POTTS my Son of the same place and also for other good causes and considerations me thereunto moving have given and granted and by these presents do give grant and confirm unto said SAMUEL POTTS one Negro Lad named Austin in a Schedule hereunto annexed mentioned. To have and to hold the said Negro Lad unto said SAMUEL POTTS his heirs and assigns forever In Witness whereof I have hereunto set my hand and Seal this 13th day of May A.D. 1771
in presence of   ANN her mark ✗ POTTS
  Memorandum the 13th day of May Anno Domini 1771. Livery and seizin was delivered by the within named ANNE POTTS unto said SAMUEL POTTS of one Shilling in name of said Negro within mentioned to hold to him said SAMUEL POTTS his heirs and assigns for ever according to the within written Deed
in the presence of   ANN her mark ✗ POTTS
  At a Court held for Loudoun County May the 13th 1771
This Deed of Gift was acknowledged by ANNE POTTS party thereto and ordered to be recorded

pp.   THIS INDENTURE made this tenth day of May in year of our Lord one thousand
2-   seven hundred and seventy one Between PHILLIP BAKER and DANIEL ADDLE-
4   MAN of Loudoun County of one part and SAMUEL RICH of same County of other part, Witnesseth that PHILLIP BAKER and DANIEL ADDLEMAN for sum of Five shillings lawful Money of England to them in hand paid by these presents do bargain and sell unto SAMUEL RICH all that tract of land lying in County of Loudoun and bounded beginning at a Stake, SAMUEL IDENs Corner, in line of MAHLON KIRKBRIDE, thence with the same East one hundred & forty poles and a half to a Stake by white Oak then S. 4 1/2 d. West one hundred and fifteen poles to a Hickory, Corner to IDEN and RICH, then S. 81 d. West one hundred and twenty eight poles to a Stake in the line of

BENJAMIN POOL then with his line and IDENs N. one hundred and twenty five poles & a quarter to the first station containing one hundred and one acres more or less, it being part of a Tract of land granted unto EDMOND SANDS by Deeds from the Proprietors Office and by said EDMOND SANDS sold and conveyed unto JOHN BERKLEY by Deeds of Lease and Release bearing date the 30th day of April and the first day of May 1751 and by him conveyed unto PHILLIP BAKER and DANIEL ADDLEMAN by Deeds of Lease and Release bearing date   Ninth and Tenth days of October 1765, And all houses Orchards and appurtenances whatsoever belonging To have and to hold unto said SAMUEL RICH his heirs and assigns for term of one whole year paying therefore one Pepper Corn in and upon the feast of St. Michael the Archangel to intent that by virtue of these presents and by force of statute for transferring uses into possession SAMUEL RICH may be in actual possession and thereby enable to accept a Release of Inheritance thereof In Witness whereof the said PHILLIP BAKER and DANIEL ADDLEMAN hath hereunto set their hands and seals the day and year first above written

in presence of SAML: IDEN,   PHILLIP his mark 𝓮 BAKER
     JOHN BISHOP, WM. DILLON   ULIONAH her mark X BAKER
                             DANIEL ADDLEMAN
                             ELIZABETH her mark ✝ ADDLEMAN

At a Court held for Loudoun County May the 13th 1771
This Indenture was proved by the Affirmation of SAMUEL IDEN and WILLIAM DILLON (Quakers) and by Oath of JOHN BISHOP Subscribing Witnesses thereto and ordered to be recorded

pp.   THIS INDENTURE made the Eleventh day of May in year of our Lord one thousand
4-   seven hundred and seventy one Between PHILLIP BAKER and ULIONAH his Wife
6   and DANIEL ADDLEMAN and ELIZABETH his Wife of County of Loudoun of one
       part and SAMUEL RICH of same County of other part Witnesseth that for sum of
Eighty pounds current money of Virginia to them in hand paid by these presents do bargain and sell unto SAMUEL RICH in his actual possession now being by virtue of a bargain and sale for one year and by force of statute for transferring uses into possession and his heirs and assigns forever all that tract of land lying in County of Loudoun .. (description of land as in Lease above) .. To have and to hold the said One hundred and one acres of land hereby granted unto SAMUEL RICH his heirs and assigns forever In Witness whereof said PHILIP BAKER and ULIANAH his Wife and DANIEL ADDLEMAN and ELIZABETH his Wife have hereunto set their hands and seals the day and year first above written

in presence of SAMUEL IDEN,   PHILLIP his mark 𝓮 BAKER
     JOHN BISHOP,   ULIANNA her mark X BAKER
     WM. DILLON   DANIEL ADDLEMAN
                             ELIZABETH her mark ✝ ADDLEMAN

At a Court held for Loudoun County May the 13th 1771
This Indenture and receipt thereon endorsed were proved by the Affirmation of SAMUEL IDEN and WILLIAM DILLON (Quakers) and by the Oath of JOHN BISHOP Subscribing witnesses thereto and ordered to be recorded
(On margin: D'd to RICH 22d Mar 82)

pp.   THIS INDENTURE made the fourth day of February in year of our Lord one thou-
7-   sand seven hundred and seventy one Between BRYAN FAIRFAX of County of
8   FAIRFAX Gentleman of one part and MATTHEW WHITE, Farmer, of other part,
       Witnesseth that said BRYAN FAIRFAX in consideration of the rents and cove-
nants herein expressed by these presents doth grant and to farm lett unto MATTHEW

WHITE of County of Loudoun one certain lott of land (being part of a Tract containing upwards of Twelve thousand acres on the West side of DIFFICULT RUN) laid off by Mr. GEORGE WEST but since altered to following bounds beginning at a small white Oak marked L thence No. 71 d. Et. 180 poles to three red or black Oak saplins one of which is marked L then the same course continued thirteen poles further thence No. 19 d. Wt. eighty seven poles to a Stake in the middle of a Glade called CAPTAIN HICKORY thence No. 29 d. Wt. 39 poles, thence South 71 d. West one hundred and eighty six poles, thence So. 19 D. Et. 122 poles to the beginning containing 150 acres together with all rights members and appurtenances thereunto belonging To have and to hold said One hundred and fifty acres during natural lives of said MATTHEW; of THOMAS, Son of said BRYAN FAIRFAX, and ROBERT WHITE, Brother to said MATTHEW paying unto BRYAN FAIRFAX before first day of December yearly sum of one shilling current money of Virginia for every acre of land hereby leased and will within three years build a Good Dwelling House at least sixteen feet Square and such other houses as his occupation may require and also plant out and keep unto good fence one hundred Apple trees and one hundred Peach trees and will not make or suffer to be made or tended any tobacco or Indian Corn in each year of aforesaid Term In Witness whereof the parties to these presents have hereunto set their hands and seals the day and year first above written in presence of JACOB HUGUELY,   BRYAN FAIRFAX
        JAMES DICKEY, JOHN DOWDALL   MATTHEW WHITE
   At a Court held for Loudoun County May the 13th 1771
This Indenture was acknowledged by BRYAN FAIRFAX Esqr. and MATTHEW WHITE parties thereto, the Court approving of the reserved Rent and is ordered to be recorded

pp.   THIS INDENTURE made the first day of January in year of our Lord one thousand
8-   seven hundred and seventy one Between BRYAN FAIRFAX of County of FAIRFAX
10   Gentleman of one part and JAMES DICKEY of Loudoun County, Farmer, of other
        part, Witnesseth that said BRYAN FAIRFAX in consideration of rents and cove-
nants herein expressed by these presents doth grant and to farm let unto JAMES DICKEY one certain lot or parcel of land (being part of a large tract containing above Twelve thousand acres on West side of DIFFICULT RUN) bounded beginning at a white Oak and running thence So. 14 d. Et. one hundred and seventy poles to a Spanish and black Oak and from thence So. 85 d. Et. one hundred and fifteen poles to a Stake in the Edge of a Glade thence No. 20 d. Et. one hundred and thirty one poles to a small red or black Oak in line of JOHN REESS's Lott thence No. 56 d. Wt. one hundred and thirty eight poles to a white Oak mark't L corner to the Patent and to WILLIAM ELLIOTTs Lot, thence So. 74 1/2 d. West 90 poles to the beginning containing one hundred and seventy two acres and a Quarter together with all rights members and appurtenances thereunto belonging To have and to hold said One hundred and seventy two acres during natural lives of said JAMES DICKEY, MARTHA his Wife and WILLIAM his Son, paying unto BRYAN FAIRFAX on the first day of December in year one thousand seven hundred and seventy one and yearly thereafter the sum of One Shilling current money of Virginia for every acre of land hereby leased and within three years build a good Dwelling House at least sixteen feet square and such other houses as his occupation may require and also plant out and keep under a good fence one hundred Apple trees and one hundred Peach trees and will not make or tend any tobacco or Indian Corn on the demised premises except about five acres of Indian Corn in each year In Witness whereof the parties to these presents have hereunto set their hands and seals the day and year first above written

in presence of JACOB HUGUELY,   BRYAN FAIRFAX
      MATTHEW WHITE,   JAMES DICKEY
      ARCHIBALD his mark ℛ McDONALD

At a Court held for Loudoun County May the 13th 1771
This Indenture was acknowledged by BRYAN FAIRFAX Esqr. and JAMES DICKEY parties
thereto, the Court approving of the reserved Rent and is ordered to be recorded

pp.   THIS INDENTURE made the Twenty seventh day of April in year of our Lord One
10-   thousand seven hundred and seventy one Between FRANCIS PEYTON and FRAN-
14   CES his Wife and CRAVEN PEYTON and ANN his Wife of County of Loudoun of one
      part and THOMAS WILLIAMS of said County of other part Witnesseth that for sum
of one hundred pounds current money of Virginia said FRANCIS and CRAVEN PEYTON in
hand paid by these presents do bargain and sell unto THOMAS WILLIAMS and his heirs
forever a certain tract of land lying in County of Loudoun and between the branches of
GOOSE CREEK and the GREAT MOUNTAIN and bounded Beginning at small white Oak in
COCK's Line and Corner to land belonging to THOMAS OWSLEY running thence North 61
d. West two hundred and two poles to three red Oaks in BRONAUGH's line thence No. 2 d.
West One hundred and eighty seven poles to two white Oaks one marked HP thence
East one hundred and twenty nine poles to a Hickory on a Stony Knowl thence South 56
d. 30' East one hundred and thirty eight poles to a Spanish Oak and Black Oak in COCK's
line thence with his line South 51 d. 30' West one hundred and thirty four poles to two
black Oaks and one double white Oak Saplin supposed to be COCK's Corner, thence still
with his line South thirty four poles to two black oaks another of COCK's Corners thence
with another of said COCK's lines South 25 d. East one hundred and two poles to the beginning containing two hundred and forty eight acres and all Houses Orchards and
appurtenances whatsoever belonging To have and to hold unto said THOMAS WILLIAMS
his heirs and assigns forever. In Witness whereof said FRANCIS PEYTON and FRANCES
his Wife and CRAVEN PEYTON and ANN his Wife have hereunto set their hands and seals
the day and year first above written

in presence of G. JOHNSTON,   FRANCIS PEYTON
      L. POWELL, CHARLES WEST   FRANCES PEYTON
                                CRAVEN PEYTON
                                ANN PEYTON

At a Court held for Loudoun County May 13th 1771
This Indenture was acknoweldged by FRANCIS PEYTON and CRAVEN PEYTON and ANN his
Wife parties thereto (the said ANN being first privately examined as the Law directs)
and the receipt thereon endors'd was likewise acknowledged by said FRANCIS and
CRAVEN and together with the said Indenture ordered to be recorded

pp.   THIS INDENTURE made the Thirteenth day of May in year of our Lord One thou-
14-   sand seven hundred and seventy one and in the Eleventh year of the Reign of
17   his Majesty GEORGE the third now King &c. Between WILLIAM NAWLES of
      County of Loudoun, Blacksmith, and SARAH his Wife of one part and ENOCH LOYD
of same County, Farmer, of other part, Witnesseth that for sum of One hundred and
twenty pounds current money of Virginia to said WILLIAM NAWLES in hand paid or
secured to be paid by these presents doth bargain and sell unto ENOCH LOYD all that lott
of land lying in County aforesaid and bounded Beginning at a small white Oak, Corner
to JOHN RAWLS extending thence North fifteen degrees and thirty minutes East three
hundred and fifty four poles to some white Oaks in the head of a Glade thence South
seventy degrees East sixty poles to three Scrubby Spanish Oaks marked WL thence
South three degrees East one hundred and ninety two poles to two white Oaks marked

WL standing in the head of a Glade thence South thirty nine degrees West eighty poles to two white Oaks land a Hickory thence South thirty one degrees West one hundred and twenty two poles to a forked black Oak marked FX on the North side of the MOUNTAIN ROAD thence West twenty five poles to a white Oak on the South side of said ROAD thence North thirty seven degrees West forty poles to the beginning containing Two hundred and two acres be the same more or less which tract of land was granted to WILLIAM LANE by the Proprietor of the Northern Neck of Virginia by Deed Poll bearing date the first day of May one thousand seven hundred and sixty four which said WILLIAM LANE by his Deed of Feoffment bearing date the fourth day of April in year one thousand seven hundred and seventy one together with NANCY his Wife sold and conveyed the same to said WILLIAM NAWLES party to these presents as by said Deed recorded in Loudoun County Court may appear And all house orchards and appurtenances whatsoever to the same belonging To have and to hold said land and premises unto said ENOCH LOYD his heirs and assigns In Witness whereof said WILLIAM NAWLES and SARAH his Wife have hereunto set their hands and affixed their seals the day and year first written in presence of HY. POTTEN, WILLIAM NALLS
JOHN GRIFFITH, SARAH her mark ∩ NALLS

At a Court lheld for Loudoun County May the 13th 1771
This Indenture was acknowledged by WILLIAM NALLS and SARAH his Wife parties thereto (the said SARAH having been first examined as the Law directs) and the receipt thereunder written was acknowledged by said WILLIAM and together with said Indenture ordered to be recorded

p. 18 Loudoun County April 30, 1771
WHEREAS I have through heat of Liquor and false insinuations of others been induced to speak sundry words tending to prejudice the Character of Mr. THOMAS OWSLEY in particular accusing him with moving a Corner of a Lott of Land which I hold under said OWSLEY which assertion I have since found to be unjust and hope that he will look upon it in the light above mentioned
Test FRANCIS PEYTON JAMES WHITLOCK
I do hereby agree to pay the cost of a suit commenced by Mr. OWSLEY against me on his Dismissing the same. Certif'd this 30th April 1771
Test F. PEYTON JAMES WHITLOCK
At a Court held for Loudoun County May the 13th 1771
This Commission was proved by the Oath of FRANCIS PEYTON Gent. the Witness thereto and on the motion of THOMAS OWSLEY ordered to be recorded

pp. 18-20 THIS INDENTURE made the XXII day of December in year of our Lord One thousand seven hundred and seventy Between BRYAN FAIRFAX of County of FAIRFAX Gentleman of one part and JOHN BALLENDINE, Merchant, of other part, Witnesseth that BRYAN FAIRFAX in consideration of rents and covenants herein expressed by these presents doth grant and to farm let unto JOHN BALLENDINE one certain lott of land being part of a large tract of 12000 acres on West side of DIFFICULT and beginning at a red Oak marked L F the beginning tree of the said Tract and the lower Southwestermost corner of the land of Mr. McCARTY's SUGARLAND TRACT and extending thence along the said McCARTYs line No. 12 d Et. 330 po: to the line of HARRISONs Patent thence along his line So. 68 1/2 d. Et. 110 poles, So. 66 d. Et. 48 poles, thence So. 42 d. Wt. 224 poles to a red Oak on a Knole to the Westward of TRAMMELS ROLLING ROAD said to be formerly marked L F but now down and by JOHN WARNER, the Surveyor, called a Corner of the land of MESSERS. EMMS, WILLIAM HARLE and JOHN HARLE and from thence in a Streight line to the beginning containing one hundred and fifty

acres more or less together with all rights members and appurtenances thereunto belonging To Have and to Hold said one hundred and fifty acres unto said JOHN BALLEN-
DINE during natural lives of him said JOHN BALLENDINE, THOMAS WILLIAM BALLEN-
DINE and RICHARD HENRY BALLENDINE, his Sons, paying unto BRYAN FAIRFAX on first
day of December in year one thousand seven hundred and seventy one the sum of five
pounds and from thence forward yearly and within three years build a good Dwelling
House at least sixteen feet square and such other houses as his occupation may require
and also plant out and keep under good fence one hundred Apple trees and one hundred Peach trees and in consideration of being allowed to tend Tobacco deliver at the
Mansion House of BRYAN FAIRFAX called TOWLSTON yearly on first day of December two
fat Turkies and six fat Ducks In Witness whereof have hereunto set their hands and
seals the day and year first above written
in presence of   BRYAN FAIRFAX
                                                            JOHN BALLENDINE
      At a Court held for Loudoun County May the 13th 1771
This Indenture was ackowledged by BRYAN FAIRFAX Esqr. a party thereto, the Court
having approved of the reserved yearly Rent as sufficient and is ordered to be recorded

pp.   THIS INDENTURE made the second day of January in year of our Lord one thou-
20-   sand seven hundred and seventy one Between WILLIAM GARDNER of County of
22   FAIRFAX, Planter, of one part and SAMUEL CHESSHIR of County of STAFFORD of
         other part WHEREAS BRYAN FAIRFAX Esqr. of County of FAIRFAX by his certain
Indenture and Lease under his hand and seal bearing date the XIII day of July 1762 for
the consideration therein mentioned did grant and to farm let unto JOSEPH GARDNER
party to these presents a certain parcel of land lying in County of Loudoun containing
three hundred and twenty acres to hold unto said JOSEPH GARDNER his heirs and
assigns during the natural lives of said JOSEPH GARDNER, JOSEPH, his Son, his Daughter,
ELONER JORDAN, and longest liver of them under yearly rent of six pounds current
money to be discharged in Cash or Tobacco at Ten shillings p Ct. Sterling or Wheat @ 2/6
per bushel to be paid BRYAN FAIRFAX yearly on first day of December NOW THIS IN-
DENTURE WITNESSETH that said WILLIAM GARDNER for sum of Ninety pounds current
money to him in hand paid by SAMUEL CHESSHIRE doth transfer and set over unto said
SAMUEL CHESHIRE his heirs all the said premises above mentioned In Witness whereof
I have hereunto set my hand and affixed my seal the day and year first above written
in presence of HENRY STODDARD,   WILLIAM GARDNER
      JOEL CHESSHIR,
      At a Court continued and held for Loudoun County May the 14th 1771
This Indenture and Receipt under written were acknowledged by WILLIAM GARDNER
party thereto and ordered to be recorded

pp.   THIS INDENTURE made the Twelfth day of May in year of our Lord One thousand
23-   seven hundred and seventy one Between JOHN HOUGH of County of Loudoun of
24   one part and SAMUEL BUTCHER of same County of other part Witnesseth that
         JOHN HOUGH for sum of Five shillings current money of Virginia to him in hand
paid by these presents doth bargain and sell unto SAMUEL BUTCHER all that tract of
land situate in County of Loudoun and bounded begining at two Hickorys the South side
of a Swamp or Drain leading into CUB RUN and corner to a Survey made for DENIS
McCARTY and Corner to a late Purchase of FRANCIS KEEN extending thence with
McCARTY's line West one hundred and twenty poles to a white and black Oak his Corner
thence with another of his lines No. 27 d. West five hundred and fifty poles thence S. 26
d. W. twenty poles to a white Oak mark't JA and a Hickory AR corner to ANDREW RUS-

SELLs survey and JOHN ELLIOTT then with ELLIOTTs lines or Survey S. 10 d. E. two hundred and eighty poles thence South 28 d. W. two hundred poles, thence S. 60 d. Wt. four hundred and two poles to a Spanish or live Oak by a Swamp the beginning Corner of said ELLIOTTs Survey thence S. 48 d. E. five hundred and eighty poles to the line of ANDREW HUTCHISONs Survey then with said line N. 40 d. E. five hundred poles to a white Oak his Corner, thence to the beginning, containing two thousand acres be the same more or less And all Houses Orchards and appurtenances whatsoever belonging To have and to hold the lands hereby conveyed paying therefore the rent of one Peper Corn on Lady Day to intent that by virtue of these presents and statute for transferring uses into possession said SAMUEL BUTCHER may be in actual possession and be thereby enabled to accept Release of inheritance thereof In Witness whereof said JOHN HOUGH hath hereunto set his hand and seal the day and year first above written

in presence of   JOHN HOUGH

At a Court continued and held for Loudoun County May the 14th 1771 This Indenture was ackowledged by JOHN HOUGH party thereto and ordered to be recorded

pp.   THIS INDENTURE made the 13th day of May in year of our Lord One thousand
24-   seven hundred and seventy one Between JOHN HOUGH of County of Loudoun of
26   one part and SAMUEL BUTCHER of same County of other part Witnesseth that
          for sum of Three hundred pounds current money of Virginia to said JOHN HOUGH in hand paid by these presents doth bargain and sell SAMUEL BUTCHER in his actual possession now being by virtue of a bargain and sale for one year and by force of statute for transferring uses into possession and his heirs all that tract of land lying in County of Loudoun bounded .. (description of land as in Lease above) .. To have and to hold the lands hereby conveyed unto said SAMUEL BUTCHER his heirs and assigns forever In Witness whereof said JOHN HOUGH hath hereunto set his hand and seal the day and year first above written

in the presence of   JOHN HOUGH

At a Court continued and held for Loudoun County May the 14th 1771 This Indenture and the Receipt thereon endorsed were acknowledged by JOHN HOUGH party thereto and ordered to be recorded

pp.   THIS INDENTURE made the fourteenth day of May in Eleventh year of the Reign
27-   of his Majesty GEORGE the Third &c. and in the year of our Lord God one thou-
29   sand seven hundred and seventy one Between JOSEPH WEST of Loudoun County,
          Farmer, and JANE his Wife, of one part and ROBERT HAMILTON of TOWN of LEES-
BURG in County aforesaid, Innholder, of other Part Witnesseth that JOSEPH WEST and JANE his Wife for sum of Twenty pounds current money of Virginia in hand paid by these presents doth bargain and sell unto ROBERT HAMILTON one certain lott or half acre of land lying in TOWN of LEESBURG and numbered (THREE) in the Plan and survey of said Town binding on and between ROYAL STREET and LOUDOUN STREET and which was formerly conveyed by NICHOLAS MINOR Gent. to ISRAEL THOMPSON who failing to improve the same according to Act of Assembly became forfeited again vested in said NICHOLAS MINOR who afterwards by Deed of Feoffment bearing date the tenth day of May in year one thousand seven hundred and sixty three for consideration therein mentioned sold same to MINOR WINN who also by his Deed of Feoffment bearing date the third day   May in year one thousand seven hundred and sixty five sold and conveyed said lott to JOHN ASHBY as by said Deeds duly acknowledged and recorded in Loudoun County Court And all houses gardens and appurtenances whatsoever belonging To have and To hold said lott or half acre of land unto said ROBERT HAMILTON his heirs and

assigns In Witness whereof said JOSEPH WEST and JANE his Wife have hereunto set
their hands and seals the day and year first above written
in presence of ANTHY. RAMSAY,   JOSEPH WEST
        WILLIAM LAUDER, WM. JOHNSTON
  At a Court held for Loudoun County May the 14th 1771
This Indenture was acknowledged by JOSEPH WEST and JANE his Wife parties thereto
(the said JANE haveing been first privately examined as the Law directs) and the Receipt under written was also acknowledged by said JOSEPH and together with said
Indenture ordered to be recorded

pp.   THIS INDENTURE made the Fourteenth day of May in year of our Lord One thou-
29-   sand seven hundred and seventy one Between ALICE GIBSON of County of Lou-
31   doun of one part and JOHN HENDREN of County of FAUQUIER of other part Wit-
         nesseth that for sum of Twenty pounds current money of Virginia said ALICE
GIBSON in hand paid by these presents doth bargain and sell unto JOHN HENDRON and
his heirs a certain parcel of land lying in County of Loudoun bounded beginning at a
white and black Oak saplin in line of said ALICE GIBSON's Land running thence No. 41 d.
Et. 30 poles to a white Oak saplin thence No. 30 d. Et. 18 poles to a white Oak in said ALICE
GIBSONs back line thence No. 72 d. Wt. 51 poles to a white Oak marked E G thence South
10 d. Et. 60 poles to the beginning containing by estimation ten acres be the same more
or less And all houses orchards and appurtenances whatsoever belonging To have and
to hold the lands hereby conveyed unto said JOHN HENDRON his heirs and assigns forever In Witness whereof said ALICE GIBSON hath hereunto set her hand and seal the
day and year first above written
in presence of   ALLICE GIBSON
  At a Court held for Loudoun County May the 14th 1771
This Indenture and receipt thereon endorsed were acknowledged by ALICE GIBSON
party thereto and ordered to be recorded
(On margin: Exd. DD to Mr. HENDRENs Son Oct. 1, 72)

pp.   THIS INDENTURE made the Fourteenth day of May in year of our Lord One thou-
31-   sand seven hundred and seventy one Between JOHN HENDRON of County of FAU-
34   QUIER and ELIZABETH his Wife of one part and JOHN GIBSON of County of Lou-
         doun of other part Witnesseth that for sum of Twenty pounds current money of
Virginia to said JOHN HENDRON in hand paid by these presents doth bargain and sell
unto JOHN GIBSON a certain parcel of land lying in County of Loudoun on the PANTHER
SKIN RUN and bounded Beginning at a Sycamore standing in the low grounds in JOSEPH
GIBSONs line upon the PANTHER SKIN running from thence So. 74 d. E. 49 poles to a
white Oak on a hill side thence South 53 d. Et. 49 poles to three white Oak saplins thence
So. 80 d. Et. 16 poles to a large black Oak thence No. 36 d. Et. 12 1/2 poles to a white and
black Oak saplins in the WIDOW GIBSONs line thence with her line So. 10 d. Et. 60 poles to
a white Oak on the bank of PANTHER SKIN RUN to a Corner of JAMES GIBSONs Land
thence with his line 87 poles to 2 Gums Corner to JOSEPH GIBSONs land thence with his
line to the beginning containing by estimation fifteen acres be the same more or less
And all houses orchards and appurtenances whatsoever belonging To have and to hold
the lands hereby conveyed unto JOHN GIBSON his heirs and assigns forever In Witness
whereof said JOHN HENDRON and ELIZABETH his Wife have hereunto set their hands and
seals the day and year first above written
in the presence of   JOHN HENDREN
                                                 ELIZABETH her mark ⌒ HENDREN

At a Court held for Loudoun County May the 14th 1771
This Indenture was acknowledged by JOHN HENDRUN and ELIZABETH his Wife parties
thereto (she having been first privately examined as the Law directs) and the receipt
endorsed was also acknowledged by said JOHN HENDRUN and together with the said Indenture ordered to be recorded
(On margin: Exam'd & dd. to MR. R. MURRAY Novr. 5th 1773)

pp.   THIS INDENTURE made this 17th day of June in year of our Lord one thousand
34-   seven hundred and seventy Between JOHN POPKINS of County of Loudoun of one
36   part and BENJAMIN JOHN of same County of other part Witnesseth that said JOHN
        POPKINS for sum of Five shillings Current money to him in hand paid by these
presents doth bargain and sell unto BENJAMIN JOHN all that parcel of land with the
rights members and appurtenances lying in County of Loudoun bounded beginning at
a red Oak marked one side standing near the MAIN ROAD being the beginning of EVAN
RICEs larger tract thence No. 11 1/2 d. Et. one hundred and twenty three poles to a Stake
thence So. 85 1/2 d. Et. one hundred & thirteen poles to two white Oaks & a Hickory in
THOMPSON MASONs line & the beginning of ROBT. POPKINS thence So. 9 1/2 d. Wt. one
hundred and ninety three poles to two white Oaks in said MASONs line thence with said
RICEs line No. 85 1/2 d. Wt. one hundred and twenty one poles to the beginning containing one hundred & forty one acres the same being part of a greater tract of land
sold to JOHN POPKINS, ROBERT POPKINS & EVAN RICE by JOSIAS CLAPHAM And all houses
orchards and appurtenances whatsoever belonging To have and to hold said premises
unto said BENJAMIN JOHN during full term of one year paying therefor one Pepper
Corn upon Feast of Saint Michael the Arch Angle to intent that by virtue of these presents and statute for transferring uses into possession said BENJAMIN JOHN may be in
actual possession and thereby enabled to accept a Release of Inheritance thereof
in presence of ROBERT HAMILTON,   JOHN POPKINS
        STEPHEN EMREY, WILLIAM LEWIS,
        JOSEPH JENNY
    At a Court held for Loudoun County May the 14th 1771
This Indenture was acknowledged by JOHN POPKINS party thereto and ordered to be
recorded

pp.   THIS INDENTURE made this Eighteenth day of June in the year of our Lord God
36-   one thousand seven hundred and seventy Between JOHN POPKINS of County of
39   Loudoun of one part and BENJAMIN JOHN of same County of other part Witnes-
        seth that for sum of Two hundred and Ten pounds PENNSYLVANIA MONEY to him
in hand paid JOHN POPKINS by these presents doth bargain and sell BENJAMIN JOHN (in
his actual possession by virtue of a bargain and sale for one year and force of statute
for transferring uses into possession) and to his heirs and assigns forever all that tract
of land lying in County of Loudoun bounded .. (description of land as in Lease above) ..
To have and to hold said parcel of land unto BENJAMIN JOHN his heirs and assigns In
Witness whereof the aforesaid JOHN POPKINS hath hereunto set his hand and affixed
his seal the day and year first above written
in presence of ROBERT HAMILTON   JOHN POPKINS
        STEPHEN EMREY, JOSEPH JENNEY,
        WILLIAM LEWIS
    At a Court held for Loudoun County May the 14th 1771
This Indenture and the receipt thereon endorsed were acknowledged by JOHN POPKINS
party thereto and ordered to be recorded

pp.   THIS INDENTURE made the 20th day of June in year of our Lord one thousand
40-   seven hundred and seventy two Between THOMAS BLACKBURN of County of
42   PRINCE WILLIAM Gent. of one part and FREDERICK CLYNE of County of Loudoun
of other part Witnesseth that THOMAS BLACKBURN in consideration of rents and
covenants hereafter mentioned by these presents doth grant and to farm let unto said
FREDERICK CLYNE a certain parcel of land lying in County of Loudoun on the BEAVER
DAM BRANCH of GOOSE CREEK and bounded beginning at a black Oak corner to DAWSON
BROWN Extending thence So. 30 East one hundred and fifty eight poles to a heap of
Stones on a Ridge by the BEAVER DAM CREEK thence So. 80 West one hundred and six
poles to THOMAS GREGGs line thence N. 49 West one hundred and sixty poles to GREGGs
Corner thence No. 72 East one hundred and forty four poles to beginning containing
One hundred and fifteen acres excepting all mines and minerals To have and to hold
said tract of land with the appurtenances unto FREDERICK CLYNE his heirs or assigns
during natural lives of him the said FREDERICK CLYNE, LYDIA CLYNE AND ANNA CLYNE
his Daughters and longest liver of them paying THOMAS BLACKBURN on first day of
November in year one thousand seven hundred and seventy four and every year the
sum of Three pounds Current money and Ten pounds of good Butter p hundred acres
and so in proportion together with Quit rents and taxes and plant at least One hundred
Apple trees and also to build a Dwelling House at least twenty feet long and sixteen feet
wide and other such houses as his way of Husbandry may require In Witness whereof
the parties to these presents have interchangeably set their hands and seals the day
and year first above written
in presence of W. ELLZEY,   T. BLACKBURN
          JOHN THORNTON, ROB. H. HARRISON,   FREDERICK CLYNE
          WM. HOUGH, SAMUEL SMITH,
          CRAVEN PEYTON, SOLOMON HOGE
  At a Court held for Loudoun County August 24th 1772
This Indenture was proved by the Oaths of JOHN THORNTON and WILLIAM ELLZEY, Gent.,
Witnesses thereto on the part of THOMAS BLACKBURN Gent., and by the Oath of CRAVEN
PEYTON Gent. and the Affirmations of WILLIAM HOUGH and SOLOMON HOGE Witnesses
thereto on the part of FREDERICK CLYNE, the Court approving the reserved yearly rent
as sufficient, & is ordered to be recorded
(On Margin: delivered to Mr. GRANT JUNR.)

pp.   TO ALL PEOPLE to whom these presents shall come We RICHARD HOCKLEY of the
42-   City of PHILADELPHIA in Province of PENNSYLVANIA Esqr. and JEREMIAH WAR-
45   DER and ABEL JAMES of same place, Merchants, send Greeting. Whereas ROBERT
          PARISH of County of FREDERICK in Province of Virginia, Merchant, by a certain
Indenture bearing date as therein mentioned did grant and confirm unto DANIEL
CLARK of the City of PHILADELPHIA, Merchant, a certain tract of land situate near WIN-
CHESTER in County of FREDERICK with the appurtenances To Hold to said DANIEL CLARK
his heirs and assigns forever in which Indenture is contained the proviso that upon
payment of the sum of One thousand and forty eight pounds fifteen shillings lawful
money of PENNSYLVANIA to said Indenture and the Estate thereby granted should become void, And Whereas said DANIEL CLARK and JANE his Wife by a certain Indenture
dated the sixth day of April 1764 did sell and set over unto said RICHARD HOCKLEY, JERE-
MIAH WARDER and ABEL JAMES and the Survivor of them (inter alia) all the Debts,
sums of money then due owing or payable unto said DANIEL CLARK from any person To
Hold unto said RICHARD HOCKLEY, JEREMIAH WARDER and ABEL JAMES their heirs And
DANIEL CLARK the better to enable (them) to execute and perform the purposes of last
recited Indenture did appoint said RICHARD HOCKLEY, JEREMIAH WARDER and ABEL

JAMES and the survivor of them to be true and Lawful attornies for DANIEL CLARK to ask demand and sue for all sums of money and debts and give acquitances as by Indentuyre recorded in Office for Recording Deeds for the City and County of PHILADELPHIA in Book H Vol. 20, page 140 &c. NOW KNOW YE that we the said RICHARD HOCKLEY, JEREMIAH WARDER and ABEL JAMES hath appointed JOSEPH JENNY of LEESBOROUGH in County of Loudoun in Province of Virginia, Merchant, our lawful Attorney as Trustees for DANIEL CLARK In Witness whereof we have hereunto set our hands and seals the twenty seventh day of September Anno Domini one thousand seven hundred and seventy one

in presence of JOHN HOUGH,   RICHD. HOCKLEY
               MAHLON JENNY   JERE:AH WARDER
                                                      ABEL JAMES

At a Court continued and held for Loudoun County August 25th 1772
This Power of Attorney was proved by the Affirmation of JOHN HOUGH and MAHLON JANNEY, the subscribing witnesses thereto, to be the acts and deeds of RICHARD HOCKLEY, JEREMIAH WARDER and ABEL JAMES, parties thereto, and is ordered to be recorded

pp.   GEORGE the Third to LEVEN POWELL, WILLIAM SMITH and SIMON TRIPLETT Gen-
45-   tlemen Greeting Whereas FRANCIS PEYTON and FRANCES his Wife have by their
47   certain deed bearing date the twenty seventh day of April in year one thousand
      seven hundred and seventy one sold and conveyed unto THOMAS WILLIAMS in
Fee simple Estate two hundred forty eight acres of land lying in County of Loudoun ..
authority given for the privy examination of said FRANCES PEYTON .. Dated 22d day of August 1771.

      Commission returned by LEVEN POWELL and WILLIAM SMITH for execution
thereof dated 22d day of August 1771
At a Court continued and held for Loudoun County August 25th 1772
This Commission with a return of Execution thereof was produced in Court and ordered to be recorded

pp.   THIS INDENTURE made the 24th day of August in year of our Lord 1772 Between
47-   JAMES HARDAGE LANE of County of FAIRFAX and Parish of Truro of one part and
49   JOHN McCOWN of County of Loudoun and Parish of Cameron of other part
      Whereas WILLOUGHBY NEWTON Gent. late of County of WESTMORELAND in his
lifetime, to wit, on the 20th day of September in year 1747 by his Indenture of Lease bearing date the day and year last mentioned and sealed with his Seal for consideration of Rents and Covenants therein expressed on part of WILLIAM REMEY of County of FAIRFAX, Planter, to be paid and performed did grant and to farm let unto WILLIAM REMEY one certain parcel of land containing One hundred and fifty acres situate in Parish of Truro and County of FAIRFAX but now in Parish of Cameron and County of Loudoun being part of a Patent granted said NEWTON and bounded according to several courses in said Lease expressed To Have and To Hold said parcel of land with all appurtenances unto WILLIAM REMEY his heirs & assigns during natural lives of him said WILLIAM REMEY, ANN OMHUNDRO his Mother and DANIEL CARROLL the Son of DEMPSEY CARROLL & the Survivor of them under yearly rent of Five hundred and sixty six pounds of good sound Merchantable top Leaf Tobacco clear of trash and ground leaves and Whereas said WILLOUGHBY NEWTON to wit on the 17th day of October 1758 by his Memorandum on the back of said Lease sealed with his Seal did agree to add the Life of WILLIAM PORTER CARROLL, Son of DEMPSEY CARROLL to said Lease but was never recorded and said WILLIAM REMEY by his Endorsement on said Lease made over the same to DEMPSEY CARROLL JUNR. and this likewise was never recorded, And Whereas

the said WILLIAM REMEY and DEMPSEY CARROLL JUNR. to wit (blank) jointly by their
Indenture of Assignment of Lease did assign their right and title of the first mentioned
Lease to the within mentioned JOHN McCOWN party to these presents and to his assigns
for the natural lives of said WM. REMEY and WILLM. PORTER CARROLL, the other lives
mentioned in said Lease being dead, he paying the yearly rent and performing the
covenants in the first recited Indenture of Lease NOW THIS INDENTURE WITNESSETH
that JOHN McCOWN for sum of Twenty pounds current money of Virginia to him in hand
paid by JAMES HARDAGE LANE by these presents doth bargain and set over unto JAMES
HARDAGE LANE and his heirs and assigns all said parcel of land containing one hundred and fifty acres with Houses rights members and appurtenances whatsoever belonging To have and to hold unto JAMES HARDAGE LANE during the life of said WIL-
LIAM REMEY and life of WILLIAM PORTER CARROLL, Son of DEMPSEY CARROLL, and the
longest liver of them under the rents and covenants in said recited Indenture of Lease
mentioned In Witness whereof the said JOHN McCOWN hath hereunto set his hand and
seal the day and year first above written
in presence of GEO. SUMMERS,   JOHN McCOWN
        FRANCIS his mark F.S SUMMERS,
        JOHN KING
    At a Court continued and held for Loudoun County August 25th 1772
This Indenture was acknowledged by JOHN McCOWN party thereto to be his act and deed
and is ordered to be recorded

pp.   THIS AGREEMENT made this 21st day of April 1772 Between WILLIAM MEAD JUNR.
49-   of Loudoun County of one part, Farmer, and PHILIP FEAZEL SENR. of County
51   aforesaid, also Farmer, of other part Witnesseth that WILLIAM MEAD JUNR. for
         the considerations hereafter reserved doth Lease to PHILIP FEAZIL one third
part of a tract of land belonging to the heirs of JOHN HAGUE deced, the said MEAD being
Executor of said HAGUE, it being the place where PHILIP FEAZIL now lives and bounded
as it is laid off to him and said PHILIP FEAZIL is to clear no more than Eighty acres of
the said land with what is already cleared which cleared ground must be divided into
four Fields which said Fields shall not be tended exceeding four years without resting
and every four years after not exceeding the Crop of Corn and a Crop of Wheat of each
Field and PHILIP FEAZIL is to have Liberty after having made a lawful fence of split
rails round every Field as he clears them to sell or dispose of as he thinks proper all the
superfluous wood that shall be left being careful not to sell or destroy any that is fit for
Board timber or shingles and he is not to have but one family living on the place at a
time and promise to pay WILLIAM MEAD 21st day of September 1772 three pounds lawfull money of Virginia and for five years afterwards the like sum annually and the
same day of September 1778 to pay Five pounds like money and so for five years and in
the year 1783 to pay Ten pounds like money until September the 21 1787 and he is to
plant 150 Apple trees within one year In confirmation whereof the parties to these
presents do bind themselves or their assigns either to other in Penal sum of One hundred and fifty pounds Lawful money of Virginia to be paid by the party failing to the
other party. As Witness our hands and seals this twenty first day of April 1772
in presence of MAJOR EVANS,   WILLIAM MEAD
        CHARLES McBRIDE, PHILLIP FEAZEL   PHILLIP FEAZEL
    At a Court continued and held for Loudoun County August 26th 1772
This Agreement was proved by Oaths of MAJOR EVANS, CHARLES McBRIDE and PHILIP
FEAZIL, the Subscribing witnesses, to be the acts and deeds of WILLIAM MEAD JUNR. and
PHILIP FEAZIL parties thereto and is ordered to be recorded

pp. | TO ALL CHRISTIAN PEOPLE to whom this present writing shall come, I VINCENT
51- | BOGGESS of Loudoun County send Greeting. Know Ye that I VINCENT BOGGESS for
52 | divers good causes and considerations me thereunto moving, more especially for
the Fatherly love and affection I have and bear towards my Children NANCY and
ROBERT BOGGESS, as also the sum of Twenty shillings Currency to me in hand paid by
said NANCY and ROBERT BOGGESS do give unto NANCY BOGGESS her heirs one Negroe
woman named Chlo and her child named Newton and all her future increase; and unto
my Son, ROBERT BOGGESS, his heirs one Negroe woman named Nell and her child named
Will and all her future increase To have and to hold the said Negro woman Chlo and
Negro woman Nell and their future increase reserving to VINCENT BOGGESS their future
increase during my natural life In Witness whereof I have hereunto set my hand and
affixed my seal this 27th day of August in year one thousand seven hundred and
seventy two
in presence of G. JOHNSTON,   VINCENT BOGGESS
     WM. GUNNELL
  At a Court continued and held for Loudoun County August 27th 1772
This Indenture was acknoweldged by VINCENT BOGGESS party thereto to be his act and
deed and is ordered to be recorded

pp. | (On margin: Dd. Mr. OWSLEY Jany 23d 1775)
52- | TO ALL CHRISTIAN PEOPLE to whom these presents shall come I JEAN COX Wife of
54 | HARMAN COX send Greeting. Know Ye that I said JEAN COX for sum of forty
shillings current money to me in hand paid by THOMAS OWSLEY of Loudoun
County by these presents for myself my heirs &c. do grant and for ever quit claim unto
said THOMAS OWSLEY his heirs and assigns in his full and peaceable possession and
seizin thereof now being by virtue of Deeds of Conveyance made by WILLIAM DAVIS
who purchased by Deeds of Conveyance also from HARMAN COX, my Husband, both
which Deeds remain of record in Court of County of Loudoun, all such right Estate and
demand which I said JEAN COX now have or have had in a certain tract of land lying on
the BEAVER DAM of GOOSE CREEK containing two hundred acres more or less which THO-
MAS OWSLEY purchased as aforesaid To have and to hold said tract of land unto said
THOMAS OWSLEY his heirs and assigns In Witness whereof said JEAN COX hath hereunto
set her hand and affixed her seal the twenty seventh day of August Seventeen hundred
and seventy two
in presence of G. JOHNSTON,   JEAN COX
     WM. GUNNELL, ROBERT ADAM
  At a Court continued and held for Loudoun County August the 27th 1772
This Indenture was acknowledged by JEAN COX, Wife of HARMAN COX, party thereto, to
be her act and deed (she having been first privately examined as the Law directs) and
is ordered to be recorded

pp. | THIS INDENTURE made the fifteenth day of April in year of our Lord One thou-
54- | sand seven hundred and seventy two Between JAMES HAMILTON of County of
55 | Loudoun Gent. of one part and JAMES KENNADY of the County afd., Weaver, of
other part, Witnesseth that said JAMES HAMILTON pursuant to a Decree of the
Honourable the General Court in Chancery dated the tenth day of October 1769 and for
sum of five shillings current money of Virginia to him in hand paid by these presents
doth bargain and sell unto JAMES KENNADY a certain parcel of land situate in County of
Loudoun whereon said JAMES KENNADY now lives being part of a larger tract of land
which formerly belonged to CATESBY COCKE and which was laid off by JOHN HOUGH into
Lotts of which the parcel of land hereby sold is one, and is bounded according to that

survey made by said HOUGH and supposed to contain two hundred and sixty acres more or less and all Houses Orchards and appurtenances whatsoever belonging To have and to hold the lands hereby conveyed for full term of one whole year paying therefore the rent of one Pepper Corn on Lady Day next to intent that by Virtue of these presents and statute for transferring uses into possession said JAMES KENNADY may be in actual possession and thereby enabled to accept a Release of Inheritance thereof In Witness whereof said JAMES HAMILTON hath hereunto set his hand and seal the day and year first above written

in presence of W. ELLZEY,   JAS. HAMILTON
           JOSEPH JANNEY, MAHLON TAYLOR
   At a Court continued and held for Loudoun County Augt. 27th 1772
This Indenture was ackoweldged by JAMES HAMILTON Gent. party thereto, to be his act and deed, and is ordered to be recorded

pp.   THIS INDENTURE made the Sixteenth day of April in year of our Lord One thou-
55-   sand seven hundred and seventy two Between JAMES HAMILTON of County of
58   Loudoun Gent. of one part and JAMES KENNADY of County aforesaid, Weaver, of
         the other part Witnesseth that for sum of Fourteen pounds Current money of
Virginia said JAMES HAMILTON in hand paid by these presents and pursuant to a decree of the Honourable the General Court in Chancery bargain and sell JAMES KENNADY (in his actual possession now being by virtue of a bargain and sale for one whole year and statute for transferring uses into possession) and his heirs a certain parcel of land situate in County of Loudoun .. (entry proceeds as in Lease above) .. In Witness whereof said JAMES HAMILTON hath hereunto set his hand and seal the day and year first above written

in presence of W. ELLZEY,   JAS. HAMILTON
           JOSEPH JANNEY, MAHLON TAYLOR
   At a Court continued and held for Loudoun County August 27th 1772
This Indenture and the Receipt under written was acknowledged by JAMES HAMILTON Gent., party thereto, to be his act and deed, and is ordered to be recorded

pp.   THIS INDENTURE made the (blank) day of October in year of our Lord one thou-
58-   sand seven hundred and seventy two Between JAMES HENDERSON of County of
59   Loudoun of one part and JOSEPH CALDWELL of same County of other part Witnes-
         seth that JAMES HENDERSON for sum of five shillings Sterling to him in hand
paid by these presents doth bargain and sell JOSEPH CALDWELL all that tract of land lying in County of Loudoun and bounded beginning at three white Oaks in a Gully, Corner of FRANCIS HAGUE bought of JOHN LESSWELL, extending thence So. 43 d. East 131 poles to a black Oak on a Mountain in a line of WILLIAM HENRY FAIRFAX thence with his line No. 43 East 116 poles to three small Oaks on said Mountain commonly called HOGG BACK, thence No. 43 d. Wt. 195 poles to two small black Oaks on a hill side Corner to land laid off for THOMAS GORE now ROBERT STRETCHBERRY, thence with his line So. 69 d. Wt. 125 poles to two white Oaks on a hill in a line of said HAGUE, thence with said Line So. 43 d. East 115 poles to the first station containing One hundred and fifty one acres of land Together with all Houses, Orchards, Meadows and appurtenances to the same belonging To have and to hold unto JOSEPH CALDWELL and his heirs for full term of one whole year paying therefore the yearly rent of one Ear of Indian Corn at the Feast of Saint Michael to intent that by virute of statute for transferring uses into possession said JOSEPH CALDWELL may be in actual possession and be enabled to accept a grant of Inheritance thereof In Witness whereof said JAMES HENDERSON hath hereunto set his

hand and seal the day and year first above written
in the presence of us   JAMES his mark ✝ HENDERSON
                                                          ANN her mark   O HENDERSON

At a Court held for Loudoun County September the 28th 1772
This Indenture was acknowledged by JAMES HENDERSON and ANN, his Wife, parties
thereto, to be their acts and deeds (the said ANN being first privately examined as the
Law directs) and is ordered to be recorded

pp.   THIS INDENTURE made this (blank) day of October in year of our Lord one thou-
59-   sand seven hundred and Seventy two Between JAMES HENDERSON and ANN his
63   Wife of County of Loudoun of one part and JOSEPH COLDWELL of the same County
         of other part Whereas there if a certain tract of land lying in County of Loudoun
bounded as followeth .. (description of land as in Lease above) .. containing one
hundred and fifty one acres being part of a tract of land granted to AMOS JENNY by a
Pattent from the Proprietors Office bearing date the Eighth day of April in the year one
thousand seven hundred and forty two and registered in the said Proprietor Office in
Book E, Folio 435, and by MAHLON JENNY, Son and Heir to said AMOS JENNY, transferred
to said JAMES HENDERSON by Deed bearing date the sixteenth day of July one thousand
seven hundred and fifty eight and recorded in Loudoun County Office NOW THIS IN-
DENTURE WITNESSETH that JAMES HENDERSON and ANN his Wife for sum of one hundred
pounds current money of Virginia to him in hand paid by these presents doth bargain
and sell unto JOSEPH COLDWELL (in his actual possession now being by Virtue of one
Indenture of bargain and sale made for one whole year and statute for transferring
uses into possession) to him his heirs and assigns forever said one hundred and fifty
one acres In Witness whereof said JAMES HENDERSON and ANN his Wife have hereunto
set their hands and seals the day and year first above written
in presence of us   JAMES his mark ✝ HENDERSON
                                                          ANN her mark   ᴐ HENDERSON

Received from JAMES CALDWELL the sum of one hundred pounds current money in
full consideration expressed in the within Deed. Witness my hand this 28th day of Sept.
1772.   JAMES his mark ✝ HENDERSON
At a Court held for Loudoun County September the 28th 1772
This Indenture and the receipt thereon endorsed was acknowledged by JAMES HENDER-
SON and ANN his Wife, parties thereto, to be their acts and deeds, (the said ANN having
been first privately examined as the Law directs and relinquished her Dower therein)
and is ordered to be recorded
(On margin: Deld. to Mr. COLDWELL 2d May 1774)

pp.   THIS INDENTURE made the Ninth and Tenth day of Sept. in year of our Lord One
63-   thousand seven hundred and seventy two Between DUNCAN GRAHAM and MARY
65   his Wife of County of CAROLINE in Colony of Virginia of one part and CHARLES
         CHINN of County of FAUQUIER in Colony aforesaid of other part Witnesseth that
for sum of five shillings current money of Virginia to them in hand paid by CHARLES
CHINN by these presents doth bargain and sell unto CHARLES CHINN all that parcel of
land situate and bounded beginning at a white Oak Corner to CHARLES BURGESS, late of
LANCASTER & RALEIGH CHINN thence North 10 d. Wt. 453 poles to a Hickory on the South
side of GOOSE CREEK thence down the said Creek the several meanders thereof which reduced to a right line is North 71 d East 430 poles to a white Oak on GOOSE CREEK in BRYAN
FAIRFAX's line, thence with his line So. 22 d. East 200 to the line of said RALEIGH CHINN,
thence with his line No. 68 d. West 90 poles to a red Oak on the side of a Hill corner to
said CHINN, thence So. 77 d. West 210 poles to a Corner of said RALEIGH CHINN thence

with his line So. 13 d. West 400 poles to the beginning, the same being contained within the bounds of a certain tract of land originally granted from the Proprietors Office to said JOHN GRAHAM and a certain JOHN GRANT (whom the said GRAHAM hath survived) by Deed dated the 23d day of May 1741 and after repattented by said JOHN GRAHAM at least the part thereof hereby intended to be conveyed by Deed from the Proprietors Office dated 28th day of July 1742, but in making out of which Deed the true Courses have been mistaken as by the said Deed recorded in said Proprietors Office will appear, and which said Tract of land by the sd last mentioned Deed according to the Courses of said Deed was by JOHN GRAHAM conveyed to said DUNCAN by Deeds of Lease & Release bearing date the 14th & 15th days of October 1745 and recorded in County Court of PRINCE WILLIAM, the said hereby conveyed and granted premises being in Loudoun County and FAUQUIER COUNTY to contain three hundred and forty nine acres of land more or less, And all houses Orchards and appurtenances whatsoever belonging To have and to hold the lands hereby conveyed unto said CHARLES CHINN during the full term of one whole year paying therefore the rent of one Pepper Corn on Lady Day next to the intent that by virtue of these presents and statute for transferring uses into possession said CHARLES CHINN may be in actual possession and be thereby enabled to accept a Release of inheritance thereof In Witness whereof said DUNCAN GRAHAM and MARY his Wife have hereunto set their hands and seals the day and year above written
in presence of ROBT. HART to DG the 10th   DUN: GRAHAM
     THOMAS FORSTER,   MARY GRAHAM
     RAWLEIG CHINN of Loudoun;
     CHAS. CHINN JUNR., ELIJAH CHINN
  At a Court held for Loudoun County September the 28th 1772
This Indenture was proved by the Oaths of RAWLEIGH CHINN, CHARLES CHINN JUNR. and ELIJAH CHINN, three of the subscribing witnesses thereto, and is ordered to be recorded

pp.   THIS INDENTURE made the ninth and tenth day of Septr. in year One thousand
65-   seven hundred and seventy two Between DUNCAN GRAHAM and MARY his Wife
70   of County of CAROLINE in Colony of Virginia of one part and CHARLES CHINN in
         County of FAUQUIER in Colony aforesaid of other part Witnesseth that for sum of one hundred pounds current money of Virginia to said DUNCAN GRAHAM and MARY his Wife in hand paid by these presents doth bargain and sell CHARLES CHINN (in his actual possession by virtue of a bargain and sale for one whole year and statute for transferring uses into possession) and his heirs all that parcel of land .. (Release proceeds as in Lease above) .. In Witness whereof said DUNCAN GRAHAM and MARY his Wife have hereunto set their hands and seals the day and year first above written
in presence of ROBT. HART to DG Sepr. 10th   DUN: GRAHAM
     THOMS. FORSTER,   MARY GRAHAM
     RAWLEIGH CHINN of Loudoun
     CHAS. CHINN JUNR., ELIJAH CHINN
  Received this thirteenth day of September 1772 of Mr. CHARLES CHINN the sum of one hundred pounds in full the within mentioned consideration as witness my hand
(Same Witnesses except THOMAS FORSTER)   DUN: GRAHAM
     (COMMISSION directed to JOHN MINOR, GEORGE GUY, ANTHONY NEW Gentlemen for privy examination of MARY GRAHAM Wife of DUNCAN GRAHAM dated (blank) day of September 1772. Return of execution thereof dated Ninth day of September 1772 signed by GEORGE GUY and ANTH: NEW.)
  At a Court held for Loudoun County September the 28th 1772
This Indenture and Receipt thereon endorsed was proved by the Oath of RAWLEIGH

CHINN, CHARLES CHINN JUNR. and ELIJAH CHINN, three of the subscribing witnesses thereto, together with a Commission for the privy Examination of the Feme with a return of Execution thereof ordered to be recorded
(On margin: Deliv'd per Order Augt. 25th 1781)

pp.   THIS INDENTURE made the sixteenth day of September Anno Domini one thou-
70-   sand seven hundred and seventy two Between RAWLEIGH DOWNMAN and ELIZA-
75   BETH his Wife of County of RICHMOND of one part and CHARLES CHINN of FAU-
QUIER COUNTY of other part Witnesseth that said RAWLEIGH DOWNMAN and ELIZABETH his Wife for sum of Forty pounds current money of Virginia in hand paid by these presents doth bargain and sell unto CHARLES CHINN his heirs and assigns forever all that tract of land lying in the Counties of Loudoun and FAUQUIER containing two hundred acres, which said Tract of land was Devised unto one BRYAN STOTT by RAW-LEIGH CHINN Gent. Deced as by the Will of said Deceased may more fully appear and conveyed by Deed of Bargain and Sale from said STOTT to WILLIAM DOWNMAN, Father to aforesaid RAWLEIGH DOWNMAN and bounded according to a Survey thereof made by JOHN BARKER Beginning at two red Oaks and a white Oak Saplins in a line of RAWLEIGH CHINN Gent. deced running along the said line So. 10 d. West 104 1/2 po: two red oak saplins & thence S. 51 d. E. 300 po: to a large white Oak on the line of GEORGE HEALE formerly CHARLES CHINN thence No. 60 1/2 d. E. 104 1/2 po: to two red Oak saplins in line of CHRISTOPHER CHINN deced, thence N. 51 d. W. 382 po: to beginning containing 200 acres Together with all houses Orchards and appurtenances to said land belonging To have and to hold said Two hundred acres of land with appurtenances unto CHARLES CHINN his heirs and assigns forever In Witness whereof said RAWLEIGH DOWNMAN and ELIZABETH his Wife have hereunto set their hands and seals the day month and year first above written
in the presence of RAWLEIGH CHINN,   RAWLEIGH DOWNMAN
        CHAS. CHINN JUNR., ELIJAH CHINN,   ELIZABETH DOWNMAN
        WILLIAM MIRKILL, CHARLES McCARTY
  September 16th 1772. Received of CHARLES CHINN the sum of Forty pounds current money being in full the consideration money mentioned in the within Deed
Witness RAWLEIGH CHINN, CHARLES CHINN JUNR.,   RAWLEIGH DOWNMAN
        ELIJAH CHINN, WILLIAM MURKILL,
        CHARLES McCARTY
  (Commission directed to JOHN SMITH, CHARLES McCARTY and WILLIAM MIRKEL Gentlemen for privy Examination of ELIZABETH, Wife of RAWLEIGH DOWNMAN, dated sixteenth day of Septr. 1772. Return of the execution thereof dated 16th day of September 1772 and signed by WILLIAM MIRKELL and CHARLES McCARTY.)
  At a Court held for Loudoun County September the 28th 1772
This Indenture and the Receipt thereon endorsed were proved by the Oath of RAW-LEIGH CHINN, CHARLES CHINN JUNR., and ELIJAH CHINN, three of the subscribing witnesses thereto, together with a Commission for the Privy Examination of the Feme with the Execution thereof annexed is ordered to be recorded
(On margin: Deliv'd p Order Augt. 25th 1781)

pp.   KNOW ALL MEN by these presents that I SUSANNA LANCE of Loudoun County,
75-   Widow, do hereby appoint my Loving Friend PHILLIP MORGERT to be my true
76   and lawful Attorney for me and in my name to ask demand sue for recover and
    receive of any person that is indebted to me by Bond Bill or otherwise with full and lawfull power to my said Attorney to give lawful discharges in as effectual manner as if I myself were personally present could do hereby ratifying and confirming all

and every thing my said Attorney shall do or cause to be done in the premises In Witness whereof I have hereunto set my hand and seal the twenty eighth day of September one thousand seven hundred and seventy two

in presence of JNO. his mark *ℓ* SIGLER, SUSANNA her mark *ɓ* LANCE
    (other witness name in German PHILIP ( ))
  At a Court held for Loudoun County September 28th 1772
This Power of Attorney was acknowledged by SUSANNA LANCE party thereto to be her act and deed and is ordered to be recorded

pp. THIS INDENTURE made the Fifteenth day of September in year of our Lord One
76- thousand seven hundred and seventy two Between MICHAEL KORTZ and SARAH
79 his Wife of County of Loudoun of one part and JOSIAH MOFFET of same County of
    other part Witnesseth that in consideration of sum of Eighty pounds current money of Virginia in hand paid MICHAEL KORTZ and SARAH his Wife by these presents doth bargain and sell unto JOSIAH MOFFETT and to his heirs and assigns a certain lot or half acre of land lying in TOWN of LEESBURG in County of Loudoun bounded on the North on MARKET STREET, on the East by a Lot or half acre of land belonging to Mr. JOHN HERYFORD, on the West by a lot or half acre of land belonging to Mr. JOHN BARTHOLOMEW RIGER and now in his possession, the said first mentioned lot being conveyed to MICHAEL KORTZ by THOMAS PRITCHARD and his Wife as will more fully appear by Deeds recorded in County Court of Loudoun and all Houses, Orchards and appurtenances whatsoever belonging To have and to hold the lands hereby conveyed unto JOSIAH MOFFET his heirs and assigns forever In Witness whereof said MICHAEL KORTZ and SARAH his Wife have hereunto set their hands and seals the day and year first above written

in the presence of WILLIAM DOUGLASS,   MICHAEL KORTZ
    JOHN THORNTON, CHARLES DAVIS,   SARAH KORTZ
    HENRY HARRIS
  At a Court continued and held for Loudoun County Sepr. 29th 1772
This Indenture was acknowledged by MICHAEL KORTZ and SARAH his Wife, parties thereto, to be their acts and deeds (the said SARAH KORTZ having been first privately examined as the Law directs and relinquished her Dower therein) and the Receipt and Memorandum of Livery and Seizin thereon endorsed was likewise acknowledged by said MICHAEL & together with the said Indenture is ordered to be recorded

pp. THIS INDENTURE made the twenty ninth day of September in year of our Lord
79- One thousand seven hundred and seventy two Between FRANCIS SCHOOLING of
81 County of Loudoun of one part and WILLIAM WILLIAMS of same County of other
    part Witnesseth that FRANCIS SCHOOLING for sum of Five shillings Sterling to him in hand paid by these presents doth bargain and sell all that tract of land lying in County of Loudoun between the SHORT HILL and BLUE RIDGE on the head Drains of PINEY RUN and bounded Beginning at a black Oak by a Swampy Marsh corner to HOWARD HAVEN extending thence So. 57 d. 30' W. one hundred and twenty four poles to a red Oak saplin, thence N. 22 d. W. one hundred and fifty four poles to three white Oaks in a Fork of a small branch (mark'd CC 1745) thence N. 56 E. one hundred and twenty poles to a Chesnut by a Swamp or Drain Corner to said HAVEN, thence with his line S. 23 E. one hundred and fifty eight poles to the first station containing One hundred acres being part of a tract of land containing 1726 acres granted to CATESBY COCKE Gent. by a Patent from the Proprietors Office and by said COCKE transferred to JOSH. GORE by his Attorney in Fact, ENEAS CAMPBELL, and said GORE transferred to ANDREW & ADAM HATFIELD and from said HATFIELDs to FRANCIS SCHOOLING, Together with all Houses Or-

chards and appurtenances whatsoever belonging To have and to hold for one year
paying therefore the rents of one Pepper Corn on Feast of St. Michael to intent that by
virtue hereof and of statute for transferring uses into possession said WM. WILLIAMS
may be in actual possession and enabled to accept a Grant of Inheritance thereof In
Witness whereof said FRANCIS SCHOOLING have hereunto set their hand and seal the
day and year first above written

in presence of   FRANCIS SCHOOLING
     At a Court continued and held for Loudoun County Sept. 30th 1772
This Indenture was acknowledged by FRANCIS SCHOOLING party thereto to be his act
and deed and is ordered to be recorded

pp.   THIS INDENTURE made the thirtieth day of September in year of our Lord one
81-   thousand seven hundred and seventy two Between FRANCIS SCHOOLING of Lou-
84   doun and ELIZABETH his Wife and WILLIAM WILLIAMS of said County of other
        part Whereas there is a certain tract of land lying in County of Loudoun Be-
tween the SHORT HILL and BLUE RIDGE on the head of PINEY RUN and bounded ..
(description of land and owners as in Lease above) .. Now this Indenture Witnesseth
that FRANCIS SCHOOLING and ELIZABETH his Wife for sum of Eighty eight pounds current money of Virginia to them in hand paid by these presents doth bargain and sell
unto WILLIAM WILLIAMS (in his actual possession now being by virtue of one Indenture of Bargain and Sale for one year and statute for transferring uses into possession)
and his heirs and assigns all the said one hundred acres of land To have and to Hold
unto said WILLIAM WILLIAMS his heirs and assigns In Witness whereof the said FRAN-
CIS SCHOOLING and ELIZABETH his Wife have hereunto set their hands and affixt their
seals the day and year first above written

in presence of   FRANCIS SCHOOLING
                                                      ELIZABETH her mark   SCHOOLING
     At a Court continued and held for Loudoun County Sept. 30th 1772
This Indenture was acknowledged by FRANCIS SCHOOLING and ELIZABETH his Wife parties thereto to be their acts and deeds (the said ELIZABETH having been first privately
examined as the Law directs and relinquished her Dower therein) and the Receipt
thereon endorsed was likewise acknowledged by the said FRANCIS and together with
said Indenture is ordered to be recorded

pp.   KNOW ALL MEN by these presents that I DAVID BLAIR, Merchant, of TOWN of
84-   FREDERICKSBURG in County of SPOTSYLVANIA, Attorney in Fact for JAMES
85   BAIRD and Company, Merchants in Glasgow, do on account of said Company
        forever discharge and release THOMAS LEWIS and JOHN TYLER, Administrators
of CHARLES TYLER deceased, and the Reverend SPENCE GRAYSON of and from all Debts
Demands duties of what kind or nature soever heretofore due from them to said BAIRD
and Company as well in their own rights as Securitys of BENJA. GRAYSON Deced or in
any right whatsoever together with all costs and Interest which have accrued on any
Judgment whatsoever and further covenant that I DAVID BLAIR at time of Executing
this Release have good power and lawfull authority from said BAIRD and Company to
sign and execute this Release as their Attorney in Fact which Release I hereby warrant
and forever defend against all persons whatsoever
Witness WILLIAM GRAYSON   DAVID BLAIR
                                                      DUMFRIES 7th September 1772
     At a Court continued and held for Loudoun County Sept. 30th 1772
This Release was proved by the Oath of WILLIAM GRAYSON Gent., a witness thereto, and
is ordered to be recorded

pp.   THIS INDENTURE made the Twenty ninth day of Sept. in year of our Lord One
85-   thousand seven hundred and seventy two Between AENEAS CAMPBELL of Pro-
87   vince of MARYLAND of one part and ALEXANDER McINTYRE of Loudoun County,
       Taylor, of other part Witnesseth that said AENEAS CAMPBELL for sum of Five
shilling current money of Virginia to him in hand paid by these presents doth bargain
and sell unto ALEXANDER McINTYRE a certain tract of land lying in Loudoun County
beginning at a white Oak by the Old MAIN ROAD on the East side of LEESBURGH TOWN
corner to LANDON CARTER and MARY FOSTER extending thence with the line of MARY
FOSTERs PATENT South seven West two hundred and forty eight poles to a white Oak, her
Corner and Corner to CATESBY COCKE then with his line South twenty West two hundred and ten poles to a large white Oak thence South fifty three East fifteen poles to a
small white Oak Corner to JOHN HAGUE, then with his line East ninety poles to said CAR-
TERs given line, then with the said Line North thirty minutes East four hundred and
fifty seven poles to the beginning containing in the whole one hundred and seven
acres And all houses Orchards and appurtenances whatseover belonging To have and to
hold the land hereby conveyed for the full term of one whole year paying therefore
the rent of one Pepper Corn on Lady Day next to the intent that said ALEXANDER
McINTYRE may be in actual possession and thereby enabled to accept a Release of inheritance thereof. In Witness whereof said AENEAS CAMPBELL hath hereunto set his
hand and seal the day and year first above written
in presence of JNO. COOPER,   AENEAS CAMPBELL
    At a Court continued and held for Loudoun County Sept. 30th 1772
This Indenture was acknowledged by AENEAS CAMPBELL party thereto to be his act and
deed and is ordered to be recorded
(On margin: Examined and deliver'd ALEXANDER McINTYRE April 26th 1773)

pp.   THIS INDENTURE made the Thirtieth day of September in year of our Lord One
87-   thousand seven hundred and seventy two Between AENEAS CAMPBELL of Pro-
90   vince of MARYLAND of one part and ALEXANDER McINTYRE of Loudoun County
       of other part Witnesseth that for sum of One hundred and fifty pounds current
money of Virginia to said AENEAS CAMPBELL in hand paid by these presents doth bargain and sell unto ALEXANDER McINTYRE (in his actual possession now being by virtue
of a bargain and sale and force of statute for transferring uses into possession) and his
heirs a certain tract of land lying in Loudoun County .. (description of land as in Lease
above) .. To have and to hold the lands hereby conveyed unto ALEXANDER McINTYRE his
heirs and assigns forever In Witness whereof said AENEAS CAMPBELL hath hereunto
set his hand and seal the day and year first above written. The Intent of above
warranty is that if ALEXANDER McINTYRE should by any Older Survey or by any ways
whatever lose any part of land hereby sold that said AENEAS CAMPBELL is to pay him at
rate of one pound Eight shillings (and if paid in Dollars at Six shillings each) per acre
in presence of JNO. COOPER   AENS. CAMPBELL
    At a Court continued and held for Loudoun County September 30th 1772
This Indenture and Receipt thereon endorsed was acknowledged by AENEAS CAMPBELL
party thereto to be his act and deed and is ordered to be recorded
(On margin: Exam'd & deld to ALEXR. McINTYRE April 26 1773)

pp.   THIS INDENTURE made the first day of April in year of our Lord one thousand
90-   seven hundred and seventy two Between HARDAGE LANE of Cameron Parish and
92   County of Loudoun of one part and WILLIAM LANE of same County and Parish of
       other part Witnesseth that HARDAGE LANE for sum of One hundred pounds to me
in hand paid by these presents doth bargain and sell unto WILLIAM LANE his heirs or

assigns forever a certain tract of land containing one hundred acres lying in County of
Loudoun and adjoining the land of BARBARA BERKLEY beginning at a red Oak thence N.
12 1/2 d. W. to a red Oak Corner marked thence East 150 poles thence South to where it
shall intersect the line of DEMSEY CARROLL, thence with the said CARROLLs line the
several Courses to the aforesaid Beginning containing one hundred acres be the same
more or less being the Lot whereon MARY PORTER now lives And all Houses Orchards
and appurtenances whatseover belonging To have and to hold said one hundred acres
of land unto said WILLIAM LANE In Witness whereof the said parties have hereunto set
their hands and seals the day and year above written
in presence of   HAR: LANE
  Recd. of WILLIAM LANE this first day of April 1772 one hundred pounds in full for the
within consideration   HAR: LANE
  At a Court continued and held for Loudoun County October the 1st 1772
This Indenture, Receipt and Memorandum were acknowledged by HARDAGE LANE party
thereto and is ordered to be recorded

pp.   THIS INDENTURE made this 24th day of April Seventeen hundred and seventy
92-   two Between JOSEPH GOING of Loudoun County, Labourer, of one part and
93   SAMUEL CANBY of same place, Merchant, of other part Witnesseth that said
         JOSEPH GOING for better securing the payment of thirty one pounds six shil-
lings and six pence at this time due and owing to said SAMUEL CANBY with lawful Interest till paid and for such farther sums of money as said JOSEPH GOING shall owe said
SAMUEL CANBY during the time of his Service, hath of his own free will and accord and
by these presents doth freely and voluntarily bind himself a Servant to said SAMUEL
CANBY his assigns and will faithfully serve in whatsoever work and employ said SAML.
CANBY shall direct at and after the rate of Fourteen pounds a year until the aforesaid
Debt and Interest shall be fully paid In Witness whereof said JOSEPH GOING hath here-
unto set his hand and seal the day and year aforesaid
in presence of MORGAN JONES.   JOSEPH his mark ✝ GOING
         GEORGE AUBERY
  At a Court continued and held for Loudoun County October 2d 1772
This Indenture was proved by the Oath of GEORGE AWBREY, a witness thereto, to be the
act and deed of JOSEPH GOING and is ordered to be recorded
(On margin: Examined & deliv'd to SAML. CANBY Feby 16th 1776)

pp.   THIS INDENTURE made the twentieth day of September in year of our Lord One
93-   thousand seven hundred and seventy two Between WILLIAM ALLEN of AMWELL
96   in County of HUNTERDON and SARAH his Wife of one part and NATHAN BEAKES of
         TRENTON in County and Province aforesaid of other part Witnesseth that WIL-
LIAM ALLEN for sum of three hundred and thirty two pounds twelve and eight pence
PROCLAMATION MONEY to said WILLIAM ALLEN by said NATHAN BEAKES to him in hand
paid doth by these presents bargain and sell unto said NATHAN BEAKES and his heirs
and assigns forever all that certain tract of land containing nine hundred acres situate
in County of Loudoun and bounded Beginning at two marked black Oaks and a white Oak
in the line of said Patent being a Corner of lands sold RICHARD KEEN and extending
thence So. 68 d. East 265 poles to a marked red Oak Corner of said Patent then So. 22 W.
545 poles to a Hickory another Corner of said Patent then No. 68 W. 265 poles to a marked
Chesnut and two black Oaks, then No. 22 d. 545 poles to beginning, Together with all
houses orchards and advantages whatsoever belonging To have and to hold the land
aforesaid PROVIDED Always that if WILLIAM ALLEN his heirs shall pay or cause to be
paid unto NATHAN BEAKES the sum aforesaid on or before the twentieth day of Septem-

ber next ensuing with lawful interest that then this present Indenture shall cease and be void In Witness whereof said WILLIAM ALLEN hath set his hand and seal the date hereof is the day and year above written
in the presence of us STACY POTTS,   WILLIAM ALLEN
            ISAAC ALLEN

I do hereby acknowledge that the sum of Three hundred and nine pounds part of the money contained in this Mortgage is included in a Mortgage given by said WILLIAM ALLEN to me upon lands in HUNTERDON COUNTY in NEW JERSEY
                                                NATHAN BEAKES

At a Court held for Loudoun County October the 26th 1772
This Indenture was acknowledged by WILLIAM ALLEN party thereto to be his act and deed and is ordered to be recorded
(On margin: Exd. & delivered to Mr. WM. ALLEN)

pp.   THIS INDENTURE made the 25th day of October in year of our Lord one thousand
96-   seven hundred and seventy two Between JOHN MARKS of County of Loudoun and
98   URIAH his Wife of one part and ELISHA MARKS of same County of other part
         Witnesseth that JOHN MARKS and URIAH his Wife for sum of five shillings to
them in hand paid by these presents doth bargain and sell unto ELISHA MARKS all that
tract of land lying in County of Loudoun on South Fork of KITTOCTON CREEK and
bounded beginning at a white Oak and Spanish Oak in a line of EPHRAIM THOMAS's lott
now in possession of JONOTHAN REED and with a lott called the DRY LOTT extending
thence So. 2 d. West one hundred and twenty poles to two small black Oaks corner to
AMOS GOODIN then with his line East two hundred poles to a small black Oak corner to
said GOODIN thence No. 2 d. East one hundred and twenty poles to a white Oak and black
Oak corner to land of EDWARD SNIGERS bought of MAHLON JENNY then with a line of
that Tract West two hundred poles to the first containing one hundred and fifty acres of
Land And all Houses orchards and advantages whatsoever to said parcel belonging To
have and to hold during full term of one whole year paying therefor one pepper Corn
upon the Feast of Saint Michael the Arch Agnel to intent that by these presents and
statute for transferring uses into possession said ELISHA MARKS may be in actual possession and thereby enable to accept a Release of Inheritance thereof In Witness
whereof said JOHN MARKS and URIAH his Wife hath hereunto set their hands and seals
the day and year first above written
in presence of   JOHN MARKS
                                                URIAHA her mark U MARKS
At a Court held for Loudoun County October the 26th 1772
This Indenture was acknowledged by JOHN MARKS and URIA his Wife parties thereto to
be their acts and deeds (the said URIA having been first privately examined as the Law
directs) and is ordered to be recorded

pp.   THIS INDENTURE made this 26th day of October in year of our Lord One thousand
98-   seven hundred and seventy two Between JOHN MARKS of County of Loudoun and
101   URIAH his Wife of one part and ELISHA MARKS of same County of other part
         Whereas there is a certain tract of land lying in County of Loudoun on South
Fork of KITTOCTON CREEK being part of a Tract of land bought of EPHRAIM THOMAS of
County of BUCKS and Province of PENNSYLVANIA of MAHLON JENNY of the County of
Loudoun and by EPHRAIM THOMAS transferred to aforesaid JOHN MARKS as by his Deed
will fully appear .. (description of land as in Lease above) .. NOW THIS INDENTURE WIT-
NESSETH that JOHN MARKS for sum of Ten pounds Virginia money to him in hand paid
by these presents doth bargain and sell unto ELISHA MARKS (in his actual possession

by virtue of one Indenture of bargain and sale and by virtue of statute for transferring uses into possession) and his heirs and assigns forever the said One hundred and
fifty acres of land being as is above set forth In Witness whereof said JOHN MARKS and
URIAH his Wife hath hereunto set their hands and seals the day and year first above
written

in the presence of us   JOHN MARKS
                                                   URIAHA her mark W MARKS

At a Court held for Loudoun County October the 26th 1772
This Indenture was acknowledged by JOHN MARKS and URIAHA his Wife parties thereto
to be their acts and deed (the said URIAHA having been first privately examined as the
Law directs and relinquished her Dower therein) and the Receipt thereon endorsed was
likewise acknowledged by said JOHN & Together with the said Indenture is ordered to be
recorded
(On margin: Examined and delivered to Mr. MARKS Sept. 14, 1778)

pp.   THIS INDENTURE made the twenty second day of November in year of our Lord
102-   One thousand seven hundred and seventy two Between JOSHUA JONES of County
103   of Loudoun, Tanner, of one part and DAVID BEATY and JOHN ELLIOTT of same
           County, Farmers, of other part, Witnesseth that said JOSHUA JONES for sum of
Five shillings current money of Virginia to him in hand paid by these presents doth
bargain and sell unto DAVID BEATY and JOHN ELLIOTT a certain parcel of land lying in
County of Loudoun being part of a larger tract of land conveyed by JOHN TODHUNTER to
WILLIAM JONES by Deeds of Lease and Release and by said WILLIAM JONES given and
bequeathed to said JOSHUA JONES by his Last Will and Testament duly proved and recorded among the records of Loudoun County bounded beginning at a Stake near two
large marked white Oaks corner to DEHAVEN extending then with his line No. 54 East
eighty one poles to a Maple in the head of a Glade in line of JOSIAS CLAPHAM thence
with his line So. 65 East twenty two poles to an old black Oak Stump, Corner to said
CLAPHAM, thence with another of his lines No. 24 East one hundred and eleven poles to
a white Oak his corner thence with another of his lines So. 69 East two hundred and
forty five poles to a white Oak lying down a Gum and an Ash in a Swamp corner to JOHN
SINCLAIR, thence with his line So. 73 West sixty six poles to a red Oak another of said
SINCLAIRs Corners, thence with another of his lines So. 5 East one hundred and fifty six
poles to a white Oak lying down in a poison field, thence with another of his lines So. 4
West fifty one poles to a Stake two poles from a red Oak, Corner to DOUGLASS, the Stake is
Corner to TODHUNTER, thence with his line to the beginning containing three hundred
and twenty four acres and all houses orchards and appurtenances whatsoever
belonging To have and to hold the full term of one whole year paying therefore the
rent of One Pepper Corn on Lady Day next to intent that by Virtue of these presents and
statute for transferring uses into possession said DAVID BEATY and JOHN ELLIOTT may
be in actual possession and thereby enabled to accept a Release of Inheritance thereof
In Witness whereof said JOSHUA JONES have hereunto set his hand and seal the day and
year first above written
in presence of   JOSHUA JONES
At a Court continued and held for Loudoun County November the 24th 1772
This Indenture was acknowledged by JOSHUA JONES party thereto to be his act and deed
and is ordered to be recorded

pp.   THIS INDENTURE made the Twenty third day of November in year of our Lord
103-   One thousand seven hundred and seventy two Between JOSHUA JONES and
106   HANNAH his Wife of County of Loudoun of one part and DAVID BEATY and JOHN

ELLIOTT of the same County, Farmers, of other part Witnesseth that for sum of Three
hundred pounds PENNSYLVANIA Currency to said JOSHUA JONES in hand paid by these
presents doth bargain and sell unto DAVID BEATY and JOHN ELLIOTT (in their actual
possession now being by virtue of a bargain and sale for one year and the statute for
transferring uses into possession) and their heirs a certain tract of land lying in
County of Loudoun .. (description of conveyances and land as in Lease above) .. containing three hundred and twenty four acres To have and to hold the lands hereby conveyed unto DAVID BEATY and JOHN ELLIOTT their heirs and assigns forever In Witness
whereof said JOSHUA JONES and HANNAH his Wife hath hereunto set their hands and
seals the day and year first above written
in the presence of   JOSHUA JONES
                                                      HANNAH JONES
   At a Court continued and held for Loudoun County November the 24th 1772
This Indenture was acknowledged by JOSHUA JONES and HANNAH his Wife parties
thereto to be their acts and deeds (the said HANNAH having been first privately examined as the Law directs and relinquished her Dower therein) and the Receipt under
written was likewise acknowledged by said JOSHUA and together with the said Indenture is ordered to be recorded

pp.   THIS INDENTURE made the 23d day of Novr. in year of our Lord one thousand
106-   seven hundred and seventy two and in the Twelfth year of the Reign of our
109   Sovereign Lord GEORGE the Third &c. Between NICHOLAS MINOR of Loudoun
         County, Gent., of one part and PHILIP NOLAND SENR. of Shelburne Parish in
County aforesaid Gent. of other part, Witnesseth that NICHOLAS MINOR for sum of Forty
five shillings current money of Virginia to him in hand paid by these presents doth
bargain and sell unto PHILIP NOLAND his heirs and assigns forever all that lott or half
acre of land and premises No. (blank) binding on ALEXR. McINTYRE's lot situate in
LEESBURG in County of Loudoun To have and to hold said lott or half acre of land unto
PHILIP NOLAND his heirs and assigns forever In Witness whereof said NICHOLAS MINOR
hath hereunto set his hand and affixed his seal the day month and year above written
in the presence of ROBT. JAMISON,   NICH: MINOR
        JOHN PETER FRYREAR, ABNER HOWELL
   At a Court continued and held for Loudoun County November 24th 1772
This Indenture Receipt and Memorandum thereon endorsed was proved by the Oaths of
ROBERT JAMISON, JOHN PETER FRYREAR and ABNER HOWELL the subscribing witnesses
thereto to be the act and deed of NICHOLAS MINOR Gent. party thereto and is ordered to
be recorded

pp.   THIS INDENTURE made the Eleventh day of November in year of our Lord One
109-   thousand seven hundred and seventy two Between JOHN GRAHAM of County of
111   PRINCE WILLIAM Gent. of one part and LEVEN POWELL of County of Loudoun
         Gent. of other part Witnesseth that JOHN GRAHAM for sum of five shillings cur-
rent money of Virginia to him in hand paid by these presents doth bargain and sell
unto LEVEN POWELL a certain tract of land situate in County of Loudoun on GOOSE CREEK
and bounded Beginning at a Poplar on the said Creek in the line of WILLIAM FAIRFAX
Esqr. and running thence So. 12 Et. three hundred and twenty poles to a red Oak corner
of said FAIRFAX, then South one hundred and sixteen poles to a red Oak in or near the
line of EDWD. HUGHS then So. 73 d. Wt. one hundred and ninety six poles to two red Oak
saplins then So. 50 d. Wt. two hundred and sixty eight poles to a white Oak in CHINNs
line then with his line No. 12 d. Wt. two hundred and fifty eight poles to a Hickory at the
mouth of a branch running into GOOSE CREEK then down the said Creek the several me-

anders thereof reduced to a straight line is No. 66 d. East four hundred and sixty six poles to the Beginning containing one thousand one hundred and seventy five acres except such part thereof as is within bounds of the sale made by said JOHN GRAHAM to DUNCAN GRAHAM and except such part as shall happen to be within the bounds of any elder Patent, the said land in this Deed described was granted to one JOHN GRANT and the said JOHN GRAHAM and by Survivorship has vested in JOHN GRAHAM as by the Patent from the Proprietors Office dated the 23d day of May 1741 may appear, And all Houses Orchards and appurtenances whatsoever belonging To have and to hold for full term of one whole year paying therefore the rent of one pepper Corn on Lady Day next to intent that by virtue of these presents and statute for transferring uses into possession LEVEN POWELL may be in actual possession and thereby enabled to accept a Release of Inheritance thereof In Witness whereof said JOHN GRAHAM hath hereunto set his hand and seal the day and year first above written
in presence of W. ELLZEY,   JOHN GRAHAM
          THOMAS CHINN, EVAN WILLIAMS,
          THOS. LAWSON
     At a Court held for Loudoun County November the 23d 1772
This Indenture was proved to be the act and deed of JOHN GRAHAM Gent. party thereto by the Oaths of EVAN WILLIAMS and THOMAS CHINN two of the Subscribing Witnesses thereto and on the 25th day of the same Month the said Indenture was fully proved by the Oaths of WILLIAM ELLZEY Gent., another of the subscribing witnesses thereto, and is ordered to be recorded

pp.   THIS INDENTURE made the twelfth day of November in year of our Lord One
111-   thousand seven hundred and seventy two Between JOHN GRAHAM of County of
114   PRINCE WILLIAM Gent. of one part and LEVEN POWELL of County of Loudoun
          Gent. of other part Witnesseth that for sum of Thirty pounds current money of
Virginia to JOHN GRAHAM in hand paid by these presents doth bargain and sell unto
LEVEN POWELL (in his actual possession by virtue of a bargain and sale for one year
and by virtue of statute for transferring uses into possession) and his heirs a certain
tract of land lying in County of Loudoun on GOOSE CREEK .. (description of land, limi-
ting terms and Patent as in Lease above) .. In Witness whereof said JOHN GRAHAM hath
hereunto set his hand and seal the day and year first above written
in presence of W. ELLZEY,   JOHN GRAHAM
          THOMAS CHINN, EVAN WILLIAMS,
          THOS. LAWSON
     At a Court held for Loudoun County November the 23d 1772
This Indenture and the Receipt under written was proved to be the act and deed of JOHN
GRAHAM Gent. party thereto by Oaths of EVAN WILLIAMS and THOMAS CHINN, two of
the subscribing witnesses thereto, and on the 25th day of the same month the said Indenture and receipt was fully proved by the Oath of WILLIAM ELLZEY Gent. another of
the subscribing witnesses thereto and is ordered to be recorded

pp.   THIS INDENTURE made the Twenty fourth day of November in year of our Lord
114-   One thousand seven hundred and seventy two Between FARLING BALL of County
115   of Loudoun and MARY his Wife of one part and THOMAS MIFFLIN of the City of
          PHILADELPHIA, Merchant, of other part Witnesseth that FARLING BALL and
MARY his Wife for sum of five shillings current money to them in hand paid by these
presents doth bargain and sell unto THOMAS MIFFLIN all that tract of land lying in
County of Loudoun being a Tract the said FARLIN BALL purchased of GEORGE GREGG
containing three hundred and three acres bounded by the lines of MATTHEW HICKSON,

RICHARD ROACH, ABRAHAM DAWSON, WILLIAM GREGG, JOHN HANBY and EDMUND SANDS and according to Courses and Expressions in Deeds of Conveyance from GEORGE GREGG to FARLING BALL which Deeds are recorded in Loudoun County Court, also another small parcel of land lying contigious and adjoining to the above described land which said FARLIN BALL purchased of ABRAHAM DAWSON containing three acres as by the Deeds of Conveyance will more fully appear, the whole being part of a larger tract formerly granted to CATESBY COCKE Esqr. by a Pattent from the Proprietors Office and by said COCKE transferred to above named GEORGE GREGG and all houses orchards and appurtenances whatsoever belonging To have and to hold for full term of one whole year paying therefore the rent of one Pepper Corn on Lady Day next to intent that by virtue of these presents and statute for transferring uses into possession THOMAS MIFFLIN may be in actual possession and thereby enabled to accept a Release of Inheritance thereof In Witness whereof FARLING BALL and MARY his Wife have hereunto set their hands and seals the day and year first above written

in presence of H. NEILSON,   FARLING BALL
      JOHN GUNNELL, WM. JOHNSTON   MARY BALL

At a Court continued and held for Loudoun County November the 25th 1772 This Indenture was acknowledged by FARLING BALL and MARY his Wife parties thereto to be their acts and deed (the said MARY having been first privately examined as the Law directs) And is ordered to be recorded

pp. THIS INDENTURE made the Twenty fifth day of November in year of our Lord One
115- thousand seven hundred and seventy two Between FARLING BALL of County of
118 Loudoun and MARY his Wife of one part and THOMAS MIFFLIN of City of PHILA-
DELPHIA, Merchant, of other part Witnesseth that for sum of Eight hundred and twenty two pounds current money of PENNSYLVANIA to the said FARLING BALL and MARY his Wife in hand paid by these presents doth bargain and sell unto THOMAS MIFFLIN (in his actual possession by virtue of a bargain and sale for one whole year and by force of statute for transferring uses into possession) all that tract of land lying in County of Loudoun on a small branch of KITTOCTON CREEK .. (purchases and bounds of neighbors as in Lease above) .. To have and to hold the lands hereby conveyed unto said THOMAS MIFFLIN his heirs and assigns forever. In Witness whereof said FARLING BALL and MARY his Wife hath hereunto set their hands and seals the day and year first above written

in the presence of H. NEILSON,   FARLING BALL
      JOHN GUNNELL, WM. JOHNSTON   MARY BALL

At a Court continued and held for Loudoun County November the 25th 1772 This Indenture was acknowledged by FARLING BALL and MARY his Wife parties thereto to be their acts and deed (the said MARY having first been privately examined as the Law directs and relinquished her Dower therein) and the Receipt thereon endorsed was likewise acknowledged by said FARLING and together with said Indenture is ordered to be recorded

pp. THIS INDENTURE made this third day of November in year of our Lord One thou-
118- sand seven hundred and seventy two and in the Thirteenth year of the Reign of
120 our Sovereign Lord GEORGE the Third &c., Between THOMAS BEST of County of
Loudoun of one part and JAMES BEST of aforesaid County of other part Witnesseth that THOMAS BEST have granted demised and to farm let unto JAMES BEST all that tract of land lying in County of Loudoun on the West side of KITTOCTON MOUNTAIN the same being part of two tracts of land granted unto WILLIAM HENRY FAIRFAX by Pattent from the Proprietor of Northern Neck of Virginia said land being bounded beginning

at a black Oak in a line of the land of Col: JOHN COLVILL Corner to JOSEPH JANNEYs, Extending thence with sd COLVILLs line So. 51 W. 140 poles to a white Oak, thence So. 62, E. 32 poles to a white Oak thence S. 36 E. 16 poles to a white Oak, thence So. 55 E. 40 poles to a red Oak saplin, thence So. 10 E. 115 poles to a red Oak sap;lin in a line of JOHN CAVENS land thence with said CAVINS line No. 85 E. 62 poles to a White Oak thence So. 70 E. 33 poles to a red Oak, thence S. 22 E. 6 poles to a black Oak thence N. 1 W. 170 poles to a Hickory Corner to JOSEPH JANNEY thence with his line West 76 poles to a stake on a hill his Corner, thence with another of his lines N. 20 Wt. 198 poles to the place of beginning containing one hundred and seventy two acres be the same more or less And all Houses Orchards and appurtenances whatsoever belonging To have and to hold the said One hundred and seventy two acres of land unto the full end of one whole year paying therefore one Ear of Indian Corn to said THOMAS BEST on last day of sd Term to the intent that by virtue of these presents and by force of statute for transferring uses into possession said JAMES BEST may be in actual possession of said tract of land and thereby enabled to accept a Release of Inheritance thereof In Witness whereof said THOMAS BEST hath hereunto set his hand and affixed his seal the day month and year first above written

in presence of JAMES RATEKIN,   THOMAS BEST
          BENJAMIN JAMESON, NATHAN LACOCK
   At a Court continued and held for Loudoun County November the 25th 1772
This Indenture was proved by the Oaths of JAMES RATEKIN, BENJAMIN JAMESON and NATHAN LACOCK the subscribing witnesses thereto to be the act and deed of THOMAS BEST party thereto and is ordered to be recorded

pp.   THIS INDENTURE made this third day of November in the year of our Lord One
120-   thousand seven hundred and seventy two and in the Twelfth year of the Reign
123   of our Sovereign Lord GEORGE the Third &c. Between THOMAS BEST of the County
         of Loudoun of one part and JAMES BEST of County of Loudoun of other part Witnesseth that said THOMAS BEST in consideration of sum of One hundred and twenty pounds current money in hand paid by these presents doth bargain and sell unto JAMES BEST (in his actual possession now being by virtue of a bargain and sale for one year and by force of statute for transferring uses into possession) and his heirs forever all that tract of land lying in County of Loudoun on West side of KITTOCTON MOUNTAIN .. (description of land and Pattents as in Lease above) .. To have and to hold said one hundred and seventy two acres of land and all the premises hereby granted unto said JAMES BEST his heirs and assigns forever. In Witness whereof said THOMAS BEST hath hereunto set his hand and affixed his seal the day month & year above written
in presence of JAMES RATEKIN,   THOMAS BEST
          BENJAMIN JAMESON, NATHAN LACOCK
   At a Court continued and held for Loudoun County Novr. 25th 1772
This Indenture and receipt thereon endorsed was proved by Oaths of RATEKIN, BENJAMIN JAMESON and NATHAN LACOCK the subscribing witnesses thereto to be the act and deed of THOMAS BEST party thereto and is ordered to be recorded
(On margin: Exd. & deld. JAS. BEST Oct 1773)

pp.   THIS INDENTURE made the first day of October in year of our Lord One thousand
123-   seven hundred and seventy two Between JAMES ROSS of County of Loudoun of
124   one part and JOHN MASON of County aforesaid of other part Witnesseth that JOHN
         CARLYLE Gent. Attorney in Fact for GEORGE WILLIAM FAIRFAX Esqr. in and by one Indenture of Lease bearing date the first day of May in year of our Lord One thousand seven hundred and sixty one for consideration therein mentioned did grant and to

farm let one tract of land situate in County of Loudoun beginning at a Hickory by a
Path the N.E. Corner of JOSEPH YEATS Lot, and farther bounded as in the said recited
Indenture of Lease, And this Indenture farther witnesseth that said JAMES ROSS for
sum of one hundred pounds lawfull money of Virginia to him in hand paid by these
presents doth bargain and sell unto JOHN MASON his assigns all that Lot of Land as more
particularly set forth in the above recited Lease To have and to hold said lott of land
unto JOHN MASON his assigns paying the rents reserved and performing the Covenants
conditions and agreements in above recited Lease contained In Witness whereof said
JAMES ROSS hath hereunto set his hand and seal the day and year first above written
in presence of   JAMES his mark ✝ ROSS
   At a Court continued and held for Loudoun County November 25th 1772
This Indenture was acknowledged by JAMES ROSS party thereto to be his act and deed
and is ordered to be recorded

pp.   THIS INDENTURE made the XVIIth day of April in year of our Lord One thousand
124-   seven hundred and seventy two Between GIDNEY CLARK of ISLAND OF BARBA-
127   DOES Esqr. by his Attorney in Fact, The Honble GEORGE WM. FAIRFAX and BRYAN
         FAIRFAX both of County of FAIRFAX and Colony of Virginia Esqrs. of one part
and HENRY FARNSWORTH of County of Loudoun of other part Witnesseth that GIDNEY
CLARK in consideration of rents and covenants hereafter mentioned doth grant and to
farm lett unto HENRY FARNSWORTH a certain parcel of land lying in County of Loudoun
and bounded as by a Survey thereof made by JOHN HOUGH begining at a white Oak corner to BENJAMIN HISKETT Lott extending thence So. 45 d. Wt. ninety eight poles to one
of the Original Lines the South side of N.W. Fork, thence with said line So. 65 E. Two
hundred and twenty poles to a white Oak thence No. 2 d. Wt. one hundred and fifty pole
to a hickory saplin by a Branch corner to said HISKETT, then with his line So. 83 Wt. one
hundred and thirty four poles to beginning containing one hundred and forty two
acres of land excepting all mines minerals and Quarries whatsoever To have and to hold
the said One hundred and forty two acres of land with the appurtenances during the
natural lives of said HENRY FARNSWORTH, JOHN FARNSWORTH and GEORGE FARNSWORTH
his Sons and longest liver of them paying unto GIDNEY CLARK every year on first day
of April the rent of four pound four shillings and six pence current money of Virginia
and that he or they plant at least one hundred good Apple trees and fifty good Peach
trees and keep same well pruned and within good fence and also cause to be built a
Dwelling House at least twenty feet long and sixteen feet wide within three years and
such other houses as his way of Husbandry may require In Witness whereof said parties to these presents have interchangeably set their hands and seals the day and year
first above written
in the presence of HENRY VAN OVER,   G. W. FAIRFAX
         HEZEKIAH HOWELL, STACY JANNEY,   BRYAN FAIRFAX
         STEPHEN JONES, HAR: LANE,   HENRY FARNSWORTH
         CHARLES WEST, STEPHEN DONALDSON
   At a Court continued and held for Loudoun County November 24th 1772
This Indenture was acknowledged by HENRY FARNSWORTH on his part and proved by
the Oaths of CHARLES WEST and STEPHEN DONALDSON, two of the subscribing witnesses
thereto, and on the day next following the same was fully proved by the Oath of HAR-
DAGE LANE, another Subscribing witness on the part and behalf of GEORGE WILLIAM
FAIRFAX and BRYAN FAIRFAX Esquires, Attornies in Fact for GIDNEY CLARK Esquire and
is ordered to be recorded
(On margin: Examined DD to Mr. FARNSWORTH)

pp.   THIS INDENTURE made the Twelfth day of October in year of our Lord God One
127-   thousand seven hundred and seventy two Between THOMAS KELLY of Parish of
131   Cameron and County of Loudoun, Planter, and MARY his Wife of one part and
       JOHN ALEXANDER of Parish of Shelburne and County aforesaid of other part
WHEREAS the Right Honble. THOMAS LORD FAIRFAX by his Deed Poll bearing date the
Twentieth day of June in year One thousand seven hundred and forty one, had granted
unto MICHAEL REGAN then of County of PRINCE WILLIAM a certain tract of land situate
in said County (now Loudoun) and on upper side of GOOSE CREEK joining to land of
JACOB LASSWELL and further bounded according to a Survey and Platt thereof given
into the Office by Mr. JOHN WARNER Beginning at A a marked white Oak standing at
the head of a Glade and in the line of JACOB LASWELL extending thence North twenty
five degrees East five hundred and fifty eight poles along the line of JACOB LASSWELL
to B a marked Oak saplin, thence South sixty eight degrees West one hundred and thirty two poles to C a marked white Oak, thence Northwest one hundred and forty four
poles to D a red Oak thence West two hundred and fifteen poles to E a red Oak, thence
South twenty degrees thirty minutes East six hundred poles to beginning containing
seven hundred and seventeen acres, be the same more or less, which said MICHAEL
REGAN being so thereof seized did by Deed duly acknowledged and recorded among the
records of the County of FAIRFAX for the consideration therein mentioned, sell and
convey all his Estate right, title and demand whatsoever of in and to said tract of land
unto said THOMAS KELLY party to these presents and to his Heirs and assigns as by the
said several Deeds remaining in the respective offices may appear NOW THIS INDEN-
TURE WITNESSETH that said THOMAS KELLY for and in consideration of sum of three
hundred pounds current money of Virginia to him paid or secured to be paid by JOHN
ALEXANDER doth by these presents bargain and sell unto JOHN ALEXANDER all that the
abovementioned parcel of land bounded and described as aforesaid, lying in County of
Loudoun (formerly PRINCE WILLIAM and afterwards FAIRFAX Counties) Together with
all houses Orchards and appurtenances to same belonging To have and to hold said
seven hundred and seventeen acres of land unto JOHN ALEXANDER his heirs and assigns
forever In Witness whereof said THOMAS KELLY and MARY his Wife have hereunto set
their hands and affixed their seals the day and year first within written
in presence of WILLIAM COTTEN,   THO. KELLY
      GEORGE TAYLOR, FRANCIS PEPTERCOE,
      JOSEPH GARDNER
Memorandum: That on this twelfth day of October in year of our Lord One thousand
seven hundred and seventy two, THOMAS KELLY, the Feoffer entered into and upon the
lands and premises hereby conveyed and gave quiet and peaceable possession livery
and Seizen thereof by the Delivery Turf and Twig to JOHN ALEXANDER, the Feoffee, To
hold to him his heirs and assigns according to the purport true intent and meaning of
the within Deed in the presence of us (Four subscribing witnesses as above).
Received the 12th day of October 1772 of JOHN ALEXANDER the sum of three hundred
pounds current money being the consideration mentioned in within Deed to be paid by
him to me on the perfection thereof
      (Same subscribing witnesses)   THO. KELLY
  At a Court continued and held for Loudoun County November 26th 1772
This Indenture, Memorandum and Receipt thereon endorsed was proved by the Oaths of
WILLIAM COTTEN, GEORGE TAYLOR and FRANCIS PEPTERCOE, three of the subscribing
witnesses thereto, to be the acts and deeds of THOMAS KELLY party to these presents,
and is ordered to be recorded
(On margin: Exam'd & dd to Mr. Alexander May 3d 1773)

pp.   THIS INDENTURE made the twenty seventh day of November in year of our Lord
131-   One thousand seven hundred and seventy two Between the Honourable GEORGE
135   WILLIAM FAIRFAX Esquire of one part and NICHOLAS OTT of County of Loudoun,
        Farmer, of other part Witnesseth that GEORGE WILLIAM FAIRFAX in considera-
tion of the rents and covenants on part of NICHOLAS OTT to be paid and performed doth
by these presents grant set and to farm let unto NICHOLAS OTT one hundred acres of
land with the appurtenances (except all mines, minerals and Quarries whatsoever),
lying in Parish of Shelburne in County of Loudoun on Branches of the DUTCHMANS
RUN being part of a tract of land of Seventeen thousand two hundred and ninety six
acres called PIEDMONT the bounds beginning at a white Oak corner to CHRISTOPHER
FEARSNER extending thence So. 60 West one hundred and thirty six poles to a red Oak on
a Hill side Corner to GRIFFIN DOBBINS thence No. 20 West ninety poles to WILLIAM
DIGGES's line thence with his line N. 4 East fourty four poles thence No. 60 East one
hundred and twenty four poles to two small Hickorys thence So. 16 East one hundred
and twenty eight poles to the beginning containing one hundred acres To have and to
hold said land and premises (except before excepted) to said NICHOLAS OTT during the
lives of him NICHOLAS OTT, MARGARET OTT his Wife and ELIZABETH OTT his Daughter,
paying unto GEORGE WILLIAM FAIRFAX yearly on first day of May rent of Two pounds
two shillings and six pence current money of Virginia and within two years plant One
hundred good Apple trees and one hundred and fifty Peach trees and build a Dwelling
House twenty feet by sixteen and a Barn twenty feet square after manner of Virginia
Building In Witness whereof said parties have hereunto interchangeably set their
hands and seals the day and year first above written
in presence of CRAVEN PEYTON,   G. W. FAIRFAX
        GEORGE EMREY, OLIVER PRICE
    At a Court continued and held for Loudoun County November 27th 1772
This Indenture was proved by the oaths of CRAVEN PEYTON, Gent., GEORGE EMREY and
OLIVER PRICE, the witnesses thereto, on the part of GEORGE WILLIAM FAIRFAX Esqr. and
acknowledged by said NICHOLAS OTT on his part And is ordered to be recorded

pp.   THIS INDENTURE made the twenty seventh day of November in year of our Lord
135-   One thousand seven hundred and seventy two Between the Honourable GEORGE
139   WILLIAM FAIRFAX Esqure of the one part and WILLIAM VERTZ of County of
        Loudoun, Farmer, of other part Witnesseth that said GEORGE WILLIAM FAIRFAX
in consideration of rents and covenants on part of WILLIAM VERTZ to be paid and performed by these presents doth grant set and to farm let unto WILLIAM VERTZ one hundred acres of land with the Appurtenances (except mines, minerals and Quarries whatsoever) lying in Parish of Shelburne in County of Loudoun on the DUTCHMANS RUN
being part of a tract of land of Seventeen thousand two hundred and ninety six acres
and called PIEDMONT the bounds beginning at two Hickorys by a Path leading to the
SHORT HILL in a line of a Survey made for SAMUEL SMITH thence No. 30. West one hundred poles to a small Hickory saplin in a poison field, thence So. 60 West one hundred
and sixty poles to two white Oaks near the head of a Glade, thence So. 30 East one hundred poles to a black Oak at the head of a Glade in the aforesaid line of SAMUEL SMITH
thence with his line No. 60 East One hundred and sixty poles to the beginning
containing one hundred acres To have and To hold the said land and premises (except
before excepted) to said WILLIAM VERTZ his heirs and assigns during natural lives of
him the said WILLIAM VERTZ, CATHARINE VERTZ his Wife and CONROD VERTZ his Son,
paying said GEORGE WILLIAM FAIRFAX yearly on first day of May the rent of two
pounds two shillings and six pence current money of Virginia and within two years
plant one hundred good Apple trees and one hundred and fifty Peach trees and build

a good Dwelling House twenty feet by sixteen and a Barn twenty feet square after the manner of Virginia building In Witness whereof the said parties to these presents have hereunto interchangeably set their hands and affixed their seals the day and year first above written

in the presence of CRAVEN PEYTON,   G. W. FAIRFAX
         GEORGE EMREY, OLIVER PRICE

  At a Court continued and held for Loudoun County November 27th 1772
This Indenture was proved by the Oath of CRAVEN PEYTON, Gent. GEORGE EMREY and OLIVER PRICE, the witnesses thereto, on the part of GEORGE WILLIAM FAIRFAX Esquire and acknowledged by WILLIAM VERTZ on his part And is ordered to be recorded
(On margin: Examined PETER VERTZ 3 Apl 87)

pp.   THIS INDENTURE made the twenty fifth day of August in year of our Lord One
139-   thousand seven hundred and seventy two Between HENRY OXLEY JUNR. of
141   County of Loudoun and JOHANNA his Wife of one part and EVERITT OXLEY of the
           County aforesaid of other part Witnesseth that said HENRY OXLEY and JOHANNA
his Wife in consideration of Five shillings current money of Virginia to them in hand paid by these presents doth bargain and sell unto EVERITT OXLEY all that tract of land in Loudoun County and bounded beginning at several small saplins Corner to JOHN OXLEY and in a line of said EVERITT OXLEYs land, extending thence with his said line So. 60 d. Et. One hundred and thirty five poles to a Locust Stake in a poison field said EVERITTs Corner, then with another of his lines So. 30 d. Wt. One hundred and twenty poles to a Locust Stake his Corner, then with another of his lines No. 60 d. Wt. one hundred and thirty four poles to a Stake, Corner to JOHN OXLEY, then with his line No. 30 d. Et. one hundred and twenty poles to the first station containing one hundred acres more or less, said land conveyed to HENRY OXLEY by his Father, HENRY OXLEY, by Deeds dated the Twelfth and Thirteenth days of December A. Dom. 1762 recorded in Loudoun County Court, And all houses Orchards and appurtenances whatsoever belonging To have and to Hold the lands hereby conveyed for full term of one whole year paying therefore the rent of one Pepper Corn on Lady Day next to intent that by virtue of these presents and statute for transferring uses into possession said EVERITT OXLEY may be in actual possession and be thereby enabled to accept a Release of Inheritance thereof In Witness whereof said HENRY OXLEY and JOHANNA his Wife hath hereunto set their hands and seals the day and year first above written

in the presence of CLARE OXLEY,   HENRY OXLEY JUNR.
         HEZEKIAH BOONE, NATHANIEL FIELD   JOANNA her mark ✚ OXLEY

  At a Court continued and held for Loudoun County November 27th 1772
This Indenture was acknowledged by HENRY OXLEY and JOANNA his Wife, parties thereto, to be their acts and deeds (the said JOHANNA having been first privately examined as the Law directs), And is ordered to be recorded
(On margin: Exam'd & d'd Mr. OXLEY at April Court 1773)

pp.   THIS INDENTURE made the twenty sixth day of August in year of our Lord One
141-   thousand seven hundred and seventy two Between HENRY OXLEY JUNR. of
143   County of Loudoun and JOHANNA his Wife of one part and EVERITT OXLEY of
           same County of other part Witnesseth that in consideration of sum of Fifty
pounds current money of Virginia to HENRY OXLEY and JOHANNA his Wife in hand paid by these presents doth bargain and sell unto EVERITT OXLEY (in his actual possession by virtue of a bargain and sale for one whole and by force of the statute for transferring uses into possession) and his heirs all that tract of land situate in County of Loudoun and bounded .. (description of land as in Lease above) .. containing one hundred acres

more or less being part of a larger tract of land formerly granted to CATESBY COCKE by
a Patten from LORD FAIRFAX's Office with other Transferrances to HENRY OXLEY, Father
to said OXLEYs, and by him conveyed to aforesaid HENRY OXLEY JUNR. by deeds bearing
date the twelfth and thirteenth days of December Anno Dom: 1762 recorded in Loudoun
County Court To have and to hold unto said EVERITT OXLEY his heirs and assigns forever
In Witness whereof said HENRY OXLEY and JOHANNA his Wife hath hereunto set their
hands and seals the day and year first above written
in presnece of CLARE OXLEY,   HENRY OXLEY JUNR.
       HEZEKIAH BOONE, NATHANIEL FIELD   JOANNA her mark ⨍ OXLEY
    At a Court continued and held for Loudoun County November 27th 1772
This Indenture was acknowledged by HENRY OXLEY JUNR. and JOANNA his Wife parties
thereto to be their acts and deeds (the said JOANNA having been first privately examined as the Law directs and relinquished her Dower therein) and the Receipt thereon
endorsed was likewise acknowledged by said HENRY and together with said Indenture
ordered to be recorded
(On margin: Exam'd and dd to Mr. OXLEY at April Court 1773)

pp.   THIS INDENTURE made the Eleventh day of June in year of our Lord One thou-
144-   sand seven hundred and seventy two Between DANIEL HUNT of (blank) of one
145   part and HENRY LOYD of Loudoun County, Farmer, of other part Witnesseth that
         said DANIEL HUNT for sum of five shillings Sterling to him in hand paid by
these presents doth bargain and sell unto HENRY LOYD all that tract of land lying in
County of Loudoun and bounded Beginning at a small white Oak in a Gully the North
side of the MAIN ROAD to LASWELL's FORD on GOOSE CREEK, in a line of JOHN MERCER's,
extending thence So. 88 Et. Two hundred and sixty five poles, thence No. 12 Wt. Ninety
five poles to a line Surveyed by CATESBY COCK, then So. 85 Wt. two hundred and forty
five poles to a white and black Oak saplin in the aforesaid line of JOHN MERCER and
Corner to JONATHAN MUNK's late purchase, then with MERCERs line South sixty poles to
the first station containing one hundred and thirty one acres more or less and all
appurtenances belonging To have and to hold the said land with appurtenances unto
HENRY LOYD for full term of one year paying therefore the rent of One Ear of Indian
Corn on first day of November to intent that by virtue hereof and statute for transfer-
ring uses into possession said HENRY LOYD may be in actual possession and be thereby
enabled to accept a Release of Inheritance thereof In Witness whereof said DANIEL
HUNT hath hereunto set his hand and seal the day and year first above written
In presents of us JAS. HAMILTON,   DANIEL HUNT
       STEPHEN DONALDSON, JASON MORLON
    At a Court continued and held for Loudoun County September 30th 1772
This Indenture was proved by the Oaths of JAMES HAMILTON and STEPEHN DONALDSON
Gent., two of the subscribing witnesses thereto, And at another Court held for said
County November the 27th in year aforesaid, the same was fully proved by the Affir-
mation of JASON MORLAN (Quaker) the other witness, And is ordered to be recorded

pp.   THIS INDENTURE made the Twelfth day of June in year of our Lord One thousand
145-   seven hundred and seventy two Between DANIEL HUNT and SUSANNAH his Wife
149   of (blank) one part and HENRY LOYD of Loudoun County, Farmer, of other part,
         Witnesseth that said DANIEL HUNT for sum of Fifty pounds current money of
Virginia to him in hand paid by these presents doth bargain and sell unto HENRY LOYD
(in his actual possession by virtue of one Indenture of bargain and sale for one year
and by force of statute for transferring uses into possession) and to his heirs and
assigns forever, all that tract of land situate in County of Loudoun and boundeth ..

(description of land as in Lease above) .. containing One hundred and thirty one acres more or less being part of a larger tract granted to JOHN HOUGH by Patent bearing date the 7th day of September 1757 which said tract of land contining one hundred and thirty one acres the said DANIEL HUNT purchased of said JOHN HOUGH by Deeds of Lease and Release bearing date the twelfth and thirteenth days of December in year one thousand seven hundred and sixty three Together with all members and appurtenances thereunto belonging To have and to hold said tract of land with appurtenances unto said HENRY LOYD his heirs and assigns forever In Witness whereof said DANIEL HUNT and SUSANNAH his Wife have hereunto set their hands and seals the day and year first above written

in presence of JAS. HAMILTON,   DANIEL HUNT
        STEPHEN DONALDSON, JASON MORLAN   SUSANNA HUNT

(Commision GEORGE the Third to JAMES HAMILTON, CRAVEN PEYTON and STEPHEN DONALDSON for privy examination of SUSANNA Wife of DANIEL HUNT dated twelfth day of June 1772, and return of execution thereof dated 12th day of June 1772 and signed by JAS. HAMILTON and STEPHEN DONALDSON)

At a Court continued and held for Loudoun County September 30th 1772
This Indenture and the receipt thereon endorsed were proved by the oaths of JAMES HAMILTON and STEPHEN DONALDSON Gent. two of the subscribing witnesses thereto, And at another Court held for said County November the 27th in year aforesaid the same was fully proved by the Affirmation of JASON MORLON, the other witness, and together with a Commission for the Privy Examination of the Feme, and the return of the Execution thereof, is ordered to be recorded
(On margin: Ex'd Deliverd to Mr. LOYD Augt. 14th 1778)

pp.   JOHN EARL of DUNMORE: Viscount Fincastle, Baron Murray of Blair of Monlin
149-   and of Tillimet, Lieutenant and Governor General of his Majestys Colony and
150   Dominion of Virginia and Vice Admiral of the same
        TO CRAVEN PEYTON

By Virtue of the Power and Authority to me given by his Majesties Lieutenant and Governor General of this Colony, I do hereby constitute and appoint you, the said CRAVEN PEYTON to be Sheriff of County of Loudoun during pleasure and that you be accordingly sworn as soon as conveniently may be and before you are sworn or admitted into the said Office you are to enter into Bond before his Majesties Justices of said County with two or more good and sufficient sureties in the sum of One thousand pounds current money; to render to the Auditor and Receiver General of his Majesties Revenues a particular perfect and true account of his Majesties rents and dues arising within your County, and also due payment to make of all other dues and Fees put into your hands to collect within said County unto the several persons to whom the same shall be due or payable and true performance to make of all matters and things relating to your Office during your continuance therein. Given under my hand and the Seal of the Colony at WILLIAMSBURG the 26th day of October 1772 and in the thirteenth year of his Majesty's Reign
                                                        DUNMORE

At a Court held for Loudoun County December the 28th 1772
This Commission was produced in Court by CRAVEN PEYTON Gent: which being Read was ordered to be recorded

pp.   KNOW ALL MEN by these presents that We CRAVEN PEYTON Gent:, Sheriff of
150-   Loudoun County and LEVEN POWELL, CHARLES WEST and FRANCIS PEYTON are
151   holden and stand firmly bound unto our Sovereign Lord GEORGE the Third now

King &c. in sum of one thousand pounds current money we bind ourselves sealed with our seals and dated this 28th day of Decr. in the Thirteenth year of his said Majesty's Reign and in year of our Lord God one thousand seven hundred and seventy two.

THE CONDITION of the above obligation is such that Whereas above bound CRAVEN PEYTON is appointed Sheriff of County of Loudoun during pleasure; Therefore if said CRAVEN PEYTON shall well and truly collect and receive all Officers Fees and Dues put into his hands to collect and duly account fir and pay the same to the Officers to whom such fees are due and faithfully perform Office of Sheriff during the time of his continuance therein That then this obligaiton to be void

in presence of The Court   CRAVEN PEYTON   LEVEN POWELL
                                   CHARLES WEST   FRANCIS PEYTON

At a Court held for Loudoun County December 28th 1772
This Bond was acknowledged by the Obligors thereto and is ordered to be recorded

pp.   Bond from CRAVEN PEYTON, LEVEN POWELL, CHARLES WEST and FRANCIS
151-   PEYTON dated 28th day of December 1772 for CRAVEN PEYTON, Sheriff, to
152   collect the levy laid and assess'd on the Tithable persons within County of Lou-
         doun (Signed and Witnessed as above) .. (Bond in sum of Fifty three thousand
four hundred and thirty pounds of Nett Tobacco) ..
At a Court held for Loudoun County December the 28th 1772
This Bond was acknowledged by the Obligors thereto and ordered to be recorded

pp.   KNOW ALL MEN by these presents that We CRAVEN PEYTON Gent., Sheriff of
152-   Loudoun County and FRANCIS PEYTON, LEVEN POWELL and CHARLES WEST of the
153   same County are holden and stand firmly bound unto our Sovereign Lord
         GEORGE the Third in Penal sum of One hundred and ten pounds Current money
of Virginia Sealed with our seals and dated the 28th day of December in the Thirteenth year of said Majesty's Reign and in year of our Lord one thousand seven hundred and seventy two

WHEREAS by an Act of the General Assembly made and passed at the Capitol in the City of WILLIAMSBURG in the Twelfth of his said Majesties Reign the sum of Fifty five pounds was thereby directed to be levied and assessed upon the Tithable persons in the County of Loudoun and collected by the Sheriff thereof and be by him paid to THOMSON MASON, FRANCIS PEYTON, JOHN HOUGH and ISRAEL THOMPSON, Trustees named and appointed by said Act, and by them disposed of in and about clearing and repairing the GREAT ROADS leading from VESTALLS and WILLIAMS GAPS to the TOWNs of ALEXANDRIA and COLCHESTER as by said Act may more fully appear

Now if said CRAVEN PEYTON shall well and truly collect of and from the several tithables within the said County the sum of Fifty five pounds and duly and faithfully account for and pay the same to the beforenamed Trustees according to the directions and true intent of said Act, That then the above obligation to be void otherwise to be in full force Power and Virtue of Law

in presence of   CRAVEN PEYTON
        The Court   FRANCIS PEYTON
                                            LEVEN POWELL
                                            CHARLES WEST

At a Court held for Loudoun County December the 28th 1772
This Bond was acknowledged by the Oligors thereto and is ordered to be recorded

p.   IN PURSUANCE and by Virtue of Acts of Parliament made and provided for the
153   more effectual transportation of Convicted Felons to his Majesties Plantations

in America, I hereby assign unto THOMAS OWSLEY, JAMES LEE a Convict within the said
Statute, to serve him his Heirs or assigns for term of Seven years commencing the 27th
Sept. 1770 being the day of the Ship *SCARSDALE's* Arrival in Virginia

THOMAS HODGE

December 14th 1772
This is to Certify that the within named JAMES LEE hath made full satisfaction for the
within time as Witness my hand

Witness Present WILLIAM SMITH,   THOS. OWSLEY
        THOS. LEWIS

At a Court held for Loudoun County December the 28th 1772
This Assignment and the acknowledgment thereon endorsed was acknowledged by
THOMAS OWSLEY, party thereto, and on his request is ordered to be recorded

pp.   KNOW ALL MEN by these presents that I GEORGE CONN of PRINCE GEORGE COUNTY
153-   in the Province of MARYLAND for the natural love which I have and bear unto
155   MARY CONN of County of Loudoun and Colony of Virginia, Widow, and her Chil-
        dren, which she had by my Brother, HUGH CONN, deceased, and for the sum of
Five shillings current money to me in hand paid by these presents do grant bargain
and sell unto MARY CONN during her natural life, one Negro man named Benn and one
Negro woman named Bett with the future increase of said Bett To have and to hold the
said two Slaves, Ben and Bett, and the future increase of said Bett, unto said MARY CONN
during her natural life and after her decease to her children which she had by my
Brother HUGH CONN forever, And I said GEORGE CONN do hereby declare the said Benn
and Bett to be two of those slaves made over to me in a Deed made by said HUGH CONN on
the sixth day of October 1758 In Testimony whereof I said GEORGE CONN have hereunto
set my hand and seal this sixteenth day of December in year of our Lord Seventeen
hundred and seventy two

in the presence of JOSA: BEALL,   GEORGE CONN JR.
        GERRARD TRAMMELL JUNR.,
        JEREMIAH THRIFT

Maryland Prince Gs. Cty. the 16th day of December 1772
Then the within named GEORGE CONN came before me one of his Lordship's Justices of
the Peace for the County aforesaid and acknowledged the two Negroes Ben and Bett to be
the right of the within named MARY CONN during her natural life and after death to
his Brothers's Children as mention'd in the within Deed. Taken before me the day and
year abovementioned

JOSA: BEALL

Received the 16th day of December 1772 of MARY CONN the sum of Five shillings it
being the consideration mentioned in the with Deed per me

Witness JOSA. BEALL,   GEORGE CONN JR.
        GERRARD TRAMELL JUNR., JEREMIAH THRIFT

At a Court held for Loudoun County December the 28th 1772
This Deed of Gift with the Certificate and Receipt thereon endorsed was proved by the
oaths of GERRARD TRAMMELL JUNR. and JEREMIAH THRIFT, two of the subscribing witnesses thereto, to be the act and deed of the within mentioned GEORGE CONN JUNR. and is
ordered to be recorded
(On margin: Examined & Deld. JOHN CONN June 6th 1788 p Order)

pp.   KNOW ALL MEN by these presents that I JOHN PATTEN of County of KENT on the
155-   RIVER DELAWARE in Province of PENNSYLVANIA for the better conveying the
156   Fee Simple Estate of and in two separate Tracts of land near MILL CREEK in

HAMSHIRE COUNTY and Colony of Virginia, the one containing One hundred and fifty seven acres the other One hundred acres taken up by and entered in the Proprietors Office in the name of JAMES PATTEN, late deceased, whose Heir at Law the said JOHN PATTEN is, to JAMES McILHANEY of County of Loudoun and to his heirs and assigns by these presents do make and appoint ALEXANDER WHITE Esquire, Attorney at Law, of TOWN of WINCHESTER, my true and lawful Attorney and Agent for me and in my name to deliver and acknowledge whatever Deeds or Instruments of Writing in the Law for the conveying the Fee simple estate of land in said two tracts to said JAMES McILHENEY hereby ratifying confirming and making valid whatever my said Attorney shall do in the Premises in my name. In Witness whereof I have hereunto set my hand and seal the Eleventh day of December Anno Domini 1772

in presence of G. JOHNSTON,   JOHN PATTEN
      WILLIAM NEILSON, ALEXANDER FRENCH
  At a Court held for Loudoun County December the 28th 1772
This Power of Attorney was proved by the Oaths of GEORGE JOHNSTON Gent., WILLIAM NEILSON and ALEXANDER FRENCH, the subscribing witnesses thereto, to be the act and deed of the within mentioned JOHN PATTEN, And is ordered to be recorded

pp.   THIS INDENTURE made the Twenty seventh day of October in year of our Lord
156-   One thousand seven hundred and seventy two Between CRAVEN PEYTON of the
157   County of Loudoun of one part and DAVID ROSS of TOWN of BLADENSBURGH,
       County of PRINCE GEORGE, MARYLAND, of other part Witnesseth that CRAVEN PEYTON for sum of five shillings current money of Virginia to him in hand paid by these presents doth bargain and sell unto DAVID ROSS all them two lotts or half acres of land situate in TOWN of LEESBURGH and County of Loudoun Numbered Fifty Nine and Sixty, the former of which was conveyed to said CRAVEN PEYTON by WILLIAM WEST by Deed of Gift bearing date the Eighth day of September One thousand seven hundred and sixty one, the latter was sold and conveyed to said CRAVEN PEYTON by Colonel NICHOLAS MINOR by Deed of Feoffment bearing date the tenth day of November one thousand seven hundred and sixty one, both which said Deeds remain of record in the Clerks Office of said County, And all houses, orchards and appurtenances whatsoever belonging To have and to hold for full term of one whole year paying therefore the rent of one Pepper Corn on Lady Day next to intent that by virtue of these presents and statute for transferring uses into possession said DAVID ROSS may be in actual possession and thereby be enabled to accept a Release of Inheritance thereof In Witness whereof said CRAVEN PEYTON hath hereunto set his hand and seal the day and year first above written

in the presence of LEVEN POWELL,   CRAVEN PEYTON
     CHARLES WEST, JONOTHAN DAVIS,
     ABEL JANNEY JUNR.
  At a Court held for Loudoun County December the 28th 1772
This Indenture was acknowledged by CRAVEN PEYTON Esqr. party thereto, to be his act and deed, And is ordered to be recorded

pp.   THIS INDENTURE made the Twenty eighth day of October in year of our Lord One
157-   thousand seven hundred and seventy two Between CRAVEN PEYTON and ANN his
160   Wife of TOWN of LEESBURGH, County of Loudoun, of one part and DAVID ROSS of
       TOWN of BLADENSBURGH, County of PRINCE GEORGE, MARYLAND of other part
Witnesseth that for sum of one hundred pounds Sterling money of Great Britain to said CRAVEN PEYTON in hand paid by these presents doth bargain and sell unto said DAVID ROSS (in his actual possession now being by virtue of a bargain and sale for one whole

year and by force of statute for transferring uses into possession) and his heirs forever
all them two lotts or half acres of land .. (description and conveyances as in Lease
above) .. To have and to hold unto said DAVID ROSS his heirs and assigns forever. In
Witness whereof said CRAVEN PEYTON and ANN his Wife have hereunto set their hands
and seals the day and year first above written
in presence of LEVEN POWELL,   CRAVEN PEYTON
      CHARLES WEST, JONOTHAN DAVIS,
      ABEL JANNEY JUNR.
 At a Court held for Loudoun County December 28th 1772
This Indenture and Receipt underwritten was acknowledged by CRAVEN PEYTON Esqr.
party thereto, to be his act and deed, and is ordered to be recorded
(On margin: Examined & del'd Mr. ELLZEY June 1786)

p.   KNOW ALL MEN by these presents that I THOMAS HAIR of Loudoun County for
160   the consideration of Twelve pounds current money of Virginia to me in hand
        paid by DAVID EVINS of same place by these presents have according to the due
form of Law bargain and sell unto DAVID EVINS one black Cow and two third parts of
Wheat now growing at JAMES DILLONs, to have and to hold said bargained premises
unto DAVID EVINS Provided Nevertheless that if THOMAS HAIR shall pay or cause to be
paid unto DAVID EVINS the sum of Twelve pounds current money at or before the first
day of March which shall be in the year of our Lord God 1773, then this obligation to be
void. In Witness whereof I have hereunto set my hand and seal this thirtieth day of
November 1772
in presence of PETER BANNER,   THOMAS HAIR
      ISRAEL THOMPSON, JOHN CHAMBERLAIN
 At a Court held for Loudoun County December the 28th 1772
This Bill of Sale was proved by the Affirmation of ISRAEL THOMPSON (a Quaker), a witness thereto, to be the act and deed of THOMAS HAIR party thereto And is ordered to be
recorded
(On margin: Exam'd & d'd to Mr. Evans the 14th June 1773)

pp.   THIS INDENTURE made the twenty fifth day of December in year of our Lord One
161-   thousand seven hundred and seventy two Between WILLIAM SMITH of Parish of
162   Shelburne and County of Loudoun, Farmer, of one part and DANIEL LUSH of the
        same Parish and County, Butcher, of other part Witnesseth that said WILLIAM
SMITH for sum of five shilings current money of Virginia to him in hand paid by these
presents doth bargain and sell unto DANIEL LUSH one lott or half acre of land lying in
TOWN of LEESBURG and Parish and County aforesaid and bounded on the East by BACK
STREET and on the North by MARKET STREET and adjoining the lot whereon WILLIAM
BAKER now Dwells, which lott or half acre of land was conveyed to WILLIAM SMITH by
aforesaid WILLIAM BAKER by his Deed of Feoffment bearing date the thirty first day of
January in year one thousand seven hundred and seventy one duly acknowledged and
recorded among the records of the Court of County of Loudoun, And all Houses, Orchards
and appurtenances thereof belonging To have and to hold unto DANIEL LUSH his
assigns for the full term of one whole year paying therefore the rent of one Pepper
Corn on Lady Day next to intent that by virtue of these presents and statute for transferring uses into possession, said DANIEL LUSH may be in actual possession and be
thereby enabled to accept a Release of the Inheritance thereof In Witness whereof the
said WILLIAM SMITH hath hereunto set his hand and seal the day and year first above
written

in presence of G. JOHNSTON,   WILLIAM his mark \X/ SMITH
    WM. BAKER, WM. JOHNSTON
   At a Court held for Loudoun County December the 28th 1772
This Indenture was acknowledged by WILLIAM SMITH party thereto to be his act and
deed and is ordered to be recorded

pp.   THIS INDENTURE made the Twenty sixth day of December in year of our Lord One
162-   thousand seven hundred and seventy two Between WILLIAM SMITH of Parish of
164   Shelburne and County of Loudoun, Farmer, and ELIZABETH his Wife of one part
        and DANIEL LUSH of same Parish and County, Butcher, of other part Witnesseth
that for sum of Eighteen pounds current money of Virginia to said WILLIAM SMITH in
hand paid by these presents doth bargain and sell unto DANIEL LUSH (in his actual possession now being by virtue of a bargain and sale for one whole year and by force of
the statute for transferring uses into possession) and to his heirs one lott or half acre
of land .. (description of land and conveyances as in Lease above) .. To have and to hold
the lands hereby conveyed unto DANIEL LUSH his heirs and assigns forever In Witness
whereof said WILLIAM SMITH and ELIZABETH his Wife have hereunto set their hands
and seals the day and year first above written
in presence of G. JOHNSTON,   WILLIAM his mark \X/ SMITH
    WM. BAKER, WM. JOHNSTON
   At a Court held for Loudoun County December the 28th 1772
This Indenture and receipt thereon endorsed was acknowledged by WILLIAM SMITH
party thereto, to be his act and deed and is ordered to be recorded
(On margin: Exam'd & del'd June 28, 1773)

pp.   THIS INDENTURE made the sixteenth day of October in year of our Lord one thou-
164-   sand seven hundred and seventy two Between CHARLES GRIFFITH of County of
166   Loudoun of one part and SIMON TRIPLETT of County aforesaid of other part Wit-
        nesseth that said CHARLES GRIFFITH for sum of Five shillings Current money of
Virginia to him in hand paid by these presents doth bargain and sell unto SIMON TRIP-
LETT all that tract of land lying on GOOSE CREEK in County of Loudoun and bound with
and by the lands of ROBT. CARTER Esqr., WILLIAM and JAMES TASSY containing four
hundred acres be the same more or less granted said GRIFFITH from the Proprietors
Office as by said Pattent and All houses Orchards and appurtenances whatsoever belonging To have and to hold the lands hereby conveyed unto SIMON TRIPLETT for full
term of one whole year paying therefore the rent of one Pepper Corn on Lady Day next
to intent that by virtue of these presents and by force of statute for transferring uses
into possession, said SIMON TRIPLETT may be in actual possession and be thereby enabled to accept a Release of inheritance thereof In Witness whereof said CHARLES
GRIFFITH have hereunto set his hand and seal the day and year first above written
in presence of JOSEPH BUTLER,   CHARLES his mark ⊂G GRIFFITH
    JNO. HERYFORD, CHARLES DAVIS,
    JAMES HERYFORD
   At a Court continued and held for Loudoun County November 24th 1772
This Indenture and Receipt were proved by the Oaths of JOHN HERYFORD and CHARLES
DAVIS, two of the subscribing witnesses thereto, And at another Court held for the said
County on the 28th day of December next following, the same was fully proved by the
Oath of JAMES HERYFORD another of the subscribing witnesses thereto, And is ordered
to be recorded

pp.   THIS INDENTURE made the 17th day of October in year of our Lord One thousand
166-   seven hundred and seventy two Between CHARLES GRIFFITH of County of Lou-
168   doun of one part and SIMON TRIPLETT of County aforesaid of other part Witnesseth that CHARLES GRIFFITH in consideration of the sum of One hundred pounds
current money to him in hand paid by these presents doth bargain and sell SIMON
TRIPLETT (in his actual possession by virtue of these presents and by force of statute
for transferring uses into possession) his heirs and assigns forever .. (description of
land and conveyances as in Lease above) .. To have and to hold unto SIMON TRIPLETT his
heirs and assigns forever. In Witness whereof I the said CHARLES GRIFFITH have hereunto set my hand and seal the day and year first above written
in presence of JOSEPH BUTLER,   CHARLES his mark Ϛ Ϛ GRIFFITH
    JNO. HERYFORD, CHARLES DAVIS,
    JAMES HERYFORD
  At a Court continued and held for Loudoun County Novr. the 28th 1772
This Indenture and the Receipt thereon endorsed was proved to be the act and deed of
CHARLES GRIFFITH party thereto by the Oaths of JOHN HERYFORD and CHARLES DAVIS,
two of the subscribing witnesses, And at another Court held for said County on the 28th
day of December in the year aforesaid, the same was fully proved by the Oath of JAMES
HERYFORD, another of the subscribing Witnesses thereto, And is ordered to be recorded

pp.   THIS INDENTURE made the Nineteenth day of March One thousand seven hun-
168-   dred and seventy three Between FRANCIS HAGUE of Loudoun County, Yeoman,
169   of one part and THOMAS HAGUE of the County aforesaid of other part Witnesseth
that FRANCIS HAGUE for sum of Five shillings Sterling to him in hand paid by
these presents doth bargain and sell unto THOMAS HAGUE all that tract or parcel of land
lying in County of Loudoun and bounded Beginning at a white Oak standing near the
Road Corner to MAHLON JANNEY's MILL LOTT, thence No. 2 1/2 d. E. 30 perches to a
Hickory on the Hill, thence S. 81 d. E. 26 perches to a white Oak Bush, thence So. 1 1/2 d.
Wt. 84 perches to a white Oak Bush by MAHLON JANNEYs Fence, thence No. 65 d. Wt. 29
perches to a small Hickory by the Race, thence down the Race No. 5 d. Wt. 20 perches to
a large white Oak standing by the Race thence No. 27 d. E. 4 perches to the beginning
containing twelve acres be the same more or less, Also one other tract of land being in
Loudoun County and bounded beginning at a white Oak standing near the SAW MILL a
corner to MAHLON JANNEY's MILL LOTT ..nd extending thence up the Race S. 20 d. E. 14
perches to a white Oak standing on the Race bank, thence continuing up the Race S. 2 d.
E. 16 perches to a small Gum bush by the Race of MAHLON JANNEYs line, thence with
said JANNEYs line No. 65 d. Wt. 22 perches, thence with said line N. 12 d. E. 9 perches,
thence with said line No. 66 d. W. 12 perches to a black Oak saplin on the West side of
South Fork of KITTOCTON CREEK on said line of MAHLON JANNEY, thence No. 18 d. E. 26
perches to a Gum tree standing near the Ford, thence across the Creek and up the Tale
Race S. 58 D. E. 39 perches to the beginning Containing Five acres and three quarters be
the same more or less Together with all Houses, orchards and appurtenances whatsoever belonging To have and to hold for full term of one whole year paying therefore
the yearly rent of one Ear of Indian Corn on the first day of November to intent that by
virtue of these presents and statute for transferring uses into possession said THOMAS
HAUGE may be in actual possession and be thereby enabled to accept a Release of Inheritance thereof In Witness whereof said FRANCIS HAGUE hath hereunto set his hand
and seal the day and year first above written
in presence of SAML. CANBY,   FRANCIS HAGUE
    AMOS HOUGH, JOHN HOUGH JUNR.

At a Court held for Loudoun County March the 22d 1773
This Indenture was acknowledged by FRANCIS HAGUE party thereto to be his act and
deed and is ordered to be recorded

pp.   THIS INDENTURE made the Twentieth day of March One thousand seven hundred
169-   and seventy three Between FRANCIS HAGUE of Loudoun County, Yeoman, of one
173   part and THOMAS HAGUE of same place, Cordwainer, of other part Witnesseth
        that Whereas there is a certain tract of land lying in County of Loudoun and on
South Fork of KITTOCTON and bounded .. (description of two parcels of land as in Lease
above) .. which two parcels of land is part of a tract of land containing Three hundred
and three acres which Tract was conveyed to FRANCIS HAGUE by JOHN MEAD by Lease
and Release which three hundred and three acres also is part of a Tract of seven hundred & three acres which tract was confirmed to CATESBY COCKE Gent: by a Pattent out
of Proprietors Office duly executed bearing date the Eight and Twentieth day of August
One thousand seven hundred and thirty one and by him conveyed to the above named
JOHN MEAD by Lease and Release duly had and executed under his hand and Seal NOW
THIS INDENTURE Witnesseth that for sum of Five pounds Sterling to him in hand paid by
these presents FRANCIS HAGUE doth bargain and sell unto THOMAS HAGUE his heirs and
assigns (in his actual possession by virtue of a bargain and sale thereof for one year
and by force of statute for transferring uses into possession) To have and to hold said
seventeen acres and three quarters of land unto said THOMAS HAGUE his heirs and
assigns In Witness whereof said FRANCIS HAGUE hath hereunto set his hand and seal
the day and year first above written
in the presence of SAML. CANBY,   FRANCIS HAGUE
        AMOS HOUGH, JOHN HOUGH JUNR.
    At a Court held for Loudoun County March the 22d 1773
This Indenture and the receipt under written were acknowledged by FRANCIS HAGUE
party thereto to be his act and deed and is ordered to be recorded

pp.   KNOW ALL MEN by these presents that We JACOB PIERCEALL and DANIEL JEN-
173-   NINGS for sum of Fifty six pounds Curt. money of Virginia to us in hand paid by
174   WILLIAM STANHOPE of County of Loudoun do bargain and sell unto said WIL-
        LIAM STANHOPE a Negro Girl named Dian and warrant and defend by these pre-
sents In Witness whereof we the said JACOB PIERCEALL and DANIEL JENNINGS hath
hereunto set our hands and seals this 28th day of July one thousand seven hundred and
seventy two
in the presence of CRAVEN PEYTON   JACOB PEARSALL
        JONOTHAN DAVIS, THOS. PRITCHARD   DANL. JENNINGS
    At a Court held for Loudoun County March the 22d 1773
This Bill of Sale was proved by the Oaths of CRAVEN PEYTON and JONATHAN DAVIS two of
the Subscribing witnesses thereto be the acts and deeds of the above mentioned JACOB
PEARSALL and DANIEL JENNINGS and is ordered to be recorded

p.   March 1st 1773
174   KNOW ALL MEN by these presents that I LASHLEY WOOD of Loudoun County do
        bargain and sell in open market unto ALEXANDER LUCAS of County aforesaid Viz.
Three mares, two cows and calves, one sow and four shoats, three beds with three fur-
nitre, two pots, one Broad Ax, one narrow Ditto, one man's Saddle, and one Womans Ditto,
one Hand saw, three Gouges, three Chizzels, two Tann'd hides and a half, Twelve barrells
and a half of Corn, one Frying pan, one Iron shovel, one raw cow hide, one Dish and
five plates, four Tin pans, one case of Knives and Forks, one Dozen of pewter spoons,

and by these presents do vest the property in aforesaid ALEXANDER LUCAS hand warranting them from the claim of any person Witness my hand and seal

    AUGUSTUS T EASTER   LASHLEY + WOOD

At a Court continued and held for Loudoun County March 22d 1773
This Bill of Sale was acknowledged by LASHLEY WOOD party thereto to be his act and deed and is ordered to be recorded

pp.   THIS INDENTURE made the Twenty seventh day of November in year of our Lord
174- One thousand seven hundred and seventy two Between JOHN RAYNES of Loudoun
176   County and Cameron Parish of one part and THOMAS LYNE of the same County of
other part Witnesseth that said JOHN RAYNES for sum of five shillings current money of Virginia to him in hand paid by these presents doth bargain and sell unto THOMAS LYNE all my right title and Interest of one certain parcel of land left to me by the Last Will and Testament of my Father, JOHN RAYNES, deced, which said Will is recorded in the Records of FAIRFAX COUNTY the said land lying in County aforesaid on the Branches of ELKLICKING Run and between the land of ANTHONY RAYNES and the land now in the Occupation of BENJAMIN HUTCHISON containing one hundred and thirty three acres more or less and all Houses orchards and appurtenances whatsoever belonging To have and to hold the lands hereby conveyed for full term of one year paying therefor the rent of One pepper Corn on Lady Day next to intent that by these presents and statute for transferring uses into possession said THOMAS LYNE may be in actual possession and be thereby enabled to accept a Release of Inheritance thereof In Witness whereof said JOHN RAYNES hath hereunto set his hand and seal the day and year first above written

in the presence of PATRICK his mark P KELLEY,   JOHN his mark + RAYNES
    CORNELIUS RINGO, FRANCIS PADGET,
    PHILIP RINGO

At a Court continued and held for Loudoun County March 23d 1773
This Indenture was acknowledged by JOHN RAYNES party thereto to be his act and deed and is ordered to be recorded

pp.   THIS INDENTURE made the Twenty Eighth day of November in year of our Lord
176- One thousand seven hundred and seventy two Between JOHN RAYNES of Loudoun
178   County and Cameron Parish of one part and THOMAS LYNE of same County of the
other part Witnesseth that for sum of Fifty pounds current money of Virginia to said JOHN RAYNES in hand paid by these presents doth bargain and sell unto THOMAS LYNE (in his actual possession now being by virtue of one bargain and sale for one whole year and by force of statute for transferring uses into possession), and to his heirs .. (description of land and how obtained as in Lease above) .. To have and to hold the lands hereby conveyed unto said THOMAS LYNE his heirs and assigns forever In Witness whereof said JOHN RAYNES hath hereunto set his hand and seal the day and year first above written

in presence of CORNELIUS RINGO,   JOHN his mark + RAYNES
    FRANCIS PADGET, PHILIP RINGO,
    PATRICK his mark P KELLEY

At a Court continued and held for Loudoun County March 23d 1773
This Indenture and the Receipt thereon endorsed was acknowledged by JOHN RAYNES party thereto to be his act and deed and is ordered to be recorded
(On margin: Exd. deld. Apl. 22. 1778)

pp.   TO ALL TO WHOM these presents shall come WILLIAM ELLZEY of County of
178-   PRINCE WILLIAM, Attorney for ROBERT BUCHAN of the Province of MARYLAND,
179   sendeth Greeting. Whereas said WILLIAM ELLZEY prosecuted a suit for said
ROBERT BUCHAN against WILLIAM WHITELY upon a Bond and recovered Judgment and sued out a Fiere Facias and Executed two slaves, Viz. Judy and Lydia, in which
SUSANNA TAYLOR claimed property and sued out a Writ of Replevin to buy the Title
thereof but upon tryal thereof it was adjudged they were liable to said ROBERT BUCHAN
to satisfy his Debt and costs afd., NOW KNOW YE that I the said WILLIAM ELLZEY as Attorney for ROBERT BUCHAN having received of JOHN TAYLOR, Son of said SUSANNA, the
full amount of said Execution being One hundred & ten pounds current money at the
desire of SUSANNA TAYLOR and WILLIAM WHITELY signified by their signing and
sealing these presents do bargain and sell unto JOHN TAYLOR said two Slaves, Judy and
Lidia, and their future increase To have and to hold said slaves unto JOHN TAYLOR his
heirs and assigns In Testimony whereof as well the said WILLIAM ELLZEY Attorney of
said ROBERT BUCHAN as the said SUSANNA TAYLOR and WILLIAM WHITELY have hereunto set their hands and seals this 24th day of November 1772
in presence of GEO: SUMMERS,   } saw W. ELLZEY   W. ELLZEY
        WILL. LANE   } and W. WHITELY   SUSANNA TAYLOR
                                     sign   WILLIAM WHITELY
        HENRY TAYLOR, JOSHUA TAYLOR
At a Court continued and held for Loudoun County March 24th 1773
This Bill of Sale was acknowledged by WILLIAM ELLZEY and WILLIAM WHITELY on
their parts to be their acts and deeds, and proved on the part of SUSANNA TAYLOR by
the Oaths of HENRY TAYLOR and JOSHUA TAYLOR, two of the Subscribing witnesses
thereto and is ordered to be recorded

pp.   THIS INDENTURE made this Eleventh day of December in year of our Lord One
179-   thousand seven hundred and seventy two Between THOMAS HUMPHREY of Lou-
181   doun County of one part and SAMUEL PEW of same County of other part Witnesseth that THOMAS HUMPHREY for sum of five shillings lawful money of England
to him in hand paid by these presents doth bargain and sell unto SAMUEL PEW all that
tract of land lying in County of Loudoun and bounded Beginning at a white Oak in a
Glade in a line of JOHN HARFORD, thence N. 63 d. West 195 poles to a black Oak on the side
of the ROUND HILL then South 33 d. West 175 poles to a black Oak in a line of HARMAN
COX then South 1 d. East 30 poles to 2 red Oaks corner to JOHN BISHOP's Land then S. 56 d.
East 304 poles to 2 small white Oaks corner to THOMAS BRYAN, then with his line No. 10
d. East 173 poles to s small white Oak and black Oak by the side of the GREAT ROAD then
South 20 d. East seventy poles to the beginning containing two hundred and twenty six
acres of land more or less and all Houses orchards and appurtenances whatsoever belonging To have and to hold said tract of land and premises unto SAMUEL PEW from first
day of April last past for one whole year paying therefore one Pepper Corn upon the
Feast of St. Michael the Arch Angel to intent that by virtue of these presents and by
force of statute for transferring uses into possession said SAMUEL PEW may be in actual
possession and be thereby enabled to accept a Release of Inheritance thereof In Witness whereof said THOMAS HUMPHREY hath hereunto set his hand and affixed his seal
the day and year first above written
in the presence of WILLIAM NEILSON,   THOMAS HUMPHREY
        HUGH NEILSON, HUGH PATTERSON   MARY HUMPHREY
At a Court held for Loudoun County April the 26th 1773
This Indenture was acknowledged by SAMUEL PEW and MARY his Wife parties thereto
to be their acts and deeds (the said MARY having been first privately examined as the

Law directs) And is ordered to be recorded

pp.   THIS INDENTURE made this twelfth day of December in year of our Lord One
181-   thousand seven hundred and seventy two Between THOMAS HUMPHREY of Lou-
183   doun County and MARY his Wife of one part and SAMUEL PEW of same County
         of other part Witnesseth that said THOMAS HUMPHREY and MARY his Wife for
sum of One hundred and fifty pounds current money of Virginia to them in hand paid
by these presents doth bargain and sell unto SAMUEL PEW (in his actual possession now
being by virtue of one bargain and sale for one year and by force of statute for transferring uses into possession) and to his heirs and assigns forever all that tract of land
lying in County of Loudoun bounded .. (description of land as in Lease above) .. containing two hundred and twenty six acres more or less To have and to hold unto said
SAMUEL PEW his heirs and assigns forever In Witness whereof said THOMAS HUM-
PHREY and MARY his Wife have hereunto set their hands and affixed their seals the
day and year first above written
in the presence of WILLIAM NEILSON,   THOMAS HUMPHREY
          HUGH NEILSON, HUGH PATTERSON   MARY   HUMPHREY
  At a Court held for Loudoun County April the 26th 1773
This Indenture was acknowledged by THOMAS HUMPHREY and MARY his Wife, parties
thereto, to be their acts and deeds (the said MARY having been first privately examined
as the Law directs and relinquished her Dower therein) and the Receipt thereon endorsed was also acknowledged by the said THOMAS and together with said Indenture is
ordered to be recorded
(On margin: Examined & d'd Capt. HUMPHREY 14 Sept. 1779)

pp.   THIS INDENTURE made the first day of December in year of our Lord One thou-
183-   sand seven hundred and seventy (blank) Between FRANCIS LIGHTFOOT LEE of the
189   Parish of LUNENBURG in County of RICHMOND Esqr. of one part and JAMES
         CLEVELAND of County of FAIRFAX, Farmer, of other part Witnesseth that said
FRANCIS LIGHTFOOT LEE for sum of five shillings to him in hand paid by these presents
doth demise grant and to farm lett unto JAMES CLEVELAND all that Tenement called the
OLD QUARTER and NEW QUARTER lying in Parish of Cameron in County of Loudoun
containing sixteen hundred and fifty acres of land whereof said FRANCIS LIGHTFOOT
LEE is now seized as Tenant in Tail and bounded Beginning at the Mouth of STALLION
BRANCH where it empties into HORSEPEN RUN and up the meanders of said Branch the
Water Course to a (blank) thence No. 85 d. W. 124 poles to (blank) corner on the said
Branch with a lott which lies in the Fork of STALLION BRANCH, thence with WILLIAM
HUMPHRIS Tenement S. 36 1/2 West 390 poles to where the NEW ROAD is to be made in
the line of another and with the same S. 36 1/2 d. E. 189 poles to a Corner for another
Lott, and with the same N. 69 1/2 d. E. 380 poles to the line of another lott and N. 11 1/2
d. E. 214 poles to three Oak in a Glade, and N. 77 E. 211 poles to JACOB RAINEY's Corner
Maple on HORSEPEN RUN and down the same to the beginning , Together with all
houses orchards and appurtenances whatsoever belonging To have and to hold unto
said JAMES CLEVELAND and his assigns for term of Twelve years to be fully compleated
and ending paying therefore yearly unto said FRANCIS LIGHTFOOT LEE and his Issue in
Tail the rent of One hundred seventy and seven pounds, Ten shillings Sterling money
of Great Britain the first payment to be made on the first day of June one thousand
seven hundred and seventy four and said JAMES CLEVELAND will out of said demised
premises reserve five hundred and fifty acres of Wood land un cut down or pillaged and
that but one crop shall be taken of the same piece of land in three years and during the
continuance of said Lease JAMES CLEVELAND shall have the use of the following negroe

slaves (to wit) York, Michael, Harry, General the Blacksmith, Bella, Sarah, Angellica, Sebinah, Susanah, Old Scilla, Shadrach, Zachary, Daniel, Billy, Arthur, Adam, Generall, Dick, John, Lidia, Lizy, Let, Peggy, Ben, Daniel, Frank, Violet, Dirt, Scilla, Grace, Rachel, Old Jenny, Little Ben, Sam, Handboy, Tom, Wallace, Jenney, Hanah, Dolly, Aggy, Winny, Penny, Easther, in all forty four who are during the said Term to work upon the said demised premises and JAMES CLEVELAND shall discharge all quitrents and taxes and will during the continuance of this Lease will and sufficiently cloath, Victual and in all other respects well use the slaves herein before named and their increase and pay all their levys and Taxes during said Term In Witness whereof the parties to these presents have hereunto interchangeably set their hands and affixed their seals the day and year first above written

It is agreed by said FRANCIS LIGHTFOOT LEE that if said JAMES CLEVELAND tend no tobacco on the said demised premises that then said JAMES CLEVELAND shall have the Liberty of working three more hands thereon, by the restriction of taking but one crop off the same piece of ground it is not intended to extend to Tobacco or preclude the said JAMES CLEVELAND's following Indian Corn with Wheat Oats or other small grain and JAMES CLEVELAND doth agree that no straw or manure shall be removed from off the said demised premises during the Term aforesaid and FRANCIS LIGHTFOOT LEE doth also agree to lend him all the stocks of horses, cattle and hogs which are now upon the said Plantation and contained in a schedule hereto annexed and leave for them the usual quantity of Corn for their present support and at end of said Lease JAMES CLEVELAND doth agree to deliver up the said Negroes fully cloathed and a sufficient quantity of Corn for their Support for the ensuing year. It is further agreed that if JAMES CLEVE-LAND shou'd die before the expiration of the Term aforesaid that his Wife his heirs shall have fifty days to consider whether they will keep the Lease and if they do keep it, then they shall not have the Liberty of working more hands than those above named which belong to said FRANCIS LIGHTFOOT LEE

in presence of GRIFFIN GARLAND,   FRANCIS LIGHTFOOT LEE
      SAMUEL HATTLY, ALEXAND. CLEVELAND,   JAMES CLEVELAND
      DANIEL SANFORD, TIMOTHY CARRINGTON,
      FRANCIS STONE, RICHARD STEPHENS, RICHARD STEPHENS
(The Schedule as mentioned follows signed by both parties)

At a Court held for Loudoun County April the 26th 1773
This Indenture was proved by the Oath of ALEXANDER CLEVELAND, TIMOTHY CARRING-TON and RICHARD STEPHENS, three of the subscribing witnesses thereto to be the acts and deeds of FRANCIS LIGHTFOOT LEE Esqr. and JAMES CLEVELAND parties thereto, together with the Schedule thereunto annexed is ordered to be recorded
(On margin: Exam'd and Deliv'd to Mr. Cleveland Augt. Court 1773)

pp.   THIS INDENTURE made the third day of December in year of our Lord one thou-
189-   sand seven hundred and seventy two Between FRANCIS LIGHTFOOT LEE of the
194   Parish of LUNENBURG in County of RICHMOND Esqr. of one part and WILLIAM
           HUMPHRIS of County of Loudoun, Farmer, of other part Witnesseth that FRANCIS
LIGHTFOOT LEE for sum of five shillings to him in hand paid and of the rents and cove-nants herein after mentioned to be paid and performed by WILLIAM HUMPRIS doth demise grant and to farm let all that Tenement commonly called BRAYS QUARTER lying in the Parish of Cameron in the County of Loudoun containing six hundred acres of land whereof FRANCIS LIGHTFOOT LEE is now seized as Tenant in Tail and bounded Beginning at a Box Oak standing at MUDDY CREEK, thence S. 11 d. 30' E. 202 pole to several small white Oaks, thence S. 36 d. 30' W. 390 pole to where the NEW ROAD is to be made and with the same road N. 36 d. 30' W. to a white Oak Corner in the out line marked L thence

N. 16 d. E. 160 pole to a Hickory near a path thence N. 79 d. 15' E. 120 pole to a large white Oak and small Hickory on the East side of MUDDY LICK BRANCH and down the meanders of said Branch the Water Course to the beginning which includes six hundred acres of land together with all houses Fences Yards Gardens Orchards profits commodities and appurtenances whatsoever belonging To have and to hold unto said WILLIAM HUMPHRIS and his Assigns during the Term of Twelve years fully to be compleated paying therefore yearly during said Term unto FRANCIS LIGHTFOOT LEE and his Issue in Tail the rent of Sixty pounds Sterling money of Great Britain the first payment to be made on the last day of June one thousand seven hundred and seventy four and said WILLIAM HUMPRHIS agrees to reserve two hundred acres of wood land uncut down or pillaged and that one crop shall be taken off the same piece of land in three years and FRANCIS LIGHTFOOT LEE doth covenant that WILLIAM HUMPHRIS shall have use of the following Negro slaves (to wit) Bray, Phil, Charity, Nan, Moll, Nelly, Beck, Sall, old Blonder, Joshua, Bryant, Sam, Jem, Joan & Peggy, Charity, Lenney, Grace, Ruth in all nineteen who are during said Term to work and live upon the demised premises and WILLIAM HUMPHRIS shall have liberty to work two hands and no more on said premises above the slaves named said WILLIAM HUMPHRIS to discharge all quit rents and taxes and sufficient Cloath Victual and in all other respects well use the slaves herein mentioned and their increase .. (This lease also contains the proviso about growing tobacco and other crops and use of stock, horses and hogs and the schedule annexed, also proviso for wife to take fifty days to decide to retain lease if said WILLIAM HUMPHRIS dies during term, as in the previous lease) ..
in the presence of GRIFFIN GARLAND,   FRANCIS LIGHTFOOT LEE
          TIMOTHY CARRINGTON, FRANCIS STONE,
          SMITH KING, BEZAIL his mark ℬ BUCKINGHAM
   At a Court held for Loudoun County April the 26th 1773
This Indenture was proved by the Oath of TIMOTHY CARRINGTON a Witness thereto and on request of WILLIAM HUMPHRIS party thereto with the approbation of the Court the same with the Schedule annexed is ordered to be recorded
(On margin: Delivered to Mr. Humphreys Sept. 24th 1778)

pp.   THIS INDENTURE made this 26th day of April in year of our Lord one thousand
194-   seven hundred and seventy three Between STEPHEN ROSZEL of County of Lou-
197   doun and SARAH his Wife of one part and WILLIAM SMITH, STEPHEN DONALDSON
          THOS. LEWIS, JAMES HAMILTON, THOMSON MASON, FRANCIS PEYTON, CRAVEN
PEYTON, JOSIAS CLAPHAM, LEVEN POWELL, JOHN LEWIS, THOMAS OWSLEY AND THOMAS
SHORE Gentlemen, Vestrymen for Parish of Shelburne, of other part Witnesseth that for
sum of Twenty pounds current money of Virginia to said STEPHEN ROSZEL in hand paid
by said Parish of Shelburne by these presents do bargain and sell unto said .. (Vestrymen above named) .. and their Successors for the use of the Parish of Shelburne and to
be at the disposal of any Vestry for said Parish, a certain lott or parcell of land whereon
is standing that is usually called the MOUNTAIN CHAPPLE beginning at about three feet
North of a small Cluster of Rocks in the said ROSZEL's field, and running thence East
ranging with the North end of said ROSZEL's buildings and crossing the GREAT ROAD
twenty poles, thence North sixteen poles, thence West twenty poles to a small Hickory
Grubb thence So. sixteen poles to the beginning containing two acres of land and all
Houses Orchards and appurtenances whatsoever belonging To have and to hold the
lands hereby conveyed unto .. (Vestrymen above named) .. In Witness whereof said
STEPHEN ROSZEL and SARAH his Wife have hereunto set their hands and seals the day
and year first above written
in presence of   STEPHEN ROSZEL
   NB It is to be understood that the above Deed is only to convey from Mr. ROSZEL a

special Warrantee which is only from him and his heirs or any person claiming under
him or them

At a Court held for Loudoun County April 26th 1773
This Indenture and the Receipt thereon endorsed were acknowledged by STEPHEN
ROSZEL party thereto and is ordered to be recorded

pp.　THIS INDENTURE made the Fourteenth day of April in year of our Lord One thou-
197-　sand seven hundred and seventy three Between the Honourable GEORGE WIL-
201　LIAM FAIRFAX Esqr. of one part and RICHARD ORSEBORNE of County of Loudoun
　　　of other part Witnesseth that GEORGE WILLIAM FAIRFAX in consideration of the
rents and covenants on part of RICHARD ORSEBORNE to be paid and performed doth by
these presents grant set and to farm let unto said RICHARD ORSEBORNE one hundred and
eighty one acres of land with the appurtenances (except all mines minerals and quarries whatsoever) lying in Parish of Shelburne in County of Loudoun on side of the
BLUE RIDGE being part of a Tract of land of Thirty thousand one hundred and eight five
acres and called SHANNANDALE the bounds Beginning at a Chesnut Oak in a line of the
ARCADIA TRACT, Corner to JOHN ORSEBORNEs Lot, extending thence with the said line
So. 22 West Eighty two poles to a red Oak Corner to said Tract, thence with another of the
said lines So. 8 West One hundred and twenty five poles to two white Oaks in the line of
JOHN ORSEBORNEs land near the Corner of RICHARD ORSEBORNEs field, thence along the
line of the said ORSEBORNEs land So. 86 West one hundred and twenty poles to a red Oak
and small Hickory, thence North 8 East two hundred and sixty five poles to a Hickory in
the line of JOHN ORSEBORNEs Lott, thence with his line So. 68 East one hundred and
forty one poles to the beginning containing One hundred and eighty one acres To have
and to hold unto said RICHARD ORSEBORNE, JOHN ORSEBORNE his Son and THOMAS ORSE-
BORNE his Son and paying unto GEORGE WILLIAM FAIRFAX the yearly rent of three
pounds seventeen shillings and nine pence current money of Virginia said RICHARD
ORSEBORNE will within one year plant one hundred good Apple trees and two hundred
Peach trees and build a good Dwelling house twenty feet by sixteen and a Barn twenty
feet square after the manner of Virginia building
in presence of JAMES ADAM,　　　　　　　　　　　　　　G. W. FAIRFAX
　　　　CRAVEN PEYTON, NATHAN POTTS
　At a Court held for Loudoun County April the 26th 1773
This Indenture was proved on the part of GEORGE WILLIAM FAIRFAX Esqr. by the Oath
of JAMES ADAM, CRAVEN PEYTON and NATHAN POTTS, and acknowledged by said
RICHARD ORSEBORNE on his part, and is ordered to be recorded

pp.　THIS INDENTURE made this twenty seventh day of April in year of our Lord One
201-　thousand seven hundred and seventy three Between THOMAS GREEN of Loudoun
203　County of one part and WILLIAM DOUGLASS Gentleman of said County of other
　　　part Witnesseth that for sum of Seventy pounds current money of Virginia to
him said THOMAS GREEN in hand paid by these presents doth bargain and sell unto said
WILLIAM DOUGLASS his heirs and assigns forever a certain tract of land which was sold
to him the said THOMAS GREEN by RICHARD ROBERTS bearing date the fourteenth day of
March in year one thousand seven hundred and fifty eight containing fifty three acres
more or less and bounded beginning at a Chesnut Tree by the edge of a Branch and
running thence South thirty degrees East thirty two perches, thence East eighty three
perches, North fifty two perches, North seventy nine degrees West twenty perches,
North twenty six degrees West seventy perches, thence West Forty perches to two white
Oak thence South fifteen degrees West to the beginning, Together with all Woods,
waters and appurtenances whatsoever belonging To have and to hold unto said WIL-

LIAM DOUGLASS his heirs and assigns In Witness whereof the said THOMAS GREEN hath
set his hand and Seal the day and year first above written

                                        THOMAS GREEN

At a Court continued and held for Loudoun County April the 27th 1773
This Indenture with the Memorandum and Receipt thereon endorsed was acknowledged
by THOMAS GREEN party thereto to be his acts and deeds And is ordered to be recorded

p.   KNOW ALL MEN by these presents that I ELISHA COMBS of County of Loudoun and
204   in consideration of FERDINANDO ONEAL's becoming my Bail in a certain suit
        brought against me at the General Court by WILLIAM ALLISON, Mercht., for Debt
I do by these presents bargain sell and make over in plain and open market the following things for his Security, Vizt. Three feather beds and furniture and bedsteads,
three pewter dishes, one cow and yearling bot. of THOMAS OWSLEY, half a dozen pewter
plates, one Leather Trunk and one Tea Table, two Iron potts, washing tubs, pails &c., and
all my effects that I am at this time possess'd of which effects by these presents I do
warrant and it is hereby agreed that said goods and effects is to be subject to pay and
Satisfie any Debt said COMBS shall owe or fall in arrear to SIMON TRIPLETT on a
Settlement of the Acct. between them at this time. In Witness whereof I have hereunto
set my hand and seal this 2d day of Novemr. 1772
Signed & delivered one Buckle in   ELISHA COMBES
  the name of the whole in presence of
      WILLIAM COOPER, MARTHA TRIPLETT
At a Court continued and held for Loudoun County April the 27th 1773
This Bill of Sale was acknowledged by ELISHA COMBS party thereto to be his act and deed
and is ordered to be recorded

pp.   TO ALL TO WHOM this may concern I JOHN GRIFFITH for sum of Twenty four
204-   pounds two shillings current money in hand paid have bargained and sold unto
205   JOSEPH STEER and JENKIN WILLIAMS the following goods and chattels Viz. Ten
        acres of Wheat in the ground, Eight ditto of Rye in the ground, one Bay Mare 13
years old, 1 Sorrell Mare 5 years old, one yearling Heifer, Six young hogs, one large
Kettle, one iron pott, four large pewter dishes, one dozn. pewter plates, two large chests,
one plough and irons, one set of Harrow Teeth, one Cart, Together with all right title
and interest I now have in the above goods In Witness whereof I have hereunto set my
hand and affixed my seal this 2d day of December 1772
Test THOMAS WARMAN,   JOHN GRIFFITH
      JOHN HOUGH JUNR.
At a Court continued and held for Loudoun County April the 27th 1773
This Bill of Sale was acknowledged by JOHN GRIFFITH party thereto to be his act and
deed and is ordered to be recorded

pp.   THIS INDENTURE made the 24th day of February in year of our Lord One thou-
205-   sand seven hundred and seventy three Between FLEMING PATTERSON late of
208   TOWN of LEESBURG in County of Loudoun, but now of County of FAIRFAX and
        ELIZABETH his Wife of one part and HENRY McCABE of TOWN of ALEXANDRIA in
FAIRFAX COUNTY of other part WHEREAS said FLEMING PATTERSON in order to secure
the payment of a considerable sum of money due and owing from himself and his deceased Brother, JOHN PATTERSON, formerly of said TOWN of LEESBURG, unto said HENRY
McCABE did on the 15th day of June 1769 among other things bargain sell and confirm
unto HENRY McCABE and his heirs all Estate, right, Title and Interest which said
FLEMING PATTERSON had and claimed of in and to two lotts containing one acre of land

situate in TOWN of LEESBURG and known by the numbers Seventeen and Eighteen, and binding on MARKET STREET and BACK STREET, subject Nevertheless to this express proviso that is said FLEMING should well and truly pay unto HENRY McCABE the full sum of Five hundred and six pounds current money of Virginia with lawful Interest thereon from date of said Deed on or before first day of October then next ensuing that said Deeds should cease and become void as by said Deed duly recorded among the records of County Court of Loudoun may appear, AND WHEREAS neither the principal sum of money or Interest been paid said HENRY McCABE by reason whereof said HENRY McCABE with some other Creditors of said JOHN and FLEMING PATTERSON did exhibit a Bill in Chancery in County Court of Loudoun against said FLEMING PATTERSON and THOMAS PATTERSON, Brother and Heir at Law of said JOHN PATTERSON, to compell among other things the payment of said sum of money and Interest or have a decree for sale of the Real Estate of said JOHN and FLEMING PATTERSON and on 14th day of August seventeen hundred and seventy one the said Bill in Chancery together with the answer of said FLEMING coming on before the Court to be heard it was on hearing the same decreed and ordered that said Real Estate mentioned in Deed of Mortgage on failure of payment of said sum and Interest shou'd on first day of November Court then next following be sold at auction to the highest bidder for ready money and FLEMING PATTERSON should convey the same to the respective purchaser in Fee Simple NOW THIS INDENTURE WITNESSETH that FLEMING PATTERSON in compliance with above recited decree and sale in consequence thereof, and in consideration of said HENRY McCABE having signed and acknowledged a receipt for the said thirty two pounds in part of his whole demand against JOHN and FLEMING PATTERSON and also for sum of five shillings to FLEMING PATTERSON in hand paid said FLEMING PATTERSON and ELIZABETH his Wife do bargin and sell unto HENRY McCABE his heirs and assigns all those two lotts of land number Seventeen and Eighteen in said TOWN of LEESBURG In Witness whereof said FLEMING PATTERSON and ELIZABETH his Wife have hereunto set their hands and seals the day and year first above written

in presence of W. ELLZEY,   FLEMING PATTERSON
          WILLIAM DOUGLASS, WILLIAM NEILSON,
          G. JOHNSTON, HUMPY. FULLERTON, JOHN ADAM
   At a Court continued and held for Loudoun County April the 28th 1773
This Indenture with the Receipt and Memorandum there under written was proved by to be the acts and deeds of the within mentioned FLEMING PATTERSON by the Oaths of WILLIAM ELLZEY, GEORGE JOHNSTON, Gent., and HUMPHREY FULLERTON, three of the Subscribing witnesses thereto and is ordered to be recorded

pp.   THIS INDENTURE made twenty sixth day of February in year of our Lord One
208-   thousand seven hundred and seventy three Between FLEMING PATTERSON of
212   TOWN of LEESBURG, Surviving Partner of JOHN PATTERSON, late of said TOWN
           deceased and ELIZABETH his Wife of one part and HENRY McCABE of TOWN of
ALEXANDRIA, Merchant, of other part. WHEREAS said FLEMING PATTERSON in order to secure the payment of a considerable sum of money due and owing by said JOHN and FLEMING PATTERSON to HENRY McCABE did among other things on Fifteenth day of June in year One thousand seven hundred and sixty nine bargain and convey unto HENRY McCABE his heirs and assigns all the right title and Estate which said FLEMING PATTERSON had in a certain lott or half acre of land lying in TOWN of LEESBURG whereon said FLEMING PATTERSON then resided, and known by the Number Thirty Two, Subject nevertheless to express proviso that if FLEMING PATTERSON should pay HENRY McCABE the just sum of Five hundred and six pounds current money of Virginia with lawfull interest thereon from date of said Deed before first day of October next ensuing that

then the said Indenture and everything therein contained should cease determine and be void as by said Indenture remaining of record in Clerks Office of County of Loudoun, And Whereas the said principal sum of money and interest or any part thereof had not been paid to HENRY McCABE by FLEMING PATTERSON said HENRY McCABE together with several other persons exhibited a Bill in Chancery in County Court of Loudoun against said FLEMING PATTERSON and a certain THOMAS PATTERSON, to compell among other things the payment of said principal sum of money and interest then due or have a decree made for sale of said Lot or half acre of land It was on the fourteenth day of November in year One thousand seven hundred and seventy one decreed, among other things. that said half acre of land should be sold on the first day of Court to be held in November then next ensuing Witnesseth that FLEMING PATTERSON in compliance with above recited decree and sale in consequence thereof and in consideration of HENRY McCABE having executed and acknowledged a Release and for sum of Five shillings to FLEMING PATTERSON in hand paid and ELIZABETH his Wife by these presents do bargain and sell unto HENRY McCABE his heirs and assigns all that lot of land lying in Town of LEESBURGH numbered Thirty two In Witness whereof said FLEMING PATTERSON and ELIZABETH his Wife have hereunto set their hands and affixed their seals the day and year first above mentioned

in presence of W. ELLZEY,   FLEMING PATTERSON
    CRAVEN PEYTON, WILLIAM DOUGLASS
    G. JOHNSTON, JOHN ADAM
  At a Court continued and held for Loudoun County April 28th 1773
This Indenture with the Receipt and Memorandum thereon endorsed was proved to be the acts and deeds of FLEMING PATTERSON by the Oaths of WILLIAM ELLZEY, CRAVEN PEYTON and GEORGE JOHNSTON Gent., three of the subscribing witnesses thereto, And is ordered to be recorded

pp.   THIS INDENTURE made the fourteenth day of April in year of our Lord One thou-
212- sand seven hundred and seventy three Between the Honourable GEORGE WIL-
217   LIAM FAIRFAX Esquire of one part and JOHN ORSBORNE of County of Loudoun of
    other part Witnesseth that GEORGE WILLIAM FAIRFAX in consideration of rents and covenants on part of said JOHN ORSEBORNE to be paid and performed by these presents doth set and to farm let unto said JOHN ORSEBORNE one hundred and thirty two acres of land with the appurtenances (except mines, minerals and Quarries whatsoever) lying in Parish of Shelburne in County of Loudoun on side of the BLUE RIDGE being part of a tract of land of Thirty thousand one hundred and eighty five acres and called SHANNANDALE, the bounds beginning at two white Oaks corner to JOHN ORSBORNEs forty acre Tract of land extending thence No. 62 West six poles to a Chesnut marked WFX corner of said ORSEBORNEs other Tract of land thence with his line No. 34 East sixteen poles to a Chesnut Oak Corner to a Lot surveyed for THOMAS LEWELLIN, thence with his line No. 68 West one hundred poles to a small Hickory saplin and three Chesnut Oaks another of said LEWELLINs Corners, thence So. 22 West One hundred and sixty poles to four Chesnut Oaks in a heap of rock Stones, thence So. 68 East One hundred and seventy seven poles to a Chesnut Oak in a line of the ARCADIA TRACT thence with said line No. 22 East forty seven poles to a white Oak in a stoney Bottom, Corner to said ORSBORNEs forty acre Tract, thence with his line No. 62 West sixty six poles to two Chesnut Oaks on a stoney Hill another of his Corners, thence with another of his lines No. 18 East ninety poles to the beginning containing One hundred and two two acres To have and to hold said land and premises (except before excepted) to said JOHN ORSE- BORNE JUNR., Son of said JOHN, MORRIS ORSEBORNE, Son of RICHARD ORSEBORNE, and SAMUEL ORSBORNE, Son of JOHN, paying unto GEORGE WILLIAM FAIRFAX every year on

first day of May the rent of Two pounds sixteen shillings and eight pence current money of Virginia and within one year plant one hundred good Apple trees and two hundred Peach trees and erect a good Dwelling House twenty feet by sixteen and a Barn twenty feet square after the manner of Virginia building In Witness whereof the said parties to these presents have hereunto interchangeably set their hands and affixed their seals the day and year first above written

in witness of JAMES ADAM,   G. W. FAIRFAX
    CRAVEN PEYTON, RICHARD ORSBORNE
  At a Court held for Loudoun County May the 10th 1773
This Indenture was proved to be the act and deed of GEORGE WILLIAM FAIRFAX Esqr. party thereto by the Oaths of JAMES ADAM, CRAVEN PEYTON and RICHARD OSBURN, the Subscribing witnesses therein mentioned and acknowledged by said JOHN OSBORNE on his part And is ordered to be recorded

pp.   THIS INDENTURE made this twenty eighth day of November in year of our Lord
217- One thousand seven hundred and seventy two Between the Honble. JOHN TAY-
219   LOE Esqr. of County of RICHMOND on one part and WILLIAM RUSSELL of Loudoun
      County, Farmer, on other part, Witnesseth that JOHN TAYLOE Esqr. in considera-
tion of rents and covenants on part of WILLIAM RUSSELL to be paid and performed doth grant and to farm let unto WILLIAM RUSSELL his heirs and assigns a certain lott of land Vizt. Lott No. 20 containing by Estimation one hundred and forty six acres or there-abouts situate in County of Loudoun being part of a larger tract of land belonging to said JOHN TAYLOE Esqr. and bounded beginning at the Corner of THOMAS PURCEL, thence running No. 114 po. to K a large Rock & Chesnut, thence So. 57 Et. 88 po. to two white Oaks thence So. 24 Wt. 11 po. to a red Oak, thence So. 57 Et. 40 po. to a red Oak a white Oak and Hickory, thence So. 34 Wt. 80 po. to two red Oaks, thence No. 59 W. 88 po. to a white Oak and two red Oak saplins, thence So. 87 W. 24 po. to a red Oak, thence to the beginning, containing one hundred and forty six acres excepting mines minerals and Quarrys To have and to hold said lott of land unto said WILLIAM RUSSELL for and during the natural lives of him said WILLIAM RUSSELL, RUTH RUSSELL his Wife and JOHN RUS-SELL his Son he or they paying unto JOHN TAYLOE upon the tenth day of November in each year the annual rent of Forty Shillings current money of Virginia to be paid at the NEABSCO FURNACE in PRINCE WILLIAM COUNTY and that he shall plant at least One hundred Apple trees and one hundred and fifty Peach trees In Witness whereof I THOMAS LAWSON by Virtue of a Power of Attorney made to me by said JOHN TAYLOE Esqr. bearing date the third day of September one thousand seven hundred and sixty four duly recorded in records of County of RICHMOND do hereunto set the name and affix the seal of said JOHN TAYLOE Esqr. in his behalf

in presence of JOHN EVANS,   JOHN TAYLOE
    SAMUEL RICH, BENJA. PHILIPS,   WM. RUSSEL
    SAMUEL RUSSELL, JAMES BROWN
  At a Court held for Loudoun County May the 10th 1773
This Indenture was proved to be the act and deed of JOHN TAYLOE Esqr. (by THOMAS LAWSON his Attorney in fact), by the oaths of JOHN EVANS, BENJAMIN PHILLIPS and SAMUEL RUSSEL three of the subscribing witnesses thereto and acknowledged by said WILLIAM RUSSEL on his part, And is ordered to be recorded

pp.   THIS INDENTURE made this Twenty Eighth day of Novr: in year of our Lord One
219- thousand seven hundred and seventy two Between the Honble. JOHN TAYLOE
221   Esqr. of RICHMOND COUNTY of one part and JOHN EVANS of Loudoun County,
      Farmer, of other part Witnesseth that JOHN TAYLOE Esqr. in consideration of

rents and covenants on part of JOHN EVANS to be paid and performed by these presents doth grant and to farm let unto JOHN EVANS and to his heirs and assigns a Certain lott of land Viz. No. 23 containing by estimation one hundred and thirty four acres or there-abouts, situate in County of Loudoun being part of a larger tract of land belonging unto JOHN TAYLOE Esqr. and bounded beginning at a red Oak in the line of the Patent, Corner to THOMAS GREGG, thence in the said Pattent No. 17 Et. 168 poles to a parcel of saplins, Corner to JOHN TREBBY thence North 64 Wt. 130 poles to a Hickory and red Oak thence So. 15 Wt. 167 poles to a white Oak thence to the beginning containing one hundred and thirty four acres excepting all mines minerals and Quarrys To have and to hold said lott of land for and during the natural lives of said JOHN EVANS, ELIZABETH EVANS his Wife and ELIAZER EVANS, his Son, he or they paying unto JOHN TAYLOE Esqr. upon the tenth day of November in each year the rent of Forty shillings current money of Virginia at the NEABSCO FURNACE in PRINCE WILLIAM COUNTY, and shall plant at least One hundred Apple trees and One hundred and fifty Peach trees In Witness whereof I THOMAS LAWSON by Virtue of a Power of Attorney made to me by said JOHN TAYLOE bearing date the third day of September One thousand seven hundred and sixty four duly recorded in the records of the County of RICHMOND do in behalf of said JOHN TAYLOE hereunto sign his name and affix his seal

in presence of WM. RUSSEL, SAMUEL RICH,   JOHN TAYLOE
    SAMUEL RUSSEL, BENJA. PHILLIPS   JOHN EVANS
    JAMES BROWN

At a Court held for Loudoun County May the 10th 1773
This Indenture was proved to be the act and deed of JOHN TAYLOE Esqr. (by THOMAS LAWSON his Attorney in Fact) by the Oaths of WILLIAM RUSSEL, SAMUEL RUSSEL and BENJAMIN PHILLIPS, three of the subscribing witnesses thereto, and acknowledged by said JOHN EVANS on his part, And is ordered to be recorded
(On margin: Exd. & d'd D. EVANS 22d Oct 1779)

pp. THIS INDENTURE made the sixteenth day of December in year of our Lord One
221- thousand seven hundred and seventy two Between the Honble. JOHN TAYLOE
223 Esqr. of County of RICHMOND of one part and THOMAS HUMPHREY of County of
   Loudoun of other part Witnesseth that JOHN TAYLOE Esqr. in consideration of
sum of five shillings current money of Virginia to him in hand paid by these presents doth bargain and sell unto THOMAS HUMPHREY all that tract of land being part of a larger tract of Twelve hundred and fourteen acres originally granted from the Proprietors Office unto a certain FRANCIS AUBREY and said AUBREY sold and conveyed to the Honble. JOHN TAYLOE of County of RICHMOND, Father to above said JOHN TAYLOE Esqr., party to these presents, situate under the BLUE RIDGE in County of Loudoun beginning at a stoney Hill on the lowermost corner of the Original Tract, where formerly stood two Chesnut Oaks which were Burnt but now some Chesnut Oak saplings growing in their Room, extending thence So. Two hundred and two poles to a small Spanish and Chesnut Oak Corner to a lot of land Leased unto a certain JOHN MARKS, thence Wt. one hundred and seventy four poles to a Hickory and Chesnut on the side of a Hill, thence No. fifty poles crossing a small branch to a Stake near a Hickory and red Oak in a line of marked trees on the said branch, thence with said line of marked trees Wt. one hundred and ninety one poles to two white Oaks in the back line of said Patent, thence with the line of said Patent NNE one hundred and thirty six poles to two red Oaks on a Barren Hill, being the Corner tree of said Patent, thence with the line of said Patent to the beginning containing by estimation three hundred and thirty two acres be the same more or less and all Houses, Orchards and appurtenances whatsoever belonging To have and to hold the lands hereby conveyed during full term of one whole year paying

therefore the rent of one Pepper Corn on Lady Day next to intent that by virtue of these presents and statute for transferring uses into possession said THOMAS HUMPHREY may be in actual possesssion and be thereby enabled to accept a Release of Inheritance thereof In Witness whereof and by Virtue of a Power of Attorney made by the Honble. JOHN TAYLOE Esqr. to me THOMAS LAWSON being date the third day of September 1764 duly recorded in the records of County of RICHMOND I THOMAS LAWSON do hereunto sign the name and affix the seal of said TAYLOE in his behalf
in presence of JOHN PRICE POSEY,   JOHN TAYLOE
        THOMAS CHAPMAN, PHIL. RD. FRANS. LEE,
        ALEX. CAMPBELL, W. ELLZEY, WILLM. GRAYSON
  At a Court held for Loudoun County May 10th 1773
This Indenture was proved by the Oaths of WILLIAM ELLZEY, WILLIAM GRAYSON and JOHN PRICE POSEY three of the subscribing witnesses to be the act and deed of JOHN TAYLOE Esqr. as Executed by THOMAS LAWSON, Attorney in Fact for said JOHN TAYLOE, party thereto, And is ordered to be recorded

pp.   THIS INDENTURE made the seventeenth day of December in year of our Lord One
223- thousand seven hundred and seventy two Between the Honourable JOHN TAYLOE
226   Esqr. of County of RICHMOND of one part and THOMAS HUMPHREY of County of
       Loudoun of other part Witnesseth that in consideration of sum of One hundred
and sixty six pounds current money of Virginia to said JOHN TAYLOE Esqr. in hand paid by these presents doth bargain and sell unto THOMAS HUMPHREY (in his actual possession by virtue of a bargain and sale for one whole year and by force of the statute for transferring uses into possession) and his heirs and assigns forever .. (amount of land, description of land and conveyances as in Lease above) .. To have and to hold unto said THOMAS HUMPHREY his heirs and assigns forever In Witness whereof and by virtue of a Power of Attorney made by the Honble JOHN TAYLOE Esqr. to me THOMAS LAWSON bearing date the third day of September 1764 duly recorded in the records of County of RICHMOND I THOMAS LAWSON do hereunto sign the name and affix the seal of the said TAYLOE in his behalf
in presence of JOHN PRICE POSEY,   JOHN TAYLOE
        THOMAS CHAPMAN, PHIL. RD. FRANS. LEE,
        ALEXR. CAMPBELL, W. ELLZEY, WILLM. GRAYSON
  At a Court held for Loudoun County May the 10th 1773
This Indenture was proved by the Oaths of WILLIAM ELLZEY, WILLIAM GRAYSON and JOHN PRICE POSEY the subscribing witnesses to be the act and deed of JOHN TAYLOE Esqr. as executed by THOMAS LAWSON, Attorney in Fact for said JOHN TAYLOE party thereto, and the Receipt thereon endorsed was also proved by the oaths of WILLIAM ELLZEY and WILLIAM GRAYSON and together with the said Indenture is ordered to be recorded
(On margin: Ex'd Deliv'd to Mr. HUMPHREYS Dec. 12th 1775)

pp.   THIS INDENTURE made the Tenth day of May in year of our Lord One thousand
226- seven hundred and seventy three Between MAHLON JANNEY of County of Lou-
228   doun and SARAH his Wife of one part and LEVEN POWELL of same County of
       other part Witnesseth that for sum of Twenty five pounds current money of
Virginia to said MAHLON JANNEY in hand paid by these presents doth bargain and sell unto LEVEN POWELL and his heirs all the residue of a certain tract of land which was taken up and Pattented by ANN JANNEY deced and descends to said MAHLON JANNEY as heirs at Law part of the said Tract being formerly sold to WILLIAM RUST and is bounded beginning at a red Oak corner to said WILLIAM RUST in the line of EDMONDSON and running thence with the said EDMONDSONs line So. 25 1/2 Wt. 56 poles thence So. 60 East

72 poles to four small Oaks thence So. 11 Et. 162 poles to a white Oak and black Oak on a Knowl marked **A I** and **H I** thence East 192 poles to the line of BENJAMIN GRAYSON deced, thence No. 30 Wt. 134 poles to a white Oak in a Glade Corner to WILLIAM RUST, thence with his line No. 56 Wt. 234 poles to the beginning containing one hundred and ninety six acres be the same more or less Except what part thereof may be taken away by any elder Survey and all Houses, Orchards and appurtenances whatsoever belonging to have and to hold the lands hereby conveyed unto LEVEN POWELL his heirs and assigns forever In Witness whereof said MAHLON JANNEY and SARAH his Wife have hereunto set their hands and seals the day and year first above written
in psence of   MAHLON JANNEY
NB It is to be understood that this Deed is only to contain a Special Warrantee
  At a Court held for Loudoun County May the 10th 1773
This Indenture and the Receipt thereon endorsed were acknowledged by MAHLON JANNEY party thereto to be his act and deed And is ordered to be recorded
(On margin: Ex'd and Del'd to Mr. HARRISON 3d May 1774)

pp.   THIS INDENTURE made the tenth day of May in year of our Lord one thousand
228-   seven hundred and seventy three Between THOMAS SMITH of County of Loudoun,
230   Farmer, of one part and WILLIAM REEDER the Younger of said County, Farmer,
        of other part Witnesseth that THOMAS BLACKBURN of PRINCE WILLIAM County
Gentleman in and by one Indenture bearing date the second day of November One thousand seven hundred and seventy one and recorded in County Court of Loudoun for the consideration therein mentioned did grant and to farm lett unto THOMAS SMITH his heirs or assigns a lot or parcel of land for and during the lives therein respectivley mentioned and the longest liver of them, NOW THIS INDENTURE WITNESSETH that said THOMAS SMITH for sum of Sixty four pounds current money of Virginia to him in hand paid by these presents doth bargain and set over unto WILLIAM REEDER his heirs or assigns all that lot or parcel of land containing one hundred and forty acres and bounded as set forth in said Lease together with all improvements thereon as also the Winter Grain now sown and all right said THOMAS SMITH now hath or ought to have in said parcel of land, as also the Indenture of Lease during lives respectively mentioned paying the rents reserved and performing the covenants and agreements in said recited Lease contained In Witness whereof said THOMAS SMITH hath hereunto set his hand and seal the day and year first above written
in presence of   THOS. SMITH
  At a Court held for Loudoun County May the 10th 1773
This Indenture was acknowledged by THOMAS SMITH party thereto to be his act and deed And is ordered to be recorded

pp.   THIS INDENTURE made this Twenty Eighth day of October in year of our Lord One
230-   thousand seven hundred and seventy two Between SIMON TRIPLETT Gent. of
232   County of Loudoun of one part and CHARLES DAVIS, Sadler, of same County of
        other part, Witnesseth that Whereas WILLIAM CARR LANE now Deceased of the
County of Loudoun in his lifetime by Indenture of Lease bearing date the Twelfth day of November in year One thousand seven hundred and sixty six sealed with his seal for the consideration of the Rents and Covenants therein expressed on part of said CHARLES DAVIS to be paid and performed did demise set and to farm let unto said CHARLES DAVIS and to his assigns &c. one certain parcel of land containing twenty five acres situate in County of Loudoun adjoining NEWGATE being part of a greater tract which said LANE bought of JOHN NEWTON late of County of WESTMORELAND and bounded according to the several courses in said above recited Deed of Lease To have and to hold said parcel of

land with all the appurtenances unto said CHARLES DAVIS his heirs and assigns during
the natural lives of said CHARLES DAVIS, ANN his Wife and CHARLES BURGESS DAVIS
and the longest liver of them under the yearly rent of ten shillings current money
Now This Indenture Witnesseth that CHARLES DAVIS for sum of thirty pounds current
money of Virginia to him in hand paid by these presents doth bargain sell and set over
unto SIMON TRIPLETT his heirs and assigns all the said parcel of land containing
twenty five acres with all Houses Orchards and appurtenances whatsoever belonging
To have and to hold during the lives of said CHARLES DAVIS, ANN his Wife and CHARLES
BURGESS DAVIS his Son and longest liver of them under the rents, reservations and
covenants in above recited Indenture of Lease In Witness whereof said CHARLES DAVIS
hath hereunto set his hand and seal the day month and year first above written
in presence of JAS. COLEMAN,   CHARLES DAVIS
          JAMES HERRYFORD, WM. GUNNELL,
          WM. GRAYSON, JOHN THORNTON
     At a Court held for Loudoun County May the 10th 1773
This Indenture was proved by the Oaths of JAMES COLEMAN, WILLIAM GRAYSON and
JOHN THORNTON, Gent., three of the subscribing witnesses thereto, to be the act and deed
of CHARLES DAVIS, the Grantor, And is ordered to be recorded

pp.   THIS INDENTURE made this twenty fourth day of April in year of our Lord One
232-   thousand seven hundred and seventy three Between CLARE OXLEY of County of
233   Loudoun of one part and EVERITT OXLEY of same County of other part Witnesseth
          that said CLARE OXLEY for sum of Twenty pounds to him in hand paid by these
presents doth bargain and sell unto EVERITT OXLEY and to his heirs and assigns forever
a certain tract of land situate in Loudoun County being part of a Tract Pattented to
CATESBY COCKE from me LORD FAIRFAX's Office and by him transferred by his Attorney
in Fact, AENEAS CAMPBELL, to JOHN HOUGH and by said HOUGH conveyed by Lease and
Release to HENRY OXLEY SENR. and by said OXLEY SENIOR to said CLARE OXLEY and
bounded beginning at a red Oak saplin an old Corner to said EVERITT OXLEY also corner
to JOHN OXLEY's the North side of a small Branch running with said EVERITTs line So. 31
Wt. thirty eight poles to a Hickory saplin on a stoney Knowl Corner to RACHEL OXLEY in
a line of EVERITT OXLEY's, thence with said RACHEL OXLEY's line N. 60 Wt. fifty four
poles to a large black Oak in said RACHELs line thence No. 20 E. Sixty seven to two white
Oak saplins growing out of one Root, thence So. 60 E. forty two poles till it intersects
JOHN OXLEY's line from thence So. 6 d. Wt. with said JOHN's line to the place of Beginning containing twenty acres but be the same more or less according to the above
boundaries and all Houses, Orchards and appurtenances whatsoever belonging To have
and to hold the tract of land abovementioned unto said EVERITT OXLEY his heirs and
assigns forever In Witness whereof said CLARE OXLEY hath hereunto set his hand and
seal the day and year first above written
in the presence of us HUGH NEILSON,   CLARE OXLEY
          THO. ROPER, THOS. SANDERS
     At a Court held for Loudoun County May the 10th 1773
This Indenture, Memorandum and Receipt thereon endorsed were acknowledged by
CLARE OXLEY party thereto to be his act and deed And is ordered to be recorded
(On margin: Delivered to JESSEE OXLEY Son & Heir to EVERITT OXLEY March 17th 1777)

pp.
234-
235

THIS INDENTURE made the XXIVth day of (blank) in year of our Lord One thousand seven hundred and (blank) Between BRYAN FAIRFAX of County of FAIR-
FAX of one part and JOHN DOWDALL of County of Loudoun of other part Witnesseth that BRYAN FAIRFAX in consideration of rents and covenants herein after
expressed doth grant and to farm let unto JOHN DOWDALL a certain parcel or lot of land
in County of Loudoun being part of a Tract containing Twelve thousand acres on West
side of DIFFICULT RUN and being bounded according to a Survey thereof made by Mr.
GEORGE WEST beginning at a Stake near a red or black Oak and running thence No. 15 d.
E. 196 poles to a Stone on No. side of a Branch in or near McCARTYs line thence with
that line So. 80 d. Et. 130 poles to two small red Oaks and a white Oak thence So. 15 d. W.
208 poles to a Spanish Oak and red Oak near a Gum No. 75 d. Wt. 130 poles to beginning
containing one hundred and sixty four acres Together with all rights members and
appurtenances thereunto belonging To have and to hold said One hundred and sixty
four acres with the appurtenances during the natural lives of said JOHN DOWDALL,
CHARLES GRIMES, his Nephew, and JOHN DOWDALL JUNIOR, his Nephew, paying unto
BRYAN FAIRFAX on or before the first day of December which shall be in year One
thousand seven hundred and seventy three the sum of one shilling current money of
Virginia for every acre of land hereby Leased and thenceforward yearly, and within
three years build a good Dwelling House at least sixteen feet square and such other
houses as his occupation may require and also plant out one hundred Apple trees and
one hundred Peach trees and will not make or tend any Tobacco or Indian Corn in the
aforesaid demised premises except about five acres of Indian Corn in each year
in the presence of us THOMAS JOHNSON,   BRYAN FAIRFAX
                                                          JOHN DOWDALL

At a Court held for Loudoun County May the 10th 1773
This Indenture was acknowledged by BRYAN FAIRFAX Esqr. and JOHN DOWDALL parties
thereto to be their acts and deeds And is ordered to be recorded
(On margin: Exam'd & D'd Augt. Court 1780)

pp.
235-
239

THIS INDENTURE made the Eleventh day of April in year of our Lord One thousand seven hundred and seventy three Between the Honourable GEORGE WIL-
LIAM FAIRFAX Esquire of one part and CHRISTOPHER FEARSNER of County of
Loudoun of other part Witnesseth that GEORGE WILLIAM FAIRFAX in consideration of the rents and covenants on part of CHRISTOPHER FEARSNER to be paid and performed doth grant and to farm let one hundred and eight acres of land with the appurtenances (except mines, mineals and Quarries) being in Parish of Shelburne in County
of Loudoun on the DUTCHMANS RUN being part of a Tract of Seventeen thousand two
hundred and ninety six acres and called PIEDMONT the bounds beginning at a white Oak
and Hickory in the line of MICHAEL USSELMAN standing near the DUTCHMANS RUN extending thence with his line So. 75 West Eighty two poles to a Hickory thence So. 30 East
seventy poles to a white Oak thence up said DUTCHMANS RUN So. 60 West seventy eight
poles to a small black Oak in a Bottom by PAYNES ROAD thence down the said Road So. 35
East eighty poles to three Spanish Oaks thence No. 75 East eighty six poles to a red Oak
by a Branch thence No. 15 West forty four poles to a Spanish Oak, thence No. 35 East sixteen poles to a Stake, thence No. 5 West forty poles in a Meadow, thence No. 84 West
seventeen poles, thence No. 5 West twenty poles, No. 72 East Eleven poles to a white Oak
thence No. 22 East forty two poles to a white Oak thence No. 57 West twenty seven poles
to the Beginning containing one hundred and eight acres To Have and to Hold said land
and premises (except before excepted) to said CHRISTOPHER FEARSNER his heirs and
assigns during lives of CHRISTOPHER FEARSNER, AGNES FRANCE, Wife of JOHN FRANCE,
and SARAH FEARSNER Wife of said CHRISTOPHER paying unto GEORGE WILLIAM FAIR-

FAX every year on the first day of May the rent of Two pounds six shillings current money of Virginia and will plant within two years one hundred good Apple trees and two hundred Peach trees and build a good Dwelling House twenty feet by sixteen and a Barn twenty feet square after the manner of Virginia building In Witness whereof the said parties to these presents have hereunto set their hands and affixed their seals the day and year first above written

in the presence of JAMES ADAM,   G. W. FAIRFAX
    JOHN ADAM, CRAVEN PEYTON   CHRISTOPHER FEARSNER

At a Court continued and held for Loudoun County May the 11th 1773
This Indenture was proved to be the act and deed of GEORGE WILLIAM FAIRFAX Esqr. the Lessor by the oaths of JAMES ADAM, JOHN ADAM and CRAVEN PEYTON, the subscribing witnesses thereto, and acknowledged by CHRISTOPHER FEARSNER on his part, and ordered to be recorded
(On margin: Examined & d'd J. FEARSNER 5 Apl: 82)

pp.   THIS INDENTURE made the thirtieth day of January in year of our Lord One
239-   thousand seven hundred and seventy three Between JAMES ABBETT and ANN his
242   Wife of County of Loudoun of one part and JOHN THORNTON, Attorney at Law, of
    TOWN of LEESBURG of other part Witnesseth that for sum of Eighty pounds current money of Virginia to said JAMES ABBETT and ANN his Wife in hand paid by these presents do bargain and sell unto JOHN THORNTON and his heirs and assigns one lot or half acre of land lying in TOWN of LEESBURG in County of Loudoun situate on MARKET STREET and adjoining one of the COURTHOUSE Lots, being numbered Twenty Six containing half an acre bound on the one side by MARKET STREET, on one other side by one of the Lots set apart for the purpose of a COURTHOUSE &c., one other side adjoining the Lot whereon BENJAMIN KEPTER now lives and all Houses Orchards and appurtenances whatsoever belonging To have and to hold the lands hereby conveyed unto said JOHN THORNTON and his heirs and assigns forever In Witness whereof said JAMES ABBETT and ANN his Wife have hereunto set their hands and seals the day and year first above written

in the presence of WILLIAM AUTON,   JAMES ABBETT
    WILLIAM DOUGLASS, JOHN LEWIS   ANN   her mark *A* ABBETT
    AMOS DAVIS

At a Court continued and held for Loudoun County May the 13th 1773
This Indenture was acknowledged by JAMES ABBETT and ANN his Wife parties thereto to be their acts and deeds (the said ANN having been first privately examined as the Law directs and relinquished her right of Dower therein) and the Receipt thereon endorsed was likewise acknowledged by the said JAMES and together with the said Indenture ordered to be recorded

pp.   THIS INDENTURE made the 27th day of May in year one thousand seven hundred
242-   and seventy three Between JOSEPH HOGE of County of Loudoun of one part and
244   SAMUEL SMITH of same County of other part Witnesseth that said JOSEPH HOGE in
    and by one Indenture of Lease for Lives obtained from Colo: THOMAS BLACK-BURN bearing date the Second day of November ADm. 1771 for the consideration therein mentioned did grant and farm let unto said JOSEPH HOGE as in recited Deed doth apper being recorded in Loudoun County Court And This Indenture further Witnesseth that said JOSEPH HOGE for sum of Forty pounds current money to him in hand paid hath sold and set over unto SAMUEL SMITH all that parcel of land containing One hundred acres on branches of GOOSE CREEK and bounded as is set forth in the Recited Indenture of Lease, And all right title interest and possession time in years to come and unexpired

which JOSEPH HOGE now hath in said premises To have and to hold the land, title and term of years sold and set over unto SAMUEL SMITH his heirs and assigns In Witness whereof said JOSEPH HOGE hath hereunto set his hand and seal the day and year first above written

in the presence of WM. HOUGH,   JOSEPH HOGE
         DANIEL LOVETT, HENRY SMITH,
         BENHARD MITINGER
   At a Court held for Loudoun County June 14th 1773
This Indenture was acknowledged by JOSEPH HOGE party thereto to be his act and deed and ordered to be recorded
(On margin: Exd. DD to Mr. Smith Jany 1775)

pp.   THIS INDENTURE made this Twenty seventh day of November in year of our Lord
244-   One thousand seven hundred and seventy two Between the Honourable JOHN
247   TAYLOE of RICHMOND COUNTY Esqr. of one part and DAVID EVANS of Loudoun
            County, Farmer, of other part Witnesseth that in consideration of the rents and
covenants on part of said DAVID EVANS to be paid and performed by these presents
JOHN TAYLOE doth grant and to farm let unto DAVID EVANS and to his heirs and assigns
a certain lot of land containing by estimation one hundred and thirty four acres or
thereabouts situate in the said County of Loudoun and bounded Beginning at a red Oak
sapling, Corner to JOHN CRAIGs lot, thence with his line No. 64 Wt. 118 po: to a white Oak
his Corner thence No. 16 East 172 po: to a white Oak Corner to JAMES NIXONs, thence So.
64 East 126 po: to a red Oak corner to AMOS GREIG in the line of the Patent, thence to the
beginning containing one hundred and thirty four acres as above To have and to hold
said lot of land with all rights members and appurtenances thereunto belonging
during natural live of him said DAVID EVANS, MARY EVANS his Wife and ABRAHAM
EVANS. his Son, paying JOHN TAYLOE upon tenth day of November in each year the
annual rents of Forty shillings to be paid at NEABSCO FURNACE in PRINCE WILLIAM
COUNTY In Witness whereof THOMAS LAWSON by virtue of a Power of Attorney to mee
made by the said JOHN TAYLOE bearing date the third day of September in year One
thousand seven hundred and sixty four and duly recorded in Records of RICHMOND
COUNTY do in the behalf of said JOHN TAYLOE hereunto set his hand and affix his seal
the day and year above written
in presence of JOHN McILHANEY,   JOHN TAYLOE
         THOS. HUMPHREY, JOSHUA his mark ⧻ GORE   DAVID EVANS
         JOHN EVANs mark ✗
   At a Court held for Loudoun County December 28th 1772 (1773 in text)
This Indenture was proved by the Oath of JOHN EVANS one of the subscribing witnesses
thereto, And at another Court held for the said County the 14th day of June 1772 the said
Indenture was fully proved by the Oaths of THOS. HUMPHREY and JOSHUA GORE, wit-
nesses thereto and then ordered to be recorded
(On margin: Ex'd & Del'd to Mr. WM. SMITH)

pp.   THIS INDENTURE made the Fifth day of December in year of our Lord One thou-
247   sand seven hundred and seventy two Between GEORGE WILLIAM FAIRFAX of
251   County of FAIRFAX Esqr. of one part and GEORGE NIXON of County of Loudoun of
            other part Witnesseth that GEO: WM. FAIRFAX in consideration of the rents and
covenants on part of GEORGE NIXON to be paid and performed by these presents doth
grant and to farm let unto said GEORGE NIXON a certain parcel of land situate in County
of Loudoun and bounded as by a Survey thereof made by JOHN HOUGH Beginning at a
white Oak corner to his former Lot extending thence So. 19 Wt. Twelve poles to a small

black Oak corner to GEORGE SHAFFER, then with his line East fifty poles to a red Oak, then South one hundred poles to a red Oak by a Road, then So. 75 Wt. one hundred and eighty four poles to a black Oak in a line of ISRAEL THOMPSON then No. 19 E. Two hundred poles to a white Oak corner to his former Lot, then So. 175 E. Ninety five poles to the beginning containing one hundred and fifty acres excepting all mines minerals and quarries To have and to hold said one hundred and fifty acres of land with the appurtenances unto GEORGE NIXON during the natural life of him said GEORGE NIXON, GEORGE NIXON JUNR., his Son, and JONAH NICKSON, his Son, and longest liver of them paying therefore unto GEO. WM. FAIRFAX on first day of May each year the rent of three pounds current money to be discharged in Cash or Tobacco at 10/ p Ct: or in Wheat at 2/6 per Bushel thats good and Merchantable to be delivered at some publick landing on the Navigable part of POTOMACK RIVER paying also the quit rents provided he or they do plant at least one hundred good Apple trees and also cause to be built a Dwelling House at least twenty feet long and sixteen feet wide the said Apple trees and house to be planted and built within two years of the date hereof and other such houses as his way of Husbandry may require In Witness whereof the parties above mentioned to these presents have interchangeably set their hands and seals the day and year first written
in presence of CRAVEN PEYTON,   G. W. FAIRFAX
          ISRAEL THOMPSON, JOHN HOWELL,
          SAM: CLANDINEN
     At a Court held for Loudoun County June 14th 1773
This Indenture was proved by the Oaths of CRAVEN PEYTON and JOHN HOWELL and by the Affirmation of ISRAEL THOMPSON, three of the subscribing witnesses thereto, to be the acts and deeds of GEORGE WILLIAM FAIRFAX Esqr. and GEORGE NIXON parties thereto and ordered to be recorded

pp.   KNOW ALL MEN by these presents that I JOHN HOPKINS of SALSBURY in County
252-   of LANCASTER and Province of PENSYLVANIA, Inn Keeper, for Divers con-
254   siderations and good causes me hereunto moving have appointed my trusty
          friend THOMAS GREGG of Loudoun County Gentleman my true and lawfull attor-
ney for me and in my name and to my use to ask demand recover and receive from JOHN HARRIS, the sum of two pounds & of DANIEL FEGAN the sum of fifteen shillings per acre for all and every acre by him calculated in both Loudoun County and Colony of Virginia granting my Attorney my sole and full power to take legal courses for such recovery as I myself might or could do were I personally present In Witness whereof I have hereunto set my hand and seal this 16th day of November in the Thirteenth year of the Reign of our Sovereign Lord George the Third &c. One thousand seven hundred and seventy two 1772.
          CALEB JOHNSON,   JOHN HOPKINS
          GEORGE BICKHAM, JAMES BUCKHAM
LANCASTER COUNTY ss.
     Before me the Subscriber one of his Majestys Justices of the peace for said County came JOHN HOPKINS and acknowledged the hereunto annexed Instrument or Power of Attorney to be his act and deed and desired that the same might be recorded. Witness my hand and seal this sixteenth day of November in year of our Lord One thousand seven hundred and seventy two
                                                 JAS. BICKHAM
LANCASTER COUNTY Ss.
     I EDWARD SHIPPEN Esqr. Clerk of the Court of General Quarter Sessions of Peace and Protonotary of the Court of Common Pleas for County of Lancaster in Province of PENSYLVANIA in North America do hereby certify that JAMES BICKHAM Esqr. is now

one of his Majestys Justices of the peace for said County Given under my hand and seal
of said County of Lancaster the Sixteenth day of November Anno Domini 1772
                              EDWARD SHIPPEN Prot.
                              & Cler Cur predict.
   At a Court held for Loudoun County June the 14th 1773
This Power of Attorney with the acknowledgment thereunto annexed under the Publick
Seal of the County of LANCASTER in the Province of PENSYLVANIA was produced in
Court and ordered to be recorded

pp.   THIS INDENTURE made the Seventh day of May in year of our Lord One thousand
254-   seven hundred and seventy three Between JOHN OSBORN SENER of County of
255   Loudoun of one part and JOHN OSBURN JUNIOR of County aforesaid of other part
         Witnesseth that JOHN OSBURN SENIOR for sum of Five shillings Sterling to him
in hand paid by these presents doth bargain and sell unto JOHN OSBURN JUNIOR all that
tract of land situate in County of Loudoun and bounded Begining at a Spanish and white
Oak saplins being the No: Et. Corner of JOHN OSBURN SENR. land and extending thence
with his line No. 62 30' Wt. three hundred and four poles to a Stake corner to said
OSBURN thence along the BLUE RIDGE No. 34 Et. Sixty five poles to a Stake corner to
THOS. PURSEL thence with his line S: 60 1/2 Et. three hundred and twenty eight poles to
a black and white Oak in a line of COLO. GEO: W. FAIRFAX thence with his line S: 52 Wt.
sixty five poles to the first station containing one hundred and sixteen and a half acres
of land and all houses orchards and appurtenances whatsoever belonging To have and
to hold the said tract of land unto said JOHN OSBORN JUNIOR his assigns for term of one
whole year paying therefore one Peper Corn in Feast of St. Michael to intent that by
virtue of these presents and by force of statute for transferring uses into possession
said JOHN OSBORN JUNR. may in actual possession and be thereby enabled to accept a
Release of Inheritance thereof In Witness whereof said JOHN OSBURN SENIOR have
hereunto set his hand and seal the day and year first above written
in the presence of us ROBT. JAMISON,   JOHN OSBURN
       RICHARD OSBORN, JOSEPH RICHARDSON   SARAH her mark α OSBURN
   At a Court held for Loudoun County June the 14th 1773
This Indenture was acknowledged by JOHN OSBURN and SARAH his Wife parties thereto
to be their acts and deeds (the said SARAH being first privately examined as the Law directs and relinquished her right of dower therein) and is ordered to be recorded

pp.   THIS INDENTURE made the Seventh day of May in year of our Lord One thousand
255-   seven hundred and seventy three Between JOHN OSBORN SENIOR of County of
259   Loudoun and SARAH his Wife of one part and JOHN OSBORN JUNIOR of the County
         aforesaid of other part Whereas there is a certain tract of land situate in County
of Loudoun on the Drains of KITTOCKTON between the SHORT HILL and the BLUE RIDGE
the above parcel of land bounded .. (description of land as in Lease above) .. containing
one hundred and sixteen and a half acres of land being part of a tract of land granted to
CATESBY COCKE Gent. by at Pattent from the Proprietors Office and by said COCK transferred to DAVID POTTS and from said POTTS to WILLIAM WILLIAMS and from sd WIL-
LIAMS to BARNARD YOUNG and from said YOUNG to THOS. LEWELLIN and JAMES JOHN
and from said THOMAS LEWELLIN to JOHN OSBORN SENR. Now This Indenture Witnesseth
that for sum of One hundred and forty pounds current money of Virginia to them in
hand paid JOHN OSBORN SENIOR and SARAH his Wife by these presents doth bargain and
sell unto JOHN OSBURN JUNR. in his actual possession now being by virtue of a bargain
and sale for one whole year and by force of statute for transferring uses into possession and his heirs and assigns all the said One hundred and sixteen and half acres of
land To have and to hold unto said JOHN OSBURN JUNR. his heirs and assigns In Wit-

ness whereof the said JOHN OSBURN SENIOR and SARAH his Wife hath hereunto set their hands and seals the day and year first above written
in presence of us ROBT: JAMISON,   JOHN OSBURN
        RICHARD OSBURN, JOSEPH RICHARDSON   SARAH her mark *Q* OSBURN
    At a Court held for Loudoun County June the 14th 1773
This Indenture was acknowledged by JOHN OSBURN SENR. and SARAH his Wife parties threto to be their acts and deeds the said SARAH having been first privately examined as the Law directs and relinquished her right of dower therein, and the receipt thereon endorsed was likewise acknowledged by said JOHN OSBURN and together with said Indenture ordered to be recorded

pp.   THIS INDENTURE made the Twelvth day of June in year of our Lord one thousand
259-   seven hundred and seventy three Between JOHN OSBURN SENIOR of County of
260   Loudoun and SARAH his Wife of one part and RICHARD OSBURN of said County
         of other part Witnesseth that JOHN OSBURN SENIOR for sum of five shillings to
him in hand paid by these presents doth bargain and sell unto RICHARD OSBURN all that tract of land situate in County of Loudoun and on South side of BLUE RIDGE on the head Draughts of KITTOCTON and bounded Beginning at a hollow white Oak and black Oak in a Valley near the foot of the BLUE RIDGE corner to GEO: W. FAIRFAX Esquire and SAMUEL JOHNSTON extending thence with JOHNSTONs line So. 26 Wt. one hundred and forty five poles to a line of COLO: JOHN TAYLOEs thence with his line West one hundred and six poles to a black Oak his Corner and Corner to THOMAS SUDONs line, No. 62 Wt. one hundred and sixty poles to a red Oak his Corner extending thence with another of his lines So. 22 30' Wst. one hundred poles thence North one hundred and twenty five poles to a line of said GEO: WM. FAIRFAX then with his line No. 86 Et. three hundred and sixty two poles to the first station containing two hundred acres of land together with all houses orchards and appurtenances to the same belonging To have and to hold during full term of one year paying therefore the rent of one Peper Corn on first day of November to intent and by virtue of these presents and force of statute for transferring uses into possession said RICHARD OSBURN may be in actual possession and be thereby enabled to except a grant of Inheritance thereof In Witness whereof JOHN OSBURN and SARAH his Wife hath hereunto set their hands and seals the day and year first above written
in the presence of us ROBERT JAMISON,   JOHN OSBURN
        JOSEPH RICHARDSON, JOHN OSBURN   SARAH her mark *U* OSBURN
    At a Court held for Loudoun County June the 14th 1773
This Indenture was acknowleged by JOHN OSBURN SENR. and SARAH his Wife parties thereto to be their acts and deeds (the said SARAH having been first privately examined as the Law directs and relinquished her right of dower therein) and is ordered to be recorded

pp.   THIS INDENTURE made the twelth day of June in year of our Lord one thousand
260-   seven hundred and seventy three Between JOHN OSBURN SENIOR of County of
263   Loudoun and SARAH his Wife of one part and RICHARD OSBURN of said County
         of other part Whereas there is a certain tract of land lying in County of Loudoun
on South side of the BLUE RIDGE on the Drafts of KITTOCTON CREEK being granted to JOHN HOUGH by a Patten from the Proprietors Office of the Northern Neck of Virginia bearing date (blank) and transferred from JOHN HOUGH to JOHN OSBURN SENIOR and bounded .. (description of land as in Lease above) .. Now This Indenture Witnesseth that JOHN OSBURN SENIOR and SARAH his Wife for sum of fourteen pounds ten shillings current money of Virginia to him in hand paid by these presents doth bargain and sell

unto RICHARD OSBURN in his actual possession now being by virtue of a bargain and
sale for one year and by virtue of the Statute for Transferring uses into possession and
his heirs and assigns all the said Two hundred acres of land In Witness whereof said
JOHN OSBURN and SARAH his Wife hath hereunto set their hands and seals the day and
year first above written
in the presence of us ROBT. JAMISON,   JOHN OSBURN
          JOSEPH RICHARDSON, JOHN OSBORN   SARAH her mark OSBURN
     At a Court held for Loudoun County June the 14th 1773
This Indenture was acknowledged by JOHN OSBORN SENR. and SARAH his Wife parties
thereto to be their acts and deeds (the said SARAH having been first privately examined
as the Law directs and relinquished her right of Dower threin) and the Receipt thereon
endorsed was likewise acknowledged by JOHN OSBORN and together with said Indenture
ordered to be recorded

pp.   THIS INDENTURE made this Tenth day of May in year of our Lord One thouand
263-   seven hundred and seventy three Between DANIEL LOVETT of County of Loudoun
265   of one part and WILLIAM BEANS of County aforesaid of other part Witnesseth
         that WILLIAM FAIRFAX Esqr. in and by one Indenture of Lease bearing date the
first day of May Domini one thouand seven hundred and fourty four for consideration
therein mentioned did grant and to farm let unto SAMUEL GREGG of County of Loudoun
one certain tract of land situate in County of Loudoun on a Branch called the BEVER
DAM BRANCH of KITTOCKTON CREEK and further bounded as in said recited Indenture of
Lease it doth more fully appear, and by him transfer'd unto JAMES CADWALLEDER by a
Lease of Assignment bearing date the Nine day of June Domini one thousand seven
hundred & sixty six and by JAMES CADWALLEDER transfer'd to DANIEL LOVATT by a
Lease of Assignment bearing date the fourth day of May Domini one thousand seven
hundred and sixty seven. And This Indenture further Witnesseth that said DANIEL
LOVATT for sum of Two hundred and twenty five pounds Virginia Currency to him in
hand paid by these presents doth bargain and sell unto WILLIAM BEANS his assigns all
that Lot of Land as more particularly set forth in the above recited Lease and all the Estate right title & Interest, possession term of years to come which said DANIEL LOVETT
now hath or should have by virtue of said recited Indenture of Lease To have and to
hold the said Lott of land and recited lease and years to come unto said WILLIAM BEANS
his assigns In Witness whereof the said DANIEL LOVETT hath hereunto set his hand and
seal the day and year first above written
in the presence of ISRAEL THOMPSON,   DANIEL LOVETT
          ISAAC THOMPSON, JNO. CHAMBERLAIN,
          JONAH THOMPSON, JOHN REDMOND
     At a Court held for Loudoun County June the 14th 1773
This Indenture was acknowledged by DANIEL LOVETT party thereto to be his act and
deed and is ordered to be recorded

pp.   THIS INDENTURE made the fourteenth day of June in year of our Lord Christ One
265-   thousand seven hundred and seventy three Between JOHN PYLES and JEMIMA
268   his Wife of Parish of Cameron in County of Loudoun of one part and JOHN SINK-
         LER and JOHN DAVIS (Trustees for the DUTCH SETTLEMENT in the said Parish of
Cameron in County aforesaid) and their Successors of other part Witnesseth that said
JOHN PYLES for sum of Twenty five shillings current money of Virginia to him in hand
paid by said JOHN SINKLER and JOHN DAVIS by these presents doth bargain and sell
unto said JOHN SINKLER and JOHN DAVIS as aforesaid and their Successors forever all
that parcel of land situate in Parish of Cameron joining the Plantation whereon said

JOHN PYLES now lives containing as by a Survey thereof by GEORGE WEST one hundred and fifty perches and bounded Beginning at a Stake by a parcel of Bushes in the line of PYLES his Tract thence No. 53 d. 45' West 25 poles to a Stone on the side of the CHURCH ROAD, thence down the same S. 87 1/2 East 22 poles to a stone on the South side thereof thence S. 7 1/2 West 14 poles to the beginning To have and to hold the said Tenement with the appurtenances unto JOHN SINKLER and JOHN DAVIS Trustees as aforesaid and their Successors In Witness whereof said JOHN PYLES and JAMIMA his Wife hath hereunto set their hands and seals the day month and year first above written
in the presence of PHILLIP MORGERT   John his mark ✝ PYLES
　　　　　HENRY SMITH,   JAMIMA her mark / PYLES
　　　　　PHILLIP MICHEL (in text "name in Dutch")
 At a Court held for Loudoun County June the 14th 1773
This Indenture was acknowledged by JOHN PYLES and JEMIMA his Wife parties thereto to be their acts and deeds (the said JEMIMA having been first privately examined as the Law directs and relinquished her right of Dower therein) and the Receipt and Memorandum thereon endorsed was likewise acknowledged by said JOHN PYLES and together with the said Indenture ordered to be recorded

pp.　　THIS INDENTURE made this 14th day of June in year of our Lord one thousand
268-　　seven hundred and seventy three Between JOHN DODD of County of Loudoun of
270　　one part and JACOB JANNY of same County of other part Witnesseth that said
　　　　JOHN DODD for sum of five shillings lawful money of England to him in hand
paid by these presents doth bargain and sell JACOB JANNEY all that tract of land situate in County of Loudoun and bounded Beginning at a black Oak at the head of a Gully marked W/Xand/A ¥ Corner to the land of CHARLES McMANNIMY purchased of BRYANT FAIRFAX Esqr. and corner to JACOB JANNEY and THOS. CARR, extending thence with CARRs line N. 80 d. Et. One hundred and sixty six poles to a white Oak his Corner in a line of Colo. JOHN CARLYLEs, thence with CARLYLEs line South one hundred and twenty poles to a red Oak and Hickory at or near the head of a Glade corner to said McMANAMY and then with his line No. 45 d. Wt. Two hundred and twenty poles to the first station containing sixty acres and a Quarter which said tract of land was conveyed to said JOHN DODD by a Pattent out of the Proprietors Office which Pattent was duly Examined and recorded in Book　　Folio 165 And all Houses orchards and advantages whatsoever belonging To have and to hold said tract of land and premises above mentioned from first day of April last past during full term of one whole year paying therefore one Pepper Corn upon Feast of St. Michael the Archangel to intent that by virtue of these presents and by force of Statute for transferring uses into possession said JACOB JANNEY may be in actual possession and be thereby enabled to accept a Release of inheritance thereof In Witness whereof said JOHN DOD hath hereunto set his hand and affixed his eal the day and year first above written
in the presence of WM. WILDMAN,   JOHN DODD
　　　　　ISAAC FOUCH, WM. WILDMAN JUNR.
 At a Court held for Loudoun County June the 14th 1773
This Indenture was ackowledged by JOHN DODD party thereto to be his act and deed and is ordered to be recorded

pp.　　THIS INDENTURE made this (blank) day of June in year of our Lord one thousand
270-　　seven hundred and seventy three Between JOHN DODD of County of Loudoun and
273　　JANE DODD his Wife of one part and JACOB JANNEY of same County of other part
　　　　Witnesseth that JOHN DODD and JANE his Wife for sum of Forty pounds current money of Virginia to them in hand paid by these presents doth bargain and sell unto

JACOB JANNEY in his actual possession now being by virtue of a bargain and sale for one whole year and by force of statute for transferring uses into possession and his heirs and assigns forever all that tract of land lying in County of Loudoun bounded .. (description of land as in Lease above) .. To have and to hold said tract of land unto said JACOB JANNEY his heirs and assigns In Witness whereof said JOHN DODD and JANE DODD his Wife have hereunto set their hands & affixt their seals the day and year first above written

in the presence of WM. WILDMAN,   JOHN DODD
      ISSAC FOUCH, WM. WILDMAN JUNR.   JANE DODD

  At a Court held for Loudoun County June the 14th 1773
This Indenture was acknowledged by JOHN DODD and JANE his Wife parties thereto to be their acts and deeds (the said JANE having been first privately examined as the Law directs and relinquished her right of Dower therein) and the Receipt thereon endorsed was likewise acknowledged by said JOHN DODD and together with the said Indenture ordered to be recorded

pp.   THIS INDENTURE made the first day of October in year of our Lord one thousand
273- seven hundred and seventy Between JOHN FITZHUGH of one part and THOMAS
276   BLINCOE of other part Witnesseth that JOHN FITZHUGH in consideration of the
       rents and covenants on part of THOMAS BLINCOE his heirs to be paid and per-
formed by these presents doth demise grant and to farm let unto THOMAS BLINCOE a certain tract of land situate in County of Loudoun commonly known by the name of FRYING PAN and bounded Beginning at a white Oak upper corner tree of PHILIP NOLANDs standing near the line of THOMAS LEE upon the bank of a branch of BROAD RUN called HORSEPEN RUN on North side thereof extending thence along said NOLANDs line North North East 248 poles to the CABBIN BRANCH thence the same Course continued 172 poles further to the corner tree of said NOLANDs, thence North 30 West 160 poles to another Corner tree of the said NOLANDs tract standing in a marshy branch thence the same Course continued 20 poles further to a black Oak on the bank of LICKING BRANCH running into HORSEPEN RUN thence up said Branch North 52 d. 30" East 140 poles to a white Oak thence South 50 d. East 116 poles to a black Oak thence South 87 East 80 poles to a black Oak thence South 80 poles to a white Oak near a ridge of Black Rocks, thence under the Ridge of Black Rocks South 30 d. West 200 poles thence South 50 East 205 poles thence South 30 d. 30" West 390 poles to the side of HORSEPEN RUN thence down said Run North 52 d. West 260 poles to the beginning excepting all mines minerals and Quarries To have and to hold the aforesaid tract of land with the appurtenances unto said THOMAS BLINCOE his heirs from date hereof untill the first day of January which shall be in the year of our Lord one thousand seven hundred and ninety one paying JOHN FITZHUGH or his heirs every year on the first day of January the sum of Thirty pounds and shall yield up unto JOHN FITZHUGH the aforesaid tract of land with appurtenances in good Tenantable repair that is to say with Four Dwelling Houses at least sixteen feet long and twelve feet wide each, also four Tobacco houses at least thirty two feet long and twenty feet wide and also plant at least four hundred Apple trees and four hundred Peach trees in good regular order and keep them well pruned and within a good fence and shall leave at expiration of said term at least three hundred acres of land uncleared in not less than one hundred acres in any one place In Witness whereof the said parties to these presents have hereunto set their hands and seals the say and year first above written

in the presence of W. PAYNE:r   JOHN FITZHUGH
      ED. DULEN, RICHARD PELL   another clause to be added that there is three
                                   hundred acres of land not to be cleared

THOS. BLINCOE

At a Court held for Loudoun County November the 12th 1770
This Indenture was proved by to be the acts and deeds of JOHN FITZHUGH and THOMAS
BLINCOE parties thereto by the Oaths of WILLIAM PAYNE Gent. one of the subscribing
witnesses thereto; At another Court held for said County the 10th day of December in
year aforesaid the same was further proved by the oath of EDWARD DULEN another subscribing witness thereto, And at another Court held for said County the 14th day of June
1773 WILLIAM PAYNE Gent. made Oath that he said RICHARD PELL deceased the other
subscribing Witness sign his name as a witness thereto and then the same was ordered
to be recorded

pp.   THIS INDENTURE made the nineteenth day of May in year of our Lord One thou-
276-   sand seven hundred and seventy two Between JAMES RUMSEY of County of Lou-
278   doun of one part and JOSHUA EVANS of County aforesaid of other part Witnesseth
         that JAMES RUMSEY for sum of One hundred pounds PENNSYLVANIA CURRENCY
to him in hand paid by these presents doth bargain and sell unto JOSHUA EVANS all that
tract of land situate and being on SUGARLAND RUN in the County of Loudoun (which
said RUMSEY leased to said EVANS forever and since he obtained said Lease hath erected
a GRIST MILL with sundry other improvements) containing three acres which is
bounded by a Survey of GEORGE WESTs, Surveyor for the County aforesaid, together with
all Houses Orchards and appurtenances thereunto belonging To have and to hold the
premises hereby bargained and sold unto JOSHUA EVANS his heirs and assigns forever
PROVIDED Always that if said JAMES RUMSEY shall truly pay JOSHUA EVANS the aforesaid sum of One hundred pounds PENNSYLVANIA CURRENCY with lawfull interest
thereon upon nineteenth day of May in year one thousand seven hundred and seventy
five without any deduction or abatement that then these presents and everything
herein contained shall cease and determine and to be void In Witness whereof said
JAMES RUMSEY hath hereunto set his hand and affixed his seal the day and year first
above written
in presence of JOHN MOSS,   JAMES RUMSEY
      JOHN DOYLE, SAMUEL SCOTT
At a Court continued and held for Loudoun County June the 15th 1773
This Indenture and the Receipt thereon endorsed was acknowledged by JAMES RUMSEY
party thereto to be his act and deed And is ordered to be recorded

pp.   THIS INDENTURE made the third day of December in year of our Lord One thou-
278-   sand seven hundred and seventy two Between CHARLES LEWIS of County of
281   Loudoun, Planter, of one part, and WILLIAM ELLZEY of County of PRINCE WIL-
         LIAM, Attorney at Law, of other part Witnesseth that for sum of Two hundred
and twenty pounds current money of Virginia to CHARLES LEWIS in hand paid by these
presents doth bargain and sell unto WILLIAM ELLZEY and his heirs all that tract of land
whereon said CHARLES LEWIS now lives situate in County of Loudoun and containing
three hundred and forty one acres and bounded as described in a Pattent granted to said
CHARLES LEWIS from the Proprietors Office dated the Sixteenth day of May 1764 except
Sixteen acres and a half which CHARLES LEWIS hath heretofore sold and conveyed to
JOHN PILES of County of Loudoun and all Houses, Orchards and appurtenances whatsoever belonging To have and to hold the lands hereby conveyed and all other the pre-
mises unto WILLIAM ELLZEY his heirs and assigns forever In Witness whereof said
CHARLES LEWIS hath hereunto set his hand and seal the day and year first written

in the presence of ALEXR. HENDERSON,
    SOLOMON The mark of $\bigcirc$ HARDEY
    EDWARD SPRIGG JUNR., SAMUEL BAYLY
    SAMUEL PEACHY JUNR., JOHN THORNTON,
    CLEON MOORE

The mark of
CHARLES $\supset$ LEWIS

At a Court continued and held for Loudoun County April 29th 1773
This Indenture and the Receipt under written was proved to be the act and deed of
CHARLES LEWIS party thereto by the Oaths of JOHN THORNTON and CLEON MOORE, Gent.,
two of the subscribing witnesses And at another Court continued and held for the
County aforesaid the 15th day of June in the year aforesaid, the said Indenture and Receipt was fully proved by the Oath of ALEXANDER HENDERSON Gent. another of the Subscribing witnesses thereto and ordered to be recorded
(On margin: Exam'd Del'd to Colo. WM. ELLZEY Oct. 15th 1833)

pp.   THIS INDENTURE made the thirteenth day of December in year of our Lord One
282-   thousand seven hundred and seventy two Between LEE MASSEY of FAIRFAX
284   COUNTY of one part and JOSEPH THOMAS of Loudoun County of other part Witnesseth that LEE MASSEY in consideration of five shillings Sterling to him in hand
paid by these presents doth bargain and sell unto JOSEPH THOMAS four tracts of land
lying and being in County of Loudoun Vizt. one tract purchased by said LEE MASSY of
JOHN POULTNEY's Executors by Deeds of Lease and Release bearing date the thirteenth
and fourteenth days of August one thousand seven hundred and fifty nine and containing by estimation three hundred and five acres; another tract purchased of PHILIP
NOLAND by Deed of Feoffment bearing date the tenth day of September one thousand
seven hundred and sixty five and containing by estimation forty five acres; another
tract purchased of ROBERT POPKINS by Deed of Feoffment bearing date the twelfth day
of September one thousand seven hundred and sixty four and containing by estimation
thirteen acres, seventy perches, and the other tract taken up as Vacant and conveyed to
LEE MASSEY by Proprietors Pattent bearing date the Sixteenth day of April one thousand seven hundred and sixty five and containing by estimation ten acres; and all
houses orchards and advantages whatsoever to said four tracts of land belonging To
have and to hold the said four tracts of land containing in the whole three hundred and
seventy three acres seventy perches be the same more or less unto said JOSEPH THOMAS
and assigns from date of these presents for full term of one whole year paying therefore one Pepper Corn upon the Feast of St. Michael the Arch Angel to intent that by
virtue of these presents and by force of statute for transferring uses into possession
said JOSEPH THOMAS may be in actual possession and thereby enabled to accept a Release of inheritance thereof In Witness whereof LEE MASSEY hath hereunto set his
hand and seal the day and year first above written
in presence of ANTHY. RAMSAY,   LEE MASSEY
    LEWIS ELLZEY, W. THOMPSON,
    WILLIAM HAMILTON, H. ROSS, SPENCE GRAYSON
At a Court held for Loudoun County April the 26th 1773
This Indenture was proved to be the act and deed of the Reverend LEE MASSEY by the
oaths of LEWIS ELLZEY Gent., and the Revd. SPENCE GRAYSON, two of the subscribing
witnesses thereto. And at another Court continued and held for said County the 15th day
of June in year aforesaid the same was fully proved by Oath of HECTOR ROSS Gent:
another of the subscribing witnesses thereto And ordered to be recorded

pp. THIS INDENTURE made the fourteenth day of December in year of our Lord One
284- thousand seven hundred and seventy two Between LEE MASSEY of FAIRFAX
288 COUNTY and MARY his Wife of one part and JOSEPH THOMAS of Loudoun County
of other part Witnesseth that LEE MASSEY and MARY his Wife for sum of Nine
hundred pounds PENNSYLVANIA CURRENCY to them in hand paid by these presents do
bargain and sell unto JOSEPH THOMAS in his actual possession by virtue of a bargain
and sale for one whole year and by force of statute for transferring uses into possession and to his heirs and assigns forever four tracts of land lying in County of Loudoun
.. (description as in Lease above) .. To have and to hold said four tracts of land containing in the whole three hundred and seventy three acres seventy perches be the
same more or less unto said JOSEPH THOMAS his heirs and assigns In Witness whereof
said LEE MASSEY and MARY his Wife have hereunto set their hands and seals the day
and year first above written

in presence of ANTHY. RAMSAY,   LEE MASSEY
      LEWIS ELLZEY, W. THOMPSON,   MARY MASSEY
      WILLIAM HAMILTON, SPENCE GRAYSON,
      H. ROSS

(COMMISSION George the Third to GEORGE MASON, DANIEL McCARTY and ALEXANDER
HENDERSON for private examination of MARY Wife of LEE MASSEY dated the fourteenth
day of December 1772; and return of Execution thereof dated same date and signed by
DANIEL McCARTY and A. HENDERSON.)
At a Court held for Loudoun County April the 26th 1773
This Indenture with the Receipt under written was proved to be the act and deed of the
REVEREND LEE MASSEY party thereto by Oaths of LEWIS ELLZEY Gent. and the REVD.
SPENCE GRAYSON two of the subscribing witnesses, And at another Court continued and
held for said County the 15th day of June in year aforesaid the same was fully proved by
the Oath of HECTOR ROSS Gent. another of the subscribing witnesses thereto and toge-
ther with a Commission for the Privy Examination of the Feme with a return of the
Execution thereof ordered to be recorded
(On Margin: Delivered to ENOCH THOMAS July 24. 78)

pp. THIS INDENTURE made the Thirty first day of May in year of our Lord One thou-
288- sand seven hundred and seventy three Between CHRISTIAN CHARLES SNYDER of
290 County of Loudoun of one part and PHILLIP BRENHOR of same County of other
part Witnesseth that Whereas the Honble. GEORGE WILLIAM FAIRFAX Esqr. by
his Indenture of Lease dated (blank) did grant and to farm let unto one HENRY ADDING-
TON a certain parcel of land containing one hundred and fifty acres under certain
covenants and reserving certain rents for and during (blank) and longest liver of
them by virtue of which demise said HENRY ADDINGTON was possessed of said Indenture
of Lease and said one hundred anf fifty acres of land and by his Assignment by Indenture bearing date the Seventeenth day of June 1768 assigned and transferred the same
unto above named CHRISTIAN CHARLES SNYDER for a valuable consideration by virtue
of which agreement CHRISTIAN CHARLES SNIDER became possessed of said one hundred
and fifty acres of land and said Indenture of Lease. Now This Indenture Witnesseth that
CHRISTIAN CHARLES SNIDER for sum of Two hundred and Eighty six pounds PENNSYL-
VANIA CURRENCEY to him in hand paid by these presents doth bargain and sell unto
PHILLIP BRENHOR and to his heirs and assigns all the said one hundred and fifty acres
of land and comprized in said Lease together with the Indenture of Lease To have and to
hold said land and Lease unto said PHILLIP BRENHOR his heirs and assigns for all the
rest and residue of said term therein mentioned In Witness whereof said CHRISTIAN
CHARLES SNIDER hath hereunto set his hand and seal the day and year first written

in presence of CRAVEN PEYTON,   CHRISTIAN CHARLES SNIDER
    ABEL JANNEY JUNR., JACOB JACOBS   (NB Wrote in Dutch)
  At a Court continued and held for Loudoun County June the 15th 1773
This Indenture was proved to be the act and deed of CHRISTIAN CHARLES SNIDER party
thereto by the Oaths of CRAVEN PEYTON and JACOB JACOBS and by the Affirmation of
ABEL JANNEY JUNR. (a Quaker) the witnesses thereto, And is ordered to be recorded

pp.   THIS INDENTURE made the Nineteenth day of May in year of our Lord One thou-
290-   sand seven hundred and seventy two Between SAMUEL SCOTT and SUSANNA his
293   Wife of County of Loudoun of one part and JOSHUA EVANS of the County afore-
      said of other part Witnesseth that SAMUEL SCOTT and SUSANNA his Wife for sum
of Sixty pounds current money of Virginia to him in hand paid by these presents doth
bargain and sell unto JOSHUA EVANS all that tract of land situate in County of Loudoun
on SUGARLAND RUN being part of a larger tract of land granted to JAMES THOMAS and
by said THOMAS conveyed to HENRY BREWER by a Deed dated the twelfth day of March
1747 recorded in FAIRFAX COUNTY COURT And by said HENRY BREWER conveyed to WIL-
LIAM FITZHUGH by a Deed dated the twenty third day of March 1751 recorded in FAIR-
FAX COUNTY COURT and by said WILLIAM FITZHUGH conveyed to WILLIAM FOX by a Deed
dated July 1766 recorded in Loudoun County Court and by said WILLIAM FOX conveyed to
aforesaid SAMUEL SCOTT by Deeds bearing date the Tenth and Eleventh days of October
1766 recorded in Loudoun County Court the above granted land beginning at two white
Oaks standing by a small branch being one of the Original Corners and extending
thence down the said Branch according to the several meanders thereof So. 78 W.
eighty poles thence No. 70. W. 97 poles thence No. 39 W. seventy poles to a Poplar
marked JT standing at the mouth of said Branch on SUGARLAND RUN then down the sd
SUGARLAND RUN the several meanders thereof to a marked Poplar at the mouth of another small branch then up said Branch the several meanders thereof to a Stake between a mark'd Chesnut and white Oak on the South Bank of said Run about thirty poles
below a marked Corner (white Oak and Gum) to JAMES COLEMAN, thence So. 22 poles to a
Hickory saplin in a thickett thence So. 63 Et. two hundred and forty three poles to a
Chesnut by a Drain, then with one of the Original Lines So. 95 poles to a scrubby red Oak
and white Oak marked JT thence So. 51 W. thirty poles to the beginning containing
three hundred and thirty five acres of land Together with all houses orchards and appurtenances thereunto belonging To Have and To Hold unto said JOSHUA EVANS his
heirs and assigns forever PROVIDED Always and upon this express condition that if
SAMUEL SCOTT and SUSANNAH his Wife shall truly pay or cause to be paid unto JOSHUA
EVANS his heirs the aforesaid sum of sixty pounds current money of Virginia with lawfull Interest thereon upon the Nineteenth day of May in year One thousand seven hundred and seventy eight without any deduction or abatement that them these presents
and everything herein contained shall cease and determine and be void In Witness
whereof said SAMUEL SCOTT and SUSANNAH his Wife hath hereunto set their hands and
affix'd their seals the day and year first above written
in the presence of JOHN MOSS,   SAMUEL SCOTT
    JAMES RUMSEY, JOHN DOYLE   SUSANNAH SCOTT
  At a Court continued and held for Loudoun County November 24th 1772
This Indenture and the Receipt thereon endorsed were proved by the Oath of JOHN
DOYLE a witness thereto, At another Court held for said County the 10th day of May 1773,
the same was further proved by the Oath of JOHN MOSS, another of the witnesses thereto. And at another Court continued and held for said County June the 15th in the year
aforesaid the same was fully proved by the Oath of JAMES RUMSEY the other subscribing witness thereto And then ordered to be recorded

pp.   THIS INDENTURE made the fourteenth day of April in year of our Lord One thou-
294-   sand seven hundred and seventy three Between JACOB JANNEY of County of
295   Loudoun and HANNAH his Wife of one part and JONAS JANNEY of same County
         of other part Witnesseth that JACOB JANNEY and HANNAH his Wife for sum of
five shillings lawfull money of England to him in hand paid by these presents doth
bargain and sell unto JONAS JANNEY all that tract of land situate in County of Loudoun
and bounded Beginning at a black Oak on the North side of a hill near the head of the
OLD MILL DAM, Corner to THOMAS CLEWS, and extending thence with his line No. 47 East
sixty perches to a Stone then No: 81 West 43 perches and a half to a black Oak then So. 68
West seventy perches and a half to two small black oaks on South side of a Hill then So:
50 1/2 West fourteen perches to a box Spanish Oak then So: 35 East sixteen perches to a
box Oak then So. 3 East twelve perches by a black Oak bush by the OLD SAW MILL then
So. 30 West twenty six perches to a saplin by the Road then So. 59 West twenty perches
to a white Oak bush then So. 78 West twenty two perches to an Ash then So: 54 West
twelve perches to two black Oaks then So. 88 1/2 West Eleven and half perches to a
white Oak then No. 79 West eighty four perches to a Stone in one of the Original Lines
then So. 1 East 83 1/2 perches to a white Oak and hickory then So. 83 East 196 perches to
a white Oak then No. 15 East 124 1/2 perches to a white Oak by the Road, Corner to THO-
MAS GORE then No. 80 West 36 perches to the beginning containing one hundred and
sixty nine acres and one hundred and fourteen perches of land more or less And all
houses Orchards and advantages whatsoever belonging To have and to hold unto said
JONAS JANNEY his assigns from first day of March last past for full term of one whole
year paying therefore one Peper Corn upon the Feast of St. Michael the Arch Angel to
intent that by virtue of these presents and by force of statute for transferring uses into
possession said JONAS JANNEY may be in actual possession thereof and be enabled to
accept a Release of inheritance thereof In Witness whereof said JACOB JANNEY hath
hereunto set his hand and affixed his seal the day and year first above written
in the presence of   JACOB JANNEY
    At a Court continued and held for Loudoun County June the 14th 1773
This Indenture was acknowledged by JACOB JANNEY party thereto to be his act and deed
and is ordered to be recorded

pp.   THIS INDENTURE made this fourteenth day of June in year of our Lord One thou-
296-   sand seven hundred and seventy three Between JACOB JANNEY of Loudoun
299   County and HANNAH his Wife of one part and JONAS JANNEY of same County of
         other part Witnesseth that JACOB JANNEY and HANNAH his Wife for sum of three
hundred and ninety seven pounds current money of Virginia to them in hand paid by
these presents doth bargain and sell unto JONAS JANNEY (in his actual possession now
being by virtue of a bargain and sale for one year and by force of statute for transferring uses into possession) all that tract of land lying in County of Loudoun bounded
.. (description of land as in Lease above) ..containing one hundred and sixty nine acres
and one hundred and fourteen perches of land To have and to hold said tract of land and
premises above mentioned unto said JONAS JANNEY his heirs and assigns In Witness
whereof said JACOB JANNEY and HANNAH his Wife have hereunto set their hands and
affixed their seals the day and year first above written
in presence of THOMAS GREGG,   JACOB JANNEY
        SAMUEL HAGUE, ISRAEL JANNEY   HANNAH JANNEY
    At a Court continued and held for Loudoun County June 14th 1773
This Indenture was acknowledged by JACOB JANNEY and HANNAH his Wife parties
thereto to be their acts and deeds (the said HANNAH having been first privately examined as the Law directs and relinquished her Dower therein) and the Receipt thereon

endorsed was also acknowledged by said JACOB & together with said Indenture ordered
to be recorded
(On margin: Examined Del'd ISRAEL JANNEY May 17, 1777)

pp.   THIS INDENTURE made the twelfth day of June in year of our Lord One thousand
299-   seven hundred and seventy two Between EDWARD HARDING of FAIRFAX COUNTY
301   and MARY his Wife of one part and HENRY McCABE of County aforesaid of other
         part Witnesseth that EDWARD HARDIN for sum of five shillings current money
of Virginia to him in hand paid by these presents doth bargain and sell unto HENRY
McCABE a certain tract of land situate in County of Loudoun bounded Begining at a
white Oak on the side of a Road marked J H 1745 Corner to GEORGE GREGG, then No. 63
1/2 Wt. 108 poles to a white Oak stump near HENRY OXLEYs Spring then So. 89 d. Wt. 280
poles to a white oak and hickory on side of the CATOCKTAN MOUNTAIN Corner to HENRY
OXLEY then North 60 poles to two red or black oaks on top of said Mountain marked N S
corner to NATHANIEL SMITH's land now ROBERT ALEXANDERs then No. 67 1/4 Et. 230
poles to a Gum then So. 61 1/2 Et. 186 poles to a Chesnutt tree then So. 102 poles to the
beginning containing two hundred and fifty acres and a half the same being part of a
larger tract of land formerly granted to CATESBY COCKE by Patent from the Proprietors
of the Northern Neck of Virginia and was afterwards by him sold and conveyed to JOHN
HOUGH who afterwards sold and conveyed the above two hundred and fifty and half
acres to the above named EDWARD HARDIN party to these presents as by the Pattens and
several Mesne conveyances of record may appear And all houses Orchards and appurtenances whatsoever belonging To have and to hold the lands hereby conveyed unto
said HENRY McCABE his assigns for term of one full year paying therefore the rent of
one Peper Corn on Lady Day next to intent that by virtue of these presents and of the
statute for transferring uses into possession said HENRY McCABE may be in actual possession and thereby enabled to accept a Release of Inheritance thereof In Witness
whereof said EDWARD HARDIN and MARY his Wife have hereunto set their hands and
seals the day and year first above written
in presence of WILLIAM ELLZEY,   The mark of EDWD. HARDIN   (none shown)
       JOHN THORTON, GEORGE WEST   MARY HARDIN
  At a Court contd. and held for Loudoun County August 26th 1772
This Indenture was proved by the Oaths of WILLIAM ELLZEY & JOHN THORNTON Gent.
two of the Subscribing witnesses thereto to be the acts and deed of EDWARD HARDING
and MARY his Wife And at another Court contd. & held for said County June 16th 1773,
the same was fully proved by Oath of GEORGE WEST Gent. another witness and then
ordered to be recorded

pp.   THIS INDENTURE made the thirteenth day of June in year of our Lord One thou-
301-   sand seven hundred and seventy three Between EDWARD HARDIN of County of
306   FAIRFAX and MARY his Wife of one part and HENRY McCABE of TOWN of ALEXAN-
         DRIA in County of FAIRFAX of other part Witnesseth that for sum of two hun-
dred and thirty one pounds current money of PENSYLVANIA to said EDWARD HARDIN in
hand paid by these presents doth bargain and sell unto HENRY McCABE in his actual
possession now being by virtue of a bargain and sale for one year and by force of
statute for transferring uses into possession and his heirs a certain tract of land situate
in County of Loudoun and bounded .. (description of land and conveyances as in Lease
above) .. To have and to hold the lands hereby conveyed unto HENRY McCABE his heirs
and assigns forever In Witness whereof said EDWARD HARDIN and MARY his Wife have
hereunto set their hands and seals the day and year first above written

in the presence of WILLIAM ELZEY,   The mark of EDWARD HARDIN   (none shown)
   JOHN THORNTON, GEORGE WEST   MARY HARDIN
(Commission George the Third to JOHN CARLYLE, JOHN WEST JUNR. WILLIAM PAYNE
and HENRY GUNNELL Gent. for privy examination of MARY the Wife of EDWARD HAR-
DIN dated the 15th day of June in XIIth year of our Reign 1772; and return of execution
dated the same date and signed by HENRY GUNNELL and WILLIAM PAYNE).
   At a Court continued and held for Loudoun County August 26th 1772
This Indenture and the Receipt under written were proved to be the acts and deeds of
EDWARD HARDING party thereto by the Oaths of WM. ELZEY & JOHN THORNTON Gent. two
of the subscribing witnesses thereto And at another Court continued and held for said
County the 16 day of June 1773, the same was fully proved by the Oath of GEORGE WEST
the other Subscribing Witness and together with a Commission for the privy Examina-
tion of the Feme with the return of execution thereof, Ordered to be recorded
(On the margins of the pages of this entry for the Release, the name is shown as HENRY
McCOMBE).

pp.   THIS INDENTURE made the seventeenth day of June in year of our Lord One
306-   thousand seven hundred and seventy three Between JOHN HEREFORD and
310   MARGARET his Wife of County of Loudoun of one part and JOHN THORNTON,
         Attorney at Law, of same County of other part Witnesseth that for sum of One
hundred and fifty pounds current money of Virginia to said JOHN HEREFORD and MAR-
GARET his Wife in hand paid by these presents do bargain and sell unto JOHN THORNTON
and his heirs and assigns forever all that lot or half acre of land situate and lying in
TOWN of LEESBURG in County of Loudoun being numbered Thirty Three in a plan and
survey thereof made by JOHN HOUGH and bounded by and on KING STREET it being the
lot or half acre of land which said HEREFORD purchased from HUGH WEST and ELIZA-
BETH his Wife, BENJAMIN GRAYSON and ELIZABETH his Wife which said lot or half acre
of land they the said HUGH WEST and BENJAMIN purchased of NICHOLAS MINOR Gent. as
appears by a Deed of Feofment made and entered into by said NICHOLAS MINOR for that
purpose bearing date the seventh day of November in year one thousand seven hundred and fifty nine admitted to record in County Court of Loudoun on Twelvth day of
March in year one thousand seven hundred and sixty, And all houses Orchards and
appurtenances whatsoever belonging To have and to hold the lands hereby conveyed
unto said JOHN THORNTON his heirs and assigns for ever In Witness whereof said JOHN
HEREFORD and MARGARET his Wife have herunto set their hands and seals the day and
year first above written
in the presence of   JOHN HERYFORD
                                                 PEGGY HERYFORD
   At a Court continued and held for Loudoun County June the 17. 1773
This Indenture was acknowledged by JOHN HERYFORD and MARGARET his Wife parties
thereto to be their acts and deeds (the said MARGARET having been first privately examined as the Law directs and relinquished her right of dower therein) and the Receipt
endorsed was likewise acknowledged by the said JOHN HERYFORD and together with the
said Indenture & ordered to be recorded

pp.   THIS INDENTURE made the Sixteenth day of June in year of our Lord One thou-
310-   sand seven hundred and seventy three Between BENJAMIN RUST of Cameron
312   Parish in County of Loudoun of one part and BENJAMIN HUTCHISON of Cameron
         Parish in Loudoun County of other part Witnesseth that BENJAMIN RUST for sum
of five shillings current money of Virginia to him in hand paid by these presents doth
bargain and sell unto BENJAMIN HUTCHISON one certain parcel of land lying in County

of Loudoun on both sides of ELK LICKING RUN being the land whereon said HUTCHISON
now lives and was granted to RICHARD MEEKS of RICHMOND COUNTY by Patent from the
Proprietors Office for Nine hundred and Ten acres bearing date the 29th day of March
1729 and in the Last Will and Testament of said RICHARD MEEKS the land was devised to
ELIZABETH WALKER and ANN SISSON and was afterwards transferred by Deeds from
THOMAS and ELIZABETH WALKER and HENRY and ANN SISSON to BENJAMIN RUST of
RICHMOND COUNTY and said BENJAMIN RUST in his last Will and Testament devised Six
hundred acres of said Tract (hereby bargained and sold) to BENJAMIN RUST party to
these presents and is bounded Beginning at a Spanish Oak Stump between two red Haw
trees in ELK LICKING RUN and extending thence So. 43 W. 100 poles to a white Oak
marked D D thence So. 1 1/2 Wt. 283 poles to several white Oaks in MEEKS PATENT line
thence with the line of the Patent No. 14 Wt. 415 poles to a white Oak in Glady land
thence S. 72 1/2 W. 180 poles to the beginning containing six hundred acres more or
less And all houses orchards and appurtenances whatsoever belonging To have and to
hold the premises hereby granted with the appurtenances unto said BENJAMIN
HUTCHISON his assigns for full term of one whole year paying therefore the rent of one
Peper Corn on Lady Day next to intent that by virtue of these presents and of the statute
for transferring uses into possession said BENJAMIN HUTCHISON may be in actual possession and thereby enabled to accept a Release of Inheritance thereof In Witness
whereof said BENJAMIN RUST hath hereunto set his hand and seal the day and year
first above written
in the presence of   BENJAMIN RUST
    At a Court continued and held for Loudoun County June the 17th 1773
This Indenture was acknowledged by BENJAMIN RUST party thereto to be his act and
deed and is ordered to be recorded

pp.   THIS INDENTURE made the Seventeenth day of June in year of our Lord One
312-   thousand seven hundred and seventy three Between BENJAMIN RUST of
315   Cameron Parish in County of Loudoun of one part and BENJAMIN HUTCHISON of
        Cameron Parish in Loudoun County of other part Witnesseth that for sum of one
hundred and fifty pounds current money of Virginia to BENJAMIN RUST in hand paid
by these presents doth bargain and sell unto BENJAMIN HUTCHISON in his actual possession now being by virtue of a bargain and sale for one whole year and by force of
statute for transferring uses into possession and to his heirs and assigns forever one
certain parcel of land being in Loudoun County on both sides of ELK LICKING RUN ..
(description of conveyances and of the land as in Lease above) .. containing Six hundred acres more or less To have and to hold the land hereby conveyed unto BENJAMIN
HUTCHISON and to his heirs and assigns forever In Witness whereof said BENJAMIN
RUST hath hereunto set his hand and seal the day and year first above written
in the presence of   BENJAMIN RUST
    At a Court continued and held for Loudoun County June 17th 1773
This Indenture and the Receipt thereon endorsed was acknowledged by BENJAMIN RUST
party thereto to be his acts and deeds and ordered to be recorded

pp.   THIS INDENTURE made the 17. day of June in year of our Lord one thousand
315-   seven hundred and seventy three Between Colonel NICHOLAS MINOR of County
318   of Loudoun and Parish of Cameron Gent. of one part and ROBERT CAMPBELL of
        Shelburn Parish and County aforesaid, Taylor, of other part Witnesseth that
NICHOLAS MINOR for sum of five pounds current money of Virginia to him in hand paid
by these presents doth bargain and sell unto ROBERT CAMPBELL his heirs and assigns
for ever all that lott or half acre of land and premises No. Forty Six binding on BACK

STREET situate in LEESBURG in County of Loudoun containing one half acre of land To
have and to hold the said half acre of land unto said ROBERT CAMPBELL his heirs and
assigns for ever with the appurtenances thereunto belonging PROVIDED Always that
said ROBERT CAMPBELL his heirs or assigns will build and finish on said lott one house
of Brick stone or wood well framed of the dimentions of twenty feet long and sixteen
feet wide and nine feet pitched at the least, with one brick or stone chimney thereto
within three years after the date of these presents and said Building to be placed agreeable to the rules orders and Directions of the Honble. PHILIP LUD. LEE, THOMPSON
MASON, FRANCIS LIGHTFOOT LEE, JAMES HAMILTON, NICHOLAS MINOR, AENEAS CAMP-
BELL, JOSIAS CLAPHAM, JOHN HOUGH and FRANCIS HAGUE or greatest part of them,
Directors and Managers of said TOWN of LEESBURG for the time being In Witness whereof said NICHOLAS MINOR hath hereunto set his hand and seal the say and date above
written
in presence of ROBERT HAMILTON,   NICH. MINOR
     SAMUEL EVANS, HENRY HARRIS
   At a Court continued and held for Loudoun County June 17th 1773
This Indenture and the Receipt and Memorandum thereon endorsed were proved by the
Oaths of ROBERT HAMILTON, SAMUEL EVANS & HENRY HARRIS, the Subscribing Witnesses thereto, and ordered to be recorded

pp.   THIS INDENTURE made this Seventeenth day of June in year of our Lord One
318-   thousand seven hundred and seventy three Between DANIEL EVANS of the
321   Province of PENSYLVANIA, Cordwinder, of one part and DAVID EVANS JUNR.
        of County of Loudoun of other part Witnesseth that Whereas JOHN TAYLOE Esqr.
in and by an Indenture of Lease bearing date the Sixteenth day of January in year of
our Lord Seventeen hundred and fifty six for the Covenants therein mentioned did
demise and to farm let unto STEPHEN EMRY his heirs a certain lot of land containing
One hundred and seventy acres as in said recited Lease may appear and by said STEPHEN
EMRY assigned and set over unto said DANIEL EVANS all his right and Interest in said
Lease or lot of land by a lawfull Lease of Assignment bearing date the third day of January in year Seventeen hundred and sixty five and admitted to record in Court of Loudoun And This Indenture Witnesseth that said DANIEL EVANS for sum of One hundred
and nine pounds current money of PENSYLVANIA to him in hand paid by these presents doth bargain and sell unto DAVID EVANS JUNIOR his heirs all that demised premises above mentioned To have and to hold said one hundred and seventy acres of land
unto said DAVID EVANS JUNIOR his assigns In Witness whereof said DANIEL EVANS have
unto these presents set my hand and seal the day and year first above written
in presence of ISRAEL THOMPSON,   DANIEL EVANS
     JOHN TREBLE, JNO. CHAMBERLAINE JUNR.
   At a Court continued and held for Loudoun County June the 18th 1773
This Indenture was acknowledged by DANIEL EVANS party thereto to be his act and deed
And is ordered to be recorded

pp.   THIS INDENTURE made the Fifteenth day of April in year of our Lord One thou-
321-   sand seven hundred and seventy three Between WILLIAM SMITH of Parish of
322   Shelburn and County of Loudoun of one part and SIMON HANCOCK of same
        Parish and County of other part Witnesseth that said WILLIAM SMITH for sum of
Five shillings to him in hand paid by these presents doth bargain and sell unto SIMON
HANCOCK a certain tract of land situate in Parish and County afsd. containing One hundred and fifty acres be the same more or less and is bounded Beginning at A a white
Oak in a Glade Corner to said WILLIAM SMITH, running thence with the line of WIL-

LIAM BRONAUGH South fifty seven degrees West one hundred and fifty poles to B Corner to BRONAUGH thence South sixty degrees East two hundred and twenty five poles to C a white Oak standing near a branch, Corner to THOMAS OWSLEY, thence North fifty seven degrees East eight six poles to D a black Oak Corner to the said WILLIAM SMITH thence with his line Reversed North forty three and a half West two hundred and seven poles to the begining which tract of land lies on the Northwest side of GOOSE CREEK and is part of a larger tract taken up and Patented by CHARLES GREEN late of County of FAIRFAX, Clerk, and sold and conveyed to said WILLIAM SMITH by WILLIAM SAVAGE of County of PRINCE WILLIAM, Surgeon, and MARGARET his Wife who was the Widow and Devise of the said CHARLES GREEN by their Deeds of Lease and Release bearing date the tenth and eleventh days of June One thousand seven hundred and sixty eight duly proved and recorded in the Records of Loudoun County and all houses orchards and appurtenances whatsoever belonging To have and to hold the lands hereby conveyed unto said SIMON HANCOCK for full term of one whole year paying therefore the rent of one Peper Corn on Lady Day next to intent that by virtue of these presents and by force of statute for transferring uses into possession said SIMON HANCOCK may be in actual possession and thereby enabled to accept a Release of Inheritance thereof In Witness whereof said WILLIAM SMITH hath hereunto set his hand and seal the day and year first above written

in presence of (the five shillings being first paid)　　　　WILLIAM SMITH
　　　　THOS. LEWIS, JOSEPH PARKER,
　　　　EDWIN his mark ✗ FURR, HY. POTTEN
　At a Court held for Loudoun County August 9th 1773
This Indenture was acknoweldged by WILLIAM SMITH party thereto to be his act and deed & is ordered to be recorded

pp.　　THIS INDENTURE made the Fifteenth day of April in year of our Lord One thou-
323-　sand seven hundred and seventy three Between WILLIAM SMITH of the Parish
326　　of Shelburn and County of Loudoun and MARGARET his Wife of one part and
　　　　SIMON HANCOCK of same Parish and County of other part Witnesseth that for sum of seventy pounds current money of Virginia to WILLIAM SMITH in hand paid by these presents do bargain and sell unto SIMON HANCOCK in his actual possession by virtue of a bargain and sale to him thereof made for one whole year and by force of the statute for transferring uses into possession and to his heirs a certain tract of land lying in Parish and County aforesaid containing One hundred and fifty acres be the same more or less and is bounded .. (description of land and conveyance to WILLIAM SMITH as in Lease above) .. To have and to hold the lands hereby conveyed unto SIMON HANCOCK his heirs and assigns forever In Witness whereof WILLIAM SMITH and MARGARET his Wife have hereunto set their hands and seals the day and year first above written

in presence of THOS. LEWIS,　　　　　　　　WILLIAM SMITH
　　　　JOSEPH PARKER, EDWIN his mark ✝ FURR,　MARGARETT SMITH
　　　　HY. POTTEN
　At a Court held for Loudoun County August 9th 1773
This Indenture was acknowledged by WILLIAM SMITH Gent. & MARGARET his Wife parties thereto to be their acts and deeds (the said MARGARET having been first privately examined as the Law directs and relinquished her right of Dower therein) the Receipt thereon endorsed also was acknowledged by said WILLIAM SMITH and together with the said Indenture ordered to be recorded
(On margin: Release dd SAML. SMITH Jany 23d 1775)

pp.
326-
328

THIS INDENTURE made this 9th day of August in year of our Lord One thousand seven hundred and seventy three By and Between JOSHUA EVANS of the Parish of Cameron County of Loudoun of one part & ARCHIBALD HAMILTON of the same Parish and County of other part Witnesseth that said JOSHUA EVANS in consideration of the yearly rent and covenants on part of ARCHIBALD HAMILTON and his heirs to be paid & performed doth grant unto ARCHIBALD HAMILTON his heirs a certain tenement of land lying in County of Loudoun and is bounded beginning at a Hiccory sapling near his Fence thence North twenty four degrees West 6 perches to a post, thence South 78 degrees West 90 perches to a post, South 10 degrees East 68 perches South 80 degrees East 102 poles to a red Oak North 10 degrees West 50 poles, South 83 1/2 degrees East 34 poles to a live Oak on SUGAR LAND RUN thence down said Run North 4 degrees West 9 poles, North 57 1/2 degrees East 12 perches to a Poplar on the bank of said Run thence North 83 1/2 degrees West 50 poles to the beginning containing fifty acres more or less with all Waters Rights and appurtenances to said Tenement belonging To have and to hold said Tenement and premises unto ARCHIBALD HAMILTON his heirs or assigns from the Seventh day of March One thousand seven hundred and seventy four for and during the term of Eighteen years with paying the Quit rents during said Term and to build a Dwelling House twenty feet by eighteen in the Clear and Shingle the same and plank the upper and lower floor and build a Stone Chimney to said House and build a barn sixteen by sixteen feet in the clear and Thatch or Shingle the same and plank the lower floor so as to make it close for Threshing and plant Eighty Apple trees and a Peach orchard and clear all low ground being Ten acres and sow seven acres of the low ground with Timothy Seed and make the same good Meadow and he shall cut no Green Timber while there is any dead Timber In Witness whereof parties first above mentioned to these presents have interchangeably set their hands and seals the day and year above written

in presence of us JAS. COLEMAN,   JOSHUA EVANS
       WILLIAM JENKINS, ROBERT POPKINS   ARCHIBLE his mark ◯ HAMILTON

At a Court held for Loudoun County August 9th 1773
This Indenture was proved to be the acts and deeds of JOSHUA EVANS and ARCHIBALD HAMILTON parties thereto by the Oaths of JAMES COLEMAN, Gent., and WILLIAM JENKINS, two of the Subscribing witnesses thereto, And on the 13th day of the same month at the Court aforesaid the same was fully proved by the Oath of ROBERT POPKIN, the other witness, And ordered to be recorded

pp.
329-
330

THIS INDENTURE made the Sixth day of August in the year of our Lord One thousand seven hundred and seventy three Between JOHN HOUGH of County of Loudoun of one part and JOSEPH JANNEY of same County of other part Witnesseth that said JOHN HOUGH in consideration of five shillings current money of Virginia to him in hand paid by these presents doth bargain and sell JOSEPH JANNEY a certain parcel of land in County of Loudoun bounded beginning at a Black Oak mark'd T J standing by the Road crossing the Mountain and the N. E. Corner of GEORGE GREGGs land and a corner to the Land said JOS. JANNEY purchased of JOHN HANBY or near the same and extending thence with a line of said HANBYs N. 23 d. Wt. one hundred poles to a Hickory Saplin by the Road to KIRKS MILL and Corner to WILLIAM HICKSON's Land, thence along the Road S. 11 d. Wt. thirty four poles to a white Oak, then So. 15 d West Eighteen poles to a Hickory then S. 10 d. Wt. thirty four poles to a black Oak, then S. 18 d. W. forty four pole to a Spanish Oak by the Road, then S. 35 d. W. fourteen poles to a Black Oak then So. 17. Wt. twenty poles to a black Oak by the South side of the first mentioned MOUNTAIN ROAD near the line of GEORGE GREGG, then binding with that Road N. 55 d. E. one hundred and sixteen poles to the beginning, containing thirty two acres being a

detached parcel lying between the two ROADS and part of a Tract the said JOHN HOUGH
purchased of JOHN MERCER and Sons and all Houses Orchards and appurtenances whatsoever belonging To have and to hold the lands hereby conveyed unto said JOSEPH
JANNEY during full term of one whole year paying therefore the rent of one Pepper
Corn on Lady Day next to intent that by virtue of these presents and of the statute for
transferring uses into possession said JOSEPH JANNEY may be in actual possession and
be thereby enabled to accept a Release of Inheritance thereof In Witness whereof said
JOHN HOUGH hath hereunto set his hand and seal the day and year first above written
in the presence of   JOHN HOUGH
  At a Court held for Loudoun County August 9th 1773
This Indenture was acknowleged by JOHN HOUGH party thereto to be his act and deed
And is ordered to be recorded

pp.   THIS INDENTURE made the Seventh day of August in year of our Lord One thou-
330-   sand seven hundred and seventy three Between JOHN HOUGH of County of Lou-
333   doun of one part and JOSEPH JANNEY of same County of other part Witnesseth
         that for sum of Sixty pounds current money of Virginia to said JOHN HOUGH in
hand paid by these presents doth bargain and sell unto JOSEPH JANNEY in his actual
possession by virtue of a bargain and sale thereof and by force of statute for transferring uses into possession and his heirs a certain parcel of land situate in County of Loudoun and bounded .. (description of land as in Lease above) .. To have and to hold the
lands hereby conveyed unto said JOSEPH JANNEY his heirs and assigns forever In Witness whereof said JOHN HOUGH hath hereunto set his hand and seal the day and year
first above written
in presence of   JOHN HOUGH
  At a Court held for Loudoun County August the 9th 1773
This Indenture and the Receipt thereon endorsed was acknowledged by JOHN HOUGH
party thereto to be his acts and deeds and ordered to be recorded

pp.   KNOW ALL MEN by these presents that I SAMUEL HOPEWELL of County of Lou-
333-   doun have bargained and sold to LEVEN POWELL of same County for sum of Fifty
334   pounds current money the following stocks, goods and Chattles, Vizt. Seven head
         of Cattle, Six head of said Cattle being mark'd with a crop and a slit in the right
ear the other being a Cow which I have from HENRY OLDACRE and the future increase
of sd Cattle, 1 small sorrell Horse with a blazed face and a small streak of white on his
near shoulder which I got of JOSEPH LONGLEY, 1 black Horse about fourteen hands high
which I got of JOHN GROVES, Eight head of hogs mark'd with a crop and a slit in the
right Ears, Three feather beds and furniture, and all my crop of Tobacco and Corn made
last year, and also every article now in my possession of which stock goods and chattels
the sd SAML. HOPEWELL hath delivered to sd LEVEN POWELL one Pennknife with an
intent that it shall be binding for the whole which sd articles SAMUEL HOPEWELL doth
Warrant In Witness whereof I have hereunto set my hand and seal this 4th day of
March 1773
Witness J. HARRISON,   SAMUEL his mark ─┼─ HOPEWELL
         VALENTINE HARRISON   │
  At a Court held for Loudoun County August the 10th 1773
This Bill of Sale was proved by the Oath of VALENTINE HARRISON to be the act and deed
of SAMUEL HOPEWELL and is ordered to be recorded

pp.   KNOW ALL MEN by these presents that I ROBERT BURWELL Esqr. for sum of One
334- hundred and fifty five pounds current money to me in hand paid by these pre-
335   sents do bargain and sell unto JAMES COLEMAN the following Slaves, to wit: Kate
      and her two children, Moll and Hannah, which said Slaves I do hereby warrant
to said JAMES COLEMAN his heirs In Witness whereof I have hereunto set my hand and
seal this 2d day of Feby 1773
in presence of FRANCIS PEYTON,   ROBERT BURWELL
   At a Court continued and held for Loudoun County Augt. 10th 1773
This Bill of Sale was proved by the Oath of FRANCIS PEYTON Gent. to be the act and deed
of ROBERT BURWELL Esqr. party thereto And is ordered to be recorded

p.   KNOW ALL MEN by these presents that I ROBERT BURWELL Esqr. for sum of One
335   hundred and thirty six pounds Ten shillings current money to me in hand paid
      by these presents do bargain and sell unto JOSIAS CLAPAHAM Gent., the fol-
lowing Slaves to wit Pegg, Marlow, Godfrey, Sarah and Boatswain which said Slaves I do
hereby warrant unto said JOSIAS CLAPHAM his heirs In Witness whereof I have hereunto set my hand and seal this 2d day of Feby 1773
in presence of FRANCIS PEYTON   ROBERT BURWELL
   At a Court continued and held for Loudoun County Augt. 10th 1773
This Bill of Sale was proved by the Oath of FRANCIS PEYTON Gent. to be the act and deed
of ROBERT BURWELL Esqr. party thereto, And is ordered to be recorded

pp.   KNOW ALL MEN by these presents that we ANTHONY BUCKNER and ANTHONY
335- SEALE of County of PRINCE WILLIAM are held and firmly bound unto CORNELIUS
336   SKINNER of County of Loudoun in full and just sum of Five hundred pounds cur-
      rent money which payment well and truly to be made we bind ourselves Sealed
with our seals and dated this 17 day of December 1772
   The Condition of the above obligation is such that whereas above bound ANTHONY
BUCKNER hath this day bargained and sold CORNELIUS SKINNER a certain tract of land
lying in Counties of Loudoun and PRINCE WILLIAM containing by Estimation Two hundred and forty acres devised to said ANTHONY BUCKNER by PEYTON BUCKNER his Father
for sum of twenty shillings for each acre the said Tract shall contain by an accurate
survey thereof. Now if said ANTHONY BUCKNER shall make over and convey to COR-
NELIUS SKINNER his heirs or assigns in Fee Simple all the aforesaid Tract of land with
appurtenances whenever said SKINNER shall make full payment of a certain Bond this
day entered into by said SKINNER and also he doth bind himself his heirs to convey the
same free and clear from any Encumbrance whatsoever on performance of above
covenants the above obligation to be void
in presence of FRANCIS PEYTON,   ANTHONY BUCKNER
              WILLIAM McCLELLAN   ANTHONY SEALE
   At a Court continued and held for Loudoun County August 13th 1773
This Bond was proved by the Oath of WILLIAM McCLELLAN one of the subscribing witnesses thereto and ordered to be recorded
(On margin: Examined D D to NATHL. SKINNER Oct. 1774)

pp.   KNOW ALL MEN by these presents that I JAMES GOLDING of County of Loudoun
337- for sum of Fifty two pounds two shillings and eight pence half penny current
338   money to me in hand paid by ALEXANDER HENDERSON, Attorney in Fact for
      GLASSFORD & HENDERSON, by these presents bargain and sell said GLASSFORD &
HENDERSON the following goods and chattels Vizt. One dark Iron Grey Horse six years
old, one black Mare with a Starr in her forehead eight years old, five Cows with white

faces mark'd with an under and overkeel, twenty head of hogs marked three slits in each ear two feather beds and furniture together with all the residue of the Household Furniture, all the Plantation Utensils, and all other the Estate of him the said GOLDING, To have and to hold to said GLASSFORD & HENDERSON their heirs and assigns In Testimony whereof I have hereunto set my hand and seal and Delivered the Black Mare in name of the other goods in presence of the subscribing Witnesses this fourth day of March Seventeen hundred and seventy three
in presence of JOHN GUNNELL,   JAMES his mark (C) GOLDING
        ROBT. DOBSON, JAS. RATTRAY,
        WILLM. GRAY
   At a Court continued and held for Loudoun County August the 13th 1773
This Bill of Sale was acknowledged by JAMES GOLDING party thereto to be his act and deed And is ordered to be recorded
(On margin: Exam'd D D Mr. H. LANE Feby 1775)

pp.   THIS INDENTURE made the 13th day of September in year of our Lord One thou-
338-   sand seven hundred and seventy three Between JOSHUA GORE JUNR. of County
341   of Loudoun of one part and WILLIAM SMITH, STEPHEN DONALDSON, THOMAS
        LEWIS, THOMSON MASON, JAMES HAMILTON, FRANCIS PEYTON, CRAVEN PEYTON,
JOSIAS CLAPHAM, LEVEN POWELL, JOHN LEWIS, THOMAS OWSLEY and THOMAS SHORES
Gentlemen, Vestrymen for the Parish of Shelburne of the other part Witnesseth that in consideration of the sum of Ten pounds current money of Virginia to JOSHUA GORE JUNR. in hand paid by these presents doth bargain and sell unto (Vestryment listed above) and their Successors for use of the Parish of Shelburne and to be at the disposal of any Vestry for said Parish a certain parcel of land Beginning at a small Spanish Oak bush on the North side of the GREAT ROAD nearly opposite the Dwelling House of THO-MAS GORE deceased and running thence West seven poles thence South six poles thence East seven poles thence North six poles to the beginning containing one quarter of an acre of land and all houses Orchards and appurtenances whatsoever belonging To have and to hold the lands hereby conveyed unto (the Vestryment above named) their Successors and the assigns of any Vestry for Parish of Shelburne In Witness whereof said JOSHUA GORE JUNR. hath hereunto set his hand and affixed his seal the day and year first above written
in presence of   JOSHUA GORE JUNR.
   At a Court held for Loudoun County September 13th 1773
This Indenture and the Receipt thereon endorsed was acknowledged by JOSHUA GORE JUNR. party thereto to be his acts and deeds And is ordered to be recorded

pp.   THIS INDENTURE made the second day of September in year of our Lord One
341-   thousand seven hundred and seventy three Between ANTHONY BUCKNER and
343   MILDRED his Wife, WILLIAM BROWN and ELIZABETH his Wife of County of
        PRINCE WILLIAM of one part and CORNELIUS SKINNER of County of Loudoun of
other part Witnesseth that said ANTHONY BUCKNER and WILLIAM BROWN for sum of five shilings current money of Virginia to them in hand paid by these presents doth bargain and sell unto CORNELIUS SKINNER all that tract or parcel of land situate in County of Loudoun and PRINCE WILLIAM and bounded Beginning at a white Oak in or near the line of ROBERT BURWELL Esqr. thence along his line No. 88 Et. 406 poles to several mark'd Hickory Grubbs on a branch side thence up said Branch and binding therewith No. 65 Wst. 260 poles to a white Oak on said branch thence with another marked line No. 48 Wt. crossing the MAIN ROAD, 60 poles to AMAPOLE on BULL RUN thence up BULL RUN according to its several meanders and binding therewith No. 54

Et. 100 poles to a stake in the place of a white Oak thence with another marked line So. 29 Wt. 160 poles to the beginning containing two hundred and thirty one acres And all houses orchards and appurtenances whatsoever belonging To have and to hold the lands hereby conveyed unto said CORNELIUS SKINNER his heirs and assigns during full term of one whole year paying therefore the rent of one pepper corn on Lady Day next to intent that by virtue of these presents and of the statute for transferring uses into possession CORNELIUS SKINNER may be in actual possession and thereby be enabled to accept a Release of inheritance thereof In Witness whereof said ANTHONY BUCKNER and MILDRED his Wife and WILLIAM BROWN and ELIZABETH his Wife have hereunto set their hands and seals the day and year first above written

in presence of FRANCIS PEYTON,   ANTHONY BUCKNER
          SIMON TRIPLETT,   MILDRED BUCKNER
          NATHANIEL SKINNER   WILLIAM his mark 𝘞 BROWN
          RICHD. SKINNER   ELIZTH. her mark / BROWN

     At a Court held for Loudoun County September the 13th 1773
This Indenture was proved by the Oaths of FRANCIS PEYTON Gent., NATHANIEL SKINNER and RICHARD SKINNER three of the subscribing witnesses thereto And is ordered to be recorded

pp.   THIS INDENTURE made the third day of September in year of our Lord One thou-
343-   sand seven hundred and seventy three Between ANTHONY BUCKNER and
346   MILDRED his Wife, WILLIAM BROWN and ELIZABETH his Wife of County of
          PRINCE WILLIAM of one part and CORNELIUS SKINNER of County of Loudoun of
other part Witnesseth that in consideration of sum of Two hundred and thirty one pounds current money of Virginia to said ANTHONY BUCKNER and WILLIAM BROWN in hand paid by these presents doth bargain and sell unto CORNELIUS SKINNER in his actual possession now being by virtue of a bargain and sale for one whole year and by force of statute for transferring uses into possession and his heirs and assigns forever all that tract of land lying in Counties of Loudoun and PRINCE WILLIAM and bounded .. (description of land as in Lease above) .. To have and to hold the lands hereby con- veyed unto said CORNELIUS SKINNER his heirs and assigns forever In Witness whereof said ANTHONY BUCKNER & MILDRED his Wife and WILLIAM BROWN and ELIZABETH his Wife have hereunto set their hands and seals the day and year first above written

in presence of FRANCIS PEYTON,   ANTHONY BUCKNER
          SIMON TRIPLETT,   MILDRED BUCKNER
          NATHANIEL SKINNER   WILLIAM his mark 𝘟 BROWN
          RICHD. SKINNER   ELIZABETH her mark / BROWN

     (COMMISSION George the Third to FRANCIS PEYTON, LEVEN POWELL & SIMON TRIPLETT Gentlemen for privy examination of MILDRED BUCKNER and ELIZABETH BROWN dated the fifth day of September 1773; Execution thereof returned dated Sixth day of Septr. 1773 and signed by FRANCIS PEYTON and SIMON TRIPLETT)
     At a Court held for Loudoun County September the 13th 1773
This Indenture and the Receipt thereon endorsed were proved by the Oaths of FRANCIS PEYTON Gent., NATHANIEL SKINNER and RICHARD SKINNER three of the subscribing witnesses thereto with a Commission for the Privy Examination of the Femes and the return of the Execution thereof together with said Indenture ordered to be recorded (On margin: D D to NATHL. SKINNER Oct. 1774)

pp.   THIS INDENTURE made the Twenty sixth day of July in year of our Lord One thou-
346-   sand seven hundred and seventy three between GEORGE MERCER late of OLD
348   ENGLAND Esqr. and JAMES MERCER of SPOTSYLVANIA COUNTY Esqr. of one part

and JOSEPH HOUGH of County of Loudoun of other part Whereas CATESBY COCKE Esqr. and JOHN MERCER Esqr. deceased obtained a grant from the Proprietors Office for the Northern Neck of Virginia for five thousand nine hundred and eighty five acres of land then in PRINCE WILLIAM now Loudoun County situate about the KITTOCTON CREEK and MOUNTAIN and a division by them made by Deeds of Partition and that said JOHN MERCER did convey two third parts of his Moiety to his two Sons, the said GEORGE MERCER and JAMES MERCER, and also that said JOHN MERCER, GEORGE MERCER and JAMES MERCER did qualify and impower JOHN HOUGH of Loudoun County by one certain power of Attorney date the third day of November ADm. 1762 and recorded in the General Court thereby impowering JOHN HOUGH to sell and convey the aforesaid tract of land (or said MERCERs part) and other lands by virtue of which power said JOHN HOUGH did bargain and unto JOSEPH HOUGH in year of our Lord 1766 a certain parcel of the aforesaid tract containing two hundred acres and enter'd in an obligation with said JOSEPH HOUGH to convey the said land to him upon his payment of the sum of Forty pounds current money of Virginia which sum being now paid the land laid off and bounded Beginning at two Hickorys in a small Valley in a dividing line Between said COCK and MERCERs and Corner to land sold BENJAMIN WILLIAMS extending thence with said WILLIAMS line So. 9 Et. one hundred and fifteen poles to a black Oak in a line of JOSEPH COX's late purchase then with his line East eighty poles to a white Oak red Oak and small Hickory his Corner, then with another of his lines South thirty poles to two Spanish Oaks and a white Oak Corner to Colo. JAMES HAMILTONs late purchase then with his line East one hundred and thirty poles to several small white Oaks on a Hill side then still East twenty five poles to a black and white Oak, then North Eighty seven poles to a white Oak on a Barren Hill then No. 28 Wt. eighty five poles to the aforesaid dividing line between COCK and MERCER then with said line So. 87 Wt. two hundred and ten poles to the first station containing two hundred acres. NOW THIS INDENTURE WITNESSETH that for sum of five shillings current money of Virginia to them said GEORGE MERCER and JAMES MERCER in hand paid by these presents do bargain and sell JOSEPH HOUGH the land above mentioned together with all houses orchards and appurtenances thereto belonging To have and to hold the said land during term of one whole year paying therefore one Peper Corn upon Feast of St. Michael to intent that by virtue of these presents and for transferring uses into possession said JOSEPH HOUGH may be in actual possession and thereby be enabled to accept a grant of Inheritance thereof In Witness whereof said GEORGE MERCER and JAMES MERCER, by their Attorney JOHN HOUGH, have hereunto set their hands and seals the day and year first above written
in presence of   ) GEORGE MERCER
                            JOHN HOUGH for   ) JAMES MERCER
    At a Court held for Loudoun County September the 13th 1773
This Indenture was acknowledged by JOHN HOUGH, Attorney in Fact for GEORGE MERCER and JAMES MERCER Esqrs. and is ordered to be recorded

pp.   THIS INDENTURE made the twenty seventh day of July in year of our Lord One
348-   thousand seven hundred and seventy three Between GEORGE MERCER lately in
352   OLD ENGLAND Esqr. and JAMES MERCER of SPOTSYLVANIA COUNTY Esqr. by their
         Attorney in Fact JOHN HOUGH of Loudoun County of one part and JOSEPH HOUGH
of County of Loudoun of other part Whereas .. (this entry proceeds as in the Lease above) .. NOW THIS INDENTURE WITNESSETH that GEORGE MERCER and JAMES MERCER by their Attorney in Fact. JOHN HOUGH, (and lately instructed by JAMES MERCER) for sum of Forty pounds current money of Virginia to them in hand paid by these presents doth sell JOSEPH HOUGH in his actual possession by virtue of a bargain and sale and by force of statute for transferring uses into possession all that tract of land situate in Loudoun

County aforesaid and bounded as is above described To have and to hold all the premises before mentioned unto JOHN HOUGH his heirs and assigns for ever In Witness whereof said GEORGE MERCER and JAMES MERCER by their Attorney in Fact, JOHN HOUGH, have hereunto set their hands and seals the day and year first above written
in the presence of   } GEORGE MERCER
                                    JOHN HOUGH for   } JAMES MERCER
  At a Court held for Loudoun County September the 13th 1773
This Indenture and Receipt thereon endorsed was acknowledged to be the acts and deeds of GEORGE MERCER and JAMES MERCER Esqrs. by JOHN HOUGH, their Attorney in Fact, and ordered to be recorded

pp.   THIS INDENTURE made the Twenty fifth day of August in year of our Lord One
352-   thousand seven hundred and seventy three Between JAMES CLEMENTS of County
354   of Loudoun and HANNAH his Wife of one part and JOHN HOUGH of same County of
           other part Witnesseth that JAMES CLEMENTS and HANNAH his Wife for sum of
five shillings current money of Virginia to them in hand paid by these presents doth bargain and sell unto JOHN HOUGH two parcels of Land joining each other one which he purchased of JOHN HAGUE by Deeds bearing date the 13th & 14th days of December ADm. 1762 bounded Beginning at a Chesnutt tree the N. E. side of a Spring Branch at or about the place called ERWINS FOLLY and Corner to GARRETT CORNELIESONs extending thence with his line So. 15 Wt. forty eight poles to a Stake near a mark'd black Oak on a Hill then N. 88 Et. forty nine poles to a small white Oak, then So. 35 d. 30" E. seventy five poles to a white Oak then N. 87 Et. Thirty poles to a small white Oak in head of a Valley, Corner to WILLIAM SCHOOLEY land then with his line N. 40 Et. One hundred and thirty poles to two red Oak saplins then No. 10 Wt. 12 poles to a red Oak then S. 87 Wt. two hundred and ten poles to the beginning containing One hundred and eight acres of land, Also the other part bounded Beginning at a red Oak saplin on a Hill side the East side of a Branch of LIMESTONE RUN corner to FRANCIS HAGUE and the above mentioned tract and extending thence with a line of that tract So. 10 Et. twelve poles to a small red Oak on said Hill side then crossing said Branch with line of said Land So. 40 Wt. one hundred and forty five poles to the dividing line of COCK and MERCER then with said line N. 87 Et. One hundred and ninety two poles to a red Oak saplin then N. 13 Et. one hundred and twenty six poles to a black oak then with a line of FRANCIS HAGUE So. 87 Wt. one hundred and eighteen poles to the beginning containing One hundred and three acres of land which parcels of Land said CLEMENT purchased of WILLIAM SCHOOLEY and Wife by Deeds bearing date the 7th and 8th days of August 1767, And all houses, orchards and appurtenances whatsoever belonging To have and to hold during full term of one whole year paying therefore the rent of one Peper Corn on Lady Day next to intent that by virtue of these presents and the statute for transferring uses into possession said JOHN HOUGH may be in actual possession and thereby be enabled to accept a release of Inheritance thereof In Witness whereof said JAMES CLEMENTS and HANNAH his Wife hath hereunto set their hands and seals the day and year first above written
in the presence of JOHN MATTHEW,   JAMES CLEMENS
        JESSE MATTHEW, ISAAC COOPER,   HANNAH CLEMENS
        WM. his mark ⋈ MARSHIL, JOHN STAPLETON
  At a Court held for Loudoun County September 13th 1773
This Indenture was acknowledged by JAMES CLEMENS and HANNAH his Wife parties thereto to be their acts and deeds the said HANNAH having been first privately examined as the Law directs and is ordered to be recorded

pp.   THIS INDENTURE made the Twenty sixth day of August in year of our Lord One
354-   thousand seven hundred and seventy three Between JAMES CLEMENTS in County
358   Loudoun and HANNAH his Wife of one part and JOHN HOUGH of same County of
other part Witnesseth that for sum of one hundred and sixty pounds current
money of Virginia to said JAMES CLEMENTS in hand paid by these presents doth bargain
and sell unto JOHN HOUGH in his actual possession by virtue of a bargain and sale and
by force of the statute for transferring uses into possession and to his heirs all them
two parcels of land situate in County of Loudoun and joining each other .. (this entry
proceeds with a description of the two parcels of land as in Lease above) .. To have and
to hold the lands hereby conveyed unto said JOHN HOUGH his heirs and assigns forever
In Witness whereof the said (blank) have hereunto set their hands and seals the day
and year first above written
in the presence of JOHN MATTHEW,   JAMES CLEMENS
    JESSE MATTHEW, WM. his mark /X\ MARSHAL   HANNAH CLEMENS
    ISAAC COOPER, JOHN STAPLETON
  At a Court held for Loudoun County September 13th 1773
This Indenture was acknowledged by JAMES CLEMENS and HANNAH his Wife parties
thereto to be their acts and deeds the said HANNAH having been first privately examined as the Law directs and relinquished her right of Dower therein the Receipt
thereon endorsed was also acknowledged by said JAMES CLEMENS and together with said
Indenture ordered to be recorded
(On margin: Examined Deliv'd to Mr. JOHN HOUGH June 8th 1774)

pp   THIS INDENTURE made the Thirteenth day of September in year of our Lord One
358-   thousand seven hundred and seventy three Between THOMAS WEST of County of
359   Loudoun of one part and CHARLES WEST of same County of other part Witnesseth
    that THOMAS WEST for sum of five shillings current money of Virginia by these
presents doth bargain and sell unto CHARLES WEST all that tract of land lying in Parish
of Cameron and County of Loudoun containing by Estimation three hundred acres be
the same more or less which land was devised to him by WILLIAM WEST Gent: deceased,
And all houses orchards and appurtenances whatsoever belonging To have and to hold
for full term of one whole year paying therefore the rent of One Peper Corn on Lady
Day next to intent that by virtue of these presents and of the statute for transferring
uses into possession said CHARLES WEST may be in actual possession and be thereby
enabled to accept a release of Inheritance thereof In Witness whereof said THOMAS
WEST have hereunto set his hand and seal the day and year first above written
in the presence of CRAVEN PEYTON,   THOS. WEST
  At a Court continued and held for Loudoun County Septr. 14th 1773
This Indenture was acknowledged by THOMAS WEST party thereto to be his act and deed
and ordered to be recorded

pp.   THIS INDENTURE made the Fourteenth day of September in year of our Lord One
359-   thousand seven hundred and seventy three Between THOMAS WEST of County of
361   Loudoun of one part and CHARLES WEST of same County of other part Witnesseth
    that for sum of Two hundred pounds current money of Virginia to said THOMAS
WEST in hand paid by these presents doth bargain and sell unto CHARLES WEST his
heirs and assigns in his actual possession now being by virtue of a bargain and sale for
one whole year and by force of statute for transferring uses into possession .. (this
entry proceeds as in Lease above) .. To have and to hold the lands hereby conveyed unto
said CHARLES WEST his heirs and assigns forever In Witness whereof THOMAS WEST

have hereunto set his hand and seal the day and year first above written
in the presence of CRAVEN PEYTON   THOS. WEST
    At a Court continued and held for Loudoun County Septr. 14th 1773
This Indenture and Receipt thereon endorsed were acknowledged by THOMAS WEST
party thereto to be his acts and deeds and is ordered to be recorded
(On margin: Exd: Del'd FRANS. PEYTON Sept. 1, 1773)

pp.   THIS INDENTURE made the XXIII day of April in year of our Lord One thousand
362-   seven hundred and seventy three Between BRYAN FAIRFAX of County of FAIR-
363   FAX of one part and THOMAS JOHNSON of other part Witnesseth that BRYAN
         FAIRFAX for sum of Five shillings current money of Virginia to him in hand
paid by these presents doth bargain and sell unto THOMAS JOHNSON a certain tract of
land situate in County of Loudoun containing One hundred and eighty eight acres be
the same more or less and is bounded beginning at three Spanish Oak saplins Corner to
a survey made for JACOB JANNEY, Blacksmith, and Extending thence with said JANNEYs
line So. 50 West one hundred and sixty nine poles to a white Oak, Corner to JOHN
GARRETTs Survey, thence with his line No. 50. Wt. Seventy poles to a Box Oak Corner to
THOMAS GREGG, Joyners, Tract thence with his line North one hundred and twenty
poles to three small black Oaks Corner to WILLIAM DODD thence with DODDs line No. 42
Et. two hundred and fifty five poles to a small Box Oak Corner to RICHARD BROWN thence
with BROWNs line So. 75 Et. one hundred and twenty poles to a black Oak thence West
sixty six poles to a Spanish Oak thence So. 70 Wt. One hundred and nine poles to a white
Oak thence So. 10 Wt. One hundred and fifty poles to three black Oaks thence So. 70 Wt.
ninety poles to the first station And all Houses Orchards and appurtenances whatsoever
belonging To have and to hold paying therefore the rent of one Pepper Corn on Lady
Day next to intent that by virtue of these presents and of the statute for transferring
uses into possession THOMAS JOHNSON may be in actual possession and thereby enabled
to accept a Release of Inheritance thereof in Witness whereof BRYAN FAIRFAX hath
hereunto set his hand and seal the day and year first above written
in presence of JOHN DOWDALL   BRYAN FAIRFAX
    At a Court continued and held for Loudoun County September the 14th 1773
This Indenture was acknowledged by BRYAN FAIRFAX Esqr. party thereto to be his act
and deed and ordered to be recorded

pp.   THIS INDENTURE made the XXIV day of April in year of our Lord One thousand
363-   seven hundred and seventy three Between BRYAN FAIRFAX and ELIZABETH his
367   Wife of County of FAIRFAX of one part and THOMAS JOHNSON of County of Lou-
         doun and Parish of Cameron of other part Witnesseth that for sum of Sixty
pounds current money of Virginia to said BRYAN FAIRFAX in hand paid by these presents doth bargain and sell unto THOMAS JOHNSON in his actual possession now being
by virtue of a bargain and sale for one whole year and by force of the statute for transferring uses into possession and his heirs a certain tract of land lying in County of
Loudoun containing One hundred and eighty eight acres be the same more or less and
bounded .. (description of land as in Lease above) .. To have and to hold the lands hereby conveyed unto THOMAS JOHNSON his heirs and assigns forever In Witness whereof
BRYAN FAIRFAX and ELIZABETH his Wife have hereunto set their hands and seals the
day and year first above written
in the presence of JOHN DOWDALL   BRYAN FAIRFAX
                                                         ELIZABETH FAIRFAX
    (COMMISSION George the Third to (names left blank) for privy examination of ELIZA-
BETH Wife of BRYAN FAIRFAX dated the 22d day of May 1773; with return of execution

thereof dated the 13th day of July 1773 signed by CHARLES BROADWATER and WILLIAM PAYNE JUNR.)

At a Court continued and held for Loudoun County September the 14th 1773 This Indenture was acknowledged by BRYAN FAIRFAX Esqr. party thereto and together with a Commission annexed for the Privy Examination of the feme with the return of execution thereof ordered to be recorded
(On margin: Deliv'd to Mr. JOHNSON June 1st 1774)

pp. 367-369   THIS INDENTURE made the Second day of September in year of our Lord One thousand seven hundred and seventy three Between BRYAN FAIRFAX of County of FAIRFAX Esqr. and WARNER WASHINGTON of County of FREDERICK and Colony of Virginia of one part and SAMUEL HARRIS of County of Loudoun of other part Witnesseth that BRYANT FAIRFAX and WARNER WASHINGTON for sum of Five shillings current money of Virginia to them in hand paid by these presents doth bargain and sell unto SAMUEL HARRIS all that tract of land situate in County of Loudoun formerly laid to JOHN WHITAKER as a tenement in order to obtain a Lease for Lives from GEORGE WILLIAM FAIRFAX Esqr. containing one hundred and fifty acres bounded beginning at a white Oak and black Oak in a line of JAMES DILWIN being also one of the Original Lines of this Intire Tract and is a Corner to a lott laid of for SAMUEL SMITH extending thence with SMITHs line So. 45 Wt. One hundred and sixty eight poles to two white Oaks corner to said SMITH and JOHN GRANTs lot then with said GRANTs lot No. 45 Wt. One hundred and forty five poles to a line of the lot formerly SAMUEL COMPTONs now the property of JOSHUA GORE then with GOREs line N. 45 Et. one hundred and sixty eight poles to the aforesaid DELWINs line then with said line So. 46 Et. One hundred and forty five poles to the first station containing one hundred and fifty acres of land being part of a larger tract formerly the property of WILLIAM FAIRFAX Esqr. deceased and called by the name of MORGAN BRYANTS, who had the same surveyed in his name and conveyed to said WILLIAM FAIRFAX Esqr. who by his Last Will and Testament did devise the said land to be sold for the benefit of his Son the said BRYANT FAIRFAX and Daughter, HANNAH. who intermarried with said WARNER WASHINGTON, the said BRYANT FAIRFAX and WARNER WASHINGTON having received the title to said land from the Execution aforesaid and all Houses orchards and appurtenances whatsoever belonging To have and to hold the lands hereby conveyed unto SAMUEL HARRIS during term of one whole year paying therefore the rent of one Peper Corn on Lady Day next to intent that by virtue of these presents and of the statute for transferring uses into possession SAMUEL HARRIS may be in actual possession and thereby enabled to accept a release of Inheritance thereof In Witness whereof BRYANT FAIRFAX and WARNER WASHINGTON hath hereunto set their hands and seals the day and year first written in the presence of   BRYANT FAIRFAX
                                                                             WARNER WASHINGTON

At a Court continued and held for Loudoun County September 14th 1773 This Indenture was ackowledged by BRYAN FAIRFAX and WARNER WASHINGTON Esqrs. parties thereto and is ordered to be recorded

pp. 369-372   THIS INDENTURE made the Third day of September in year of our Lord One thousand seven hundred and seventy three Between BRYANT FAIRFAX of County of FAIRFAX Esqr. and WARNER WASHINGTON of County of FREDERICK in Colony of Virginia Esqr. and HANNAH his Wife of one part and SAMUEL HARRIS of County of Loudoun of other part Witnesseth for sum of One hundred and thirty eight pounds current money of Virginia to said BRYANT FAIRFAX and WARNER WASHINGTON in hand paid by these presents doth bargain and sell SAMUEL HARRIS in his actual possession

now being by virtue of a bargain and sale for one whole year and by force of statute for transferring uses into possession all that tract of land situate in County of Loudoun and formerly laid off to JOHN WHITAKER as a Tenement in order to Obtain a Lease for Lives from GEORGE WILLIAM FAIRFAX Esqr, containing one hundred and fifty acres bounded .. (description of land as in Lease above) .. To have and to hold the lands hereby conveyed unto SAMUEL HARRIS his heirs and assigns forever In Witness whereof BRYAN FAIRFAX and WARNER WASHINGTON and HANNAH his Wife have hereunto set their hands and seals the day and year first above written
in the presence of   BRYAN FAIRFAX
                                                          WARNER WASHINGTON
   At a Court continued and held for Loudoun County September the 14th 1773
This Indenture and Receipt thereon endorsed were acknowledged by BRYAN FAIRFAX and WARNER WASHINGTON Esqrs, parties thereto to be their acts and deeds and ordered to be recorded
(On margin: Examined & delivered to SAML. HARRIS April 23. 1779)

pp.   THIS INDENTURE made the 9th day of June in year of our Lord One thousand
372-   seven hundred and seventy three Between JOHN ANDERSON of County of FAU-
374   QUIER of one part and WILLIAM HUTCHISON of County of Loudoun of other part
        Witnesseth that said JOHN ANDERSON for sum of five shillings to him in hand
paid by these presents doth bargain and sell unto WILLIAM HUTCHISON his heirs and assigns all that tract of land situate in County of Loudoun and bounded beginning at a white Oak Corner to JOHN HANBY thence with his line N. 25 W. 74 poles to two black Oaks thence N: 80 Et. 184 poles to an Elm thence So. 1 d. Et. 126 pos. to the beginning containing one hundred acres more or less together with all houses profits and appurtenances to said premises belonging To have and to hold during term of one whole year paying therefore the rent of one Ear of Indian Corn on the Feast of St. Michael the Arch Angel to intent by that by virtue of these presents and of statute for transferring uses into possession WILLIAM HUTCHISON may be in actual possession and thereby enabled to accept a Release of Inheritance thereof In Witness whereof JOHN ANDERSON hath hereunto put his hand and seal the day and year first above written
in presence of FRANCIS PEYTON,   JOHN ANDERSON
        ALEXANDER McPHERSON, JOHN WALKER,
        NATH. McPHERSON, HENRY his mark A/D PARKER
   At a Court continued and held for Loudoun County September 14th 1773
This Indenture was proved by Oaths of FRANCIS PEYTON, NATHANIEL McPHERSON and HENRY PARKER three of the subscribing witnesses thereto and ordered to be recorded
(On margin: Exd. & del'd COLO. PERVICE Oct. 22. 1795)

pp.   THIS INDENTURE made the Tenth day of June in year of our Lord One thousand
374-   seven hundred and seventy three Between JOHN ANDERSON of County of FAU-
376   QUIER of one part and WILLIAM HUTCHISON of County of Loudoun of other part
        Witnesseth that JOHN ANDERSON for sum of Fifty pounds current money to him
in hand paid by these presents doth bargain and sell unto WILLIAM HUTCHISON in his actual possession now being by virute of a bargain and sale for one whole year and by force of statute for transferring uses into possession and to his heirs and assigns forever all that parcel of land situate in County of Loudoun bounded .. (description of land as in Lease above) .. To have and to hold said One hundred acres of land and premises with appurtenances unto WILLIAM HUTCHISON his heirs and assigns forever In Witness whereof JOHN ANDERSON hath hereunto set his hand and seal the day and year first above written

in the presence of FRANCIS PEYTON,   JOHN ANDERSON
         NATH: McPHERSON, ALEXANDER McPHERSON,
         JNO. WALKER, HENRY his mark /\/) PARKER
   At a Court continued and held for Loudoun County September the 14th 1773
This Indenture and the Receipt thereon endorsed was proved by the Oath of FRANCIS
PEYTON, NATHANIEL McPHERSON and HENRY PARKER three of the subscribing wit-
nesses thereto and ordered to be recorded

pp.   THIS INDENTURE made the Second day of September in year of our Lord one
377-   thousand seven hundred and seventy three Between BRYANT FAIRFAX of County
379   of FAIRFAX Esqr. and WARNER WASHINGTON of County of FREDERICK and Colony
         of Virginia Esqr. of one part and JOSHUA GORE of County of Loudoun of other
part Witnesseth that BRYAN FAIRFAX and WARNER WASHINGTON for sum of five shillings current money of Virginia to them in hand paid by these presents doth bargain
and sell unto JOSHUA GORE that tract of land situate in County of Loudoun formerly
granted to SAMUEL COMPTON and JOHN COMPTON by a Lease for Lives from GEORGE WIL-
LIAM FAIRFAX Esqr. containing three hundred acres and bounded beginning at a large
Spanish Oak standing by the South Fork of KITTOCKTON CREEK near the line of Colo.
JOHN TAYLOE's and is the Original Beginning tree of the land now Bargained for and
extending thence So. 45 Wt. Three hundred and thirty five poles to a white Oak another
Original Corner then So. 43 Et. with another Original Line one hundred and forty five
poles to a white Oak Corner to JOHN GRANTs Lott then with said GRANTs lott and JOHN
WHITAKERs Lot No. 45 Et. three hundred and thirty five poles to one of the Original
Lines the N: side of said KITTOCTON CREEK in a line formerly granted to JOHN MEAD now
in possession of JAMES DILWIN or Brothers then with said line N: 45 Wt. one hundred
and forty five poles to beginning containing three hundred acres being part of a larger tract formerly the property of WILLIAM FAIRFAX Esqr. deceased and called by the
name of MORGAN BRYANT who had the same surveyed in his name and conveyed to said
WILLIAM FAIRFAX who by his Last Will and Testament did devise the said land to be sold
by his Executors for the benefit of his Son the said BRYANT FAIRFAX and his Daughter,
HANNAH, who intermarried with said WARNER WASHINGTON the said BRYANT FAIRFAX
and WARNER WASHINGTON having received a Title to said land from the Executors
aforesaid And all houses Orchards and appurtenances whatsoever belonging To have
and to hold the lands hereby conveyed unto JOSHUA GORE his assigns for full term of
one whole year paying therefore the rent of one Peper Corn on Lady Day next to intent
that by virtue of these presents and of the statute for transferring uses into possession
said JOSHUA GORE may be in actual possession and thereby enabled to accept a Release
of Inheritance thereof In Witness whereof BRYANT FAIRFAX and WARNER WASHING-
TON have hereunto set their hands and seals the day and year first above written
in presence of   BRYAN FAIRFAX
                                                        WARNER WASHINGTON
   At a Court continued and held for Loudoun County September the 14th 1773
This Indenture was acknowledged by BRYAN FAIRFAX and WARNER WASHINGTON Esqrs.
parties thereto and is ordered to be recorded

pp.   THIS INDENTURE made the third day of September in year of our Lord One thou-
379-   sand seven hundred and seventy three Between BRYAN FAIRFAX of County of
3S2   FAIRFAX Esqr. and WARNER WASHINGTON of County of FREDERICK and Colony of
         Virginia Esqr. and HANNAH his Wife of one part and JOSHUA GORE of County of
Loudoun of other part Witnesseth that for sum of Three hundred and forty pounds current money of PENSYLVANIA to said BRYANT FAIRFAX and WARNER WASHINGTON in

hand paid by these presents doth bargain and sell unto JOSHUA GORE in his actual possession now being by virtue of a bargain and sale for one whole and by force of statute
for transferring uses into possession and to his heirs all that tract of land situate in
County of Loudoun formerly granted to SAMUEL COMPTON and JOHN COMPTON by a Lease
for Lives containing three hundred acres bounded .. (description of land, conveyance
and descent as in Lease above).. To have and to hold the lands hereby conveyed unto
JOSHUA GORE and his heirs and assigns for ever In Witness whereof BRYANT FAIRFAX
and WARNER WASHINGTON have hereunto set their hands and seals the day and year
first above written
in the presence of   BRYAN FAIRFAX
                                                WARNER WASHINGTON
   At a Court continued and held for Loudoun County September the 14th 1773
This Indenture and receipt thereon endorsed was acknowledged by BRYAN FAIRFAX
and WARNER WASHINGTON Esqrs. parties thereto to be their acts and deeds and ordered
to be recorded

pp.   THIS INDENTURE made the Fourth day of September in year of our Lord One
382-   thousand seven hundred and seventy three Between RICHARD GRAHAM of
385   DUMFRIES in County of PRINCE WILLIAM of one part and WILLIAM LATIMORE of
           County of Loudoun of other part Witnesseth that said RICHARD GRAHAM in con-
sideration of the rents and covenants on part of WILLIAM LATIMORE to be paid and performed doth grant and to farm let a certain tract of land lying in County of Loudoun
about a mile above the GREAT FALLS of POTMACK RIVER and bounded by a survey made
by JOHN GUNNELL Beginning at some red Oak saplins being the second corner of
DANIEL MACRAEs Lease then along said MACRAEs N:W: line to BRUESTERs line thence to
POTOMACK RIVER then down said River to Mr. JOHN SEMPLEs Corner then along said
SEMPLEs line to the beginning Containing about 150 acres under the reservations
hereafter mentioned and excepting all mines minerals and Quarries whatsoever To
have and to hold said 150 acres of land with the appurtenances unto WILLIAM LATI-
MORE his heirs during natural lives of said WILLIAM LATAMORE, EDY LATAMORE and
WILLIAM LATAMORE paying therefore to RICHARD GRAHAM on or before twenty fifth
day of June every year the annual rent of seven pounds ten shillings lawful money of
Virginia together with the quit rents of said lands In Witness whereof the partys above
mentioned to these presents have interchangeably set their hands and seals the day
and year above written, the said GRAHAM agreeing that said LATAMORE may assign
over these premises provided it is a person agreeable to him said GRAHAM and WIL-
LIAM LATAMORE Oblidges himself to plant within four years at least one hundred Apple
trees and two hundred Peach trees and have Liberty of taking a Sub tenant while he
remains himself on the premises
in presence of JOHN NODING,   RICHARD GRAHAM
       HUGH his mark ⌣⌣CORN, HENRY BOGGESS JUNR.
   At a Court continued and held for Loudoun County September 15th 1773
This Indenture was proved by the Oaths of JOHN NODING, HUGH CORN and HENRY BOG-
GESS JUNR. the subscribing witnesses thereto And is ordered to be recorded
(On margin: Deliv'd to JNO. CHATTAM by Order of the Lessee May 19th 1774)

pp.   THIS INDENTURE made the twenty fifth day of May in year of our Lord One thou-
385-   sand seven hundred and seventy three Between JOSEPH JANNEY and MAHLON
387   TAYLOR of County of Loudoun of one part and JONATHAN MYRES of County
           aforesaid of other part Witnesseth that JOSEPH JANNEY and MAHLON TAYLOR for
sum of five shillings to them in hand paid by these presents doth bargain and sell unto

JONATHAN MYRES all that tract of land situate in County of Loudoun on a small branch of KITTOCKTON CREEK Two hundred and forty acres of which is part of a tract granted to COCK and MERCER the remainder is part of a tract granted to WILLIAM HENRY FAIRFAX and by several Patentees transferred to others and in Course and due form said JANNY and TAYLOR the whole bounded Beginning at two white oaks by MAHLON JANNYs fence mark'd C M E A (C M F A in Release) corner to land taken up by FRANCIS AWBRY and COCK and MERCER extending thence with MAHLON JANNEYs line in part East one hundred and sixty eight poles to a small Hickory and red Oak saplin on hill side Corner to JOHN BALL thence with his lines So: 5 Et. One hundred and twenty four poles to two small Hickorys from one root then So. 1 Et. one hundred and sixty eight poles to a Hickory in the dividing line of COCKE and MERCER then being with said line So. 87 Wt. One hundred and twelve poles to a white Oak in one of the Original lines of COCKE and MERCER then with the same N: 3 W. forty poles to a Hickory at the head of a great Gulley then So. 89 Wt. One hundred and fifteen poles to a Stake near a mark't white Oak then N: 21 Wt. Two hundred and one poles to a black Oak on hill side joining the aforesaid Land of AWBRY then with a line of that tract N: 50 Et. one hundred and two poles to the beginning containing three hundred and ninety five acres And all houses orchards and appurtenances whatsoever belonging To have and to hold the lands hereby conveyed unto JONATHAN MYRES and assigns during the full term of one whole year paying therefore the rent of one Peper Corn to intent that by virtue of these presents and of the statute for transferring uses into possession JONATHAN MYRES may be in actual possession and thereby enabled to accept a Release of Inheritance thereof In Witness whereof said JOSEPH JANNEY and MAHLON TAYLOR hath hereunto set their hands and seals the day and year first above written
in the presence of   JOSEPH JANNEY
                                                            MAHLON TAYLOR

At a Court continued and held for Loudoun County June the 14th 1773
This Indenture was acknowledged by JOSEPH JANNEY and MAHLON TAYLOR parties thereto And is ordered to be recorded

pp.   THIS INDENTURE made the Twenty sixth day of May in year of our Lord One thou-
387-   sand seven hundred and seventy three Between JOSEPH JANNEY and HANNAH
391   his Wife and MAHLON TAYLOR of the County of Loudoun of one part and JONA-
           THAN MYRES of County aforesaid of other part Witnesseth that for sum of three
hundred pounds current money of Virginia to said JOSEPH JANNEY and MAHLON TAY-
LOR in hand paid by these presents doth bargain and sell unto JONATHAN MYRES in his
actual possession now being by virtue of a bargain and sale for one whole year and of
the statute for transferring uses into possession all that parcel of land lying in County
of Loudoun on a small branch of KITTOCKTON CREEK (description of land and conveyances as in Lease above) .. To have and to hold the lands hereby conveyed unto said
JONATHAN MYRES his heirs and assigns for ever In Witness whereof JOSEPH JANNEY
and HANNAH his Wife and MAHLON TAYLOR hath hereunto set their hands and seals the
day and year first above written
in the presence of   JOSEPH JANNEY
                                                            MAHLON TAYLOR
                                                            HANNAH JANNEY

At a Court held for Loudoun County June 14th 1773
This Indenture and the Receipt thereon endorsed were acknowledged by JOSEPH JANNEY and MAHLON TAYLOR parties thereto And at another Court continued and held for the said County on the 15th day of September in the year aforesaid HANNAH JAN-NEY Wife of said JOSEPH being privately examined as the Law directs and relinquished

her right of Dower therein and likewise acknowledged the said Indenture to be her act and deed and then ordered to be recorded

pp.   MEMO. It is agreed between B. FAIRFAX Esqr. on the part of GIDNEY CLARKE Esqr
391-   and JOHN GARRETT that said FAIRFAX will as soon as he conveniently can pro-
392   cure a good and sufficient Power of Attorney legally executed and recorded en-
         abling him to Lease to said GARRETT 200 acres of said CLARKEs land in Loudoun
where said GARRETT now lives to the said GARRETT for three lives at and for the Rent of
L 3..0 p cent. acres and said GARRETT agrees to accept of a Lease on the above Terms and
immediately pay the Rent now in arrear for the time he has occupied said 150 acres at
the above rate. It is farther agreed that said GARRETT may have a Subtenant on said 200
acres that Subtenant makeing Improvements proportionble to the Quantity of land he
occupies September 16th 1773.
         G. JOHNSTON   BRYAN FAIRFAX
         W. ELZEY   JOHN JARED
   We the Subscribers do agree to accept of Leases on the above terms and pay the said
Rents of L 3..0 p cent. acres in proportion to what we hold in our Lotts as already laid off
and occupied by us with the proviso that such of us as have more than 150 acres of land
in the lot may have leave to place a Subtenant on the same on the same terms with the
said JARRETTs is and we farther agree to pay the rents in arrear for 150 acres if we
have enjoyed as much. Witness our hands this 16th day of Septr. 1773
                                                   BRYAN FAIRFAX

         STEPHEN JONES sold to JOHN WHITACRE,
         JOHN PALMER, JONATHAN MILLASON,
         BENJA. HISKETTS mark B SHADRACH LEWALLEN,
         HENRY VAN OVER, SAMUEL BONHAM
   At a Court continued and held for Loudoun County September the 16th 1773
This Memorandum of Agreement was acknowledged by the parties and ordered to be
recorded

pp.   KNOW ALL MEN by these presents that I ELIZABETH EVANS Exetx. of DAVID
392-   EVANS deceased of FREDIFFRIN in County of CHESHIRE and Province of PENSYL-
393   VANIA for divers good causes and considerations me hereunto moving have
         appointed my trusty friend JAMES COLEMAN Gent. of Loudoun County in the
Colony of Virginia my true and lawfull Attorney for me and to my use to ask demand
recover and receive of and from all persons in Colony of Virginia and follow such legal
courses for the recovery and obtaining of same as I myself might or could do were I
personally present and upon Receipt of the same Acquittance or other sufficient dis-
charges for me to make sign seal and deliver Rattifying and allowing whatsoever my
said Attorney shall lawfully do or cause to be done in the execution of the premises by
virtue of these presents. In Witness whereof I have hereunto set my hand and seal the
Eleventh day of October in the Thirteenth year of the Reign of our Sovereign Lord
George the third &c. and in the year of our Lord one thousand seven hundred and
seventy three 1773.
in the presence of   ELIZABETH EVANS
   At a Court held for Loudoun County October the 11th 1773
This Power of Attorney was acknowledged by ELIZABETH EVANS party thereto and
ordered to be recorded

pp.   THIS INDENTURE made the Thirty first day of July in year of our Lord One thou-
393-   sand seven hundred and seventy One between ELIZABETH ASKREN of Loudoun
395   County and EVAN THOMAS her Son of one part and THOMAS DOUGHTY of FAU-
        QUIRE COUNTY of other part Witnesseth that ELIZABETH ASKREN hath and said
EVAN THOMAS doth consent and of his own free will and accord bind himself apprentice to said THOMAS DOUGHTY to serve him and his heirs until said EVAN THOMAS who is
now sixteen years five months and nine days old shall arrive to the full age of Twenty
one years during which term said EVAN THOMAS his said Master faithfully shall serve
his secrets keep and all his lawfull commands every where gladly obey he shall not
waste his masters goods nor lend them unlawfully to any he shall do no damage to his
Master nor see it done by others without giving Notice thereof to his Master he shall
not contract marriage nor commit fornication during said term nor haunt Taverns nor
play houses nor any other places of bad resort he shall not absent himself day nor
night from his Masters house without his Masters leave but in all things behave himself as a good and faithfull Apprentice ought to do And THOMAS DOUGHTY for himself
and his heirs promise and agree to and with ELIZABETH ASKREN and EVAN THOMAS her
Son that he said THOMAS DOUGHTY shall to the utmost of his power and endeavour teach
or cause to be taught in the art trade and Mystery of a Blacksmith and also to find and
provide sufficient meat drink washing lodging and apparell fit for an apprentice according to the custom of the Country and shall also cause him to be Learned to read and
write English and to Cypher as far as the rule of three and shall at the expiration of said
term give him a freedom Suit from head to foot or five pounds Virginia currency and
his wearing apparel and shall give him all the necessary small tools to carry on the
Blacksmiths trade and help him make a new pair of Bellows for the trade but EVAN
THOMAS is to find the material for it the parties to these presents have interchangeably
set their hands and seals the day month and year first above mentioned
in presence of THOS. ASKREN,   ELIZABETH her mark ⟨ ASKREN
        JER. HUTCHISON,   EVAN THOMAS
        THOS. ASKREN JUNR., JOHN ASKREN   THOMAS DOUGHTY
    At a Court held for Loudoun County October 11th 1773
This Indenture was proved by the Oaths of THOMAS ASKREN and JOHN ASKREN, two of
the subscribing witnesses, and is ordered to be recorded

pp.   THIS INDENTURE made the Fourth day of October in year of our Lord One thou-
395-   sand seven hundred and seventy three Between JOSIAS SUTTLE and ELIZABETH
397   his Wife of County of Loudoun of one part and STEPHEN McPHERSON of County of
        CHESTER in Province of PENSYLVANIA of other part Witnesseth that JOSIAS SUT-
TLE and ELIZABETH his Wife for sum of five shilling current money of Virginia to them
in hand paid by these presents doth bargain and sell unto STEPHEN McPHERSON a parcel of land situate in County of Loudoun containing two hundred and eighty five acres
bounded according to a Survey thereof made by WILLIAM WEST JUNIOR Beginning at a
red Oak corner to JOSEPH ALLEN and extending So. 70 Et. 128 poles to a small Gum and
white Oak corner to ALLEN in the Fork of two branches thence N. 65 Et. 90 poles to a
large Gum another Corner to said ALLEN thence N: 75 Et. 120 poles to a small Gum near
the BEAVER DAM also ALLENs Corner thence So: 12 Wt. 180 poles binding with a small
branch to three red Oaks in CARTERs line thence N: 84 Wt. 410 poles to a Chesnut and
two black Oaks thence N: 42 Et. along WARNERs line 140 poles to the beginning being
part of a larger tract of land formerly the property of Mr. CHARLES GREEN, Minister of
Truro Parish in County of FAIRFAX, And all houses Orchards and appurtenances whatsoever belonging To have and to hold unto STEPHEN McPHERSON his heirs and assigns
for the full term of one whole year paying therefore the rent of one Peper Corn on

Lady Day next to intent that by virtue of these presents and of the statute for transferring uses into possession STEPHEN McPHERSON may be in actual possession and be
thereby enabled to accept a release of Inheritance thereof In Witness whereof said
JOSIAH SUTTLE and ELIZABETH his Wife have hereunto set their hands and seals this day
and year first above written

in presence of JOHN GIBSON,   JOSIAH SETTLE
    ISAAC GIBSON, MOSES GIBSON   ELIABETH her mark ⟨ SUTTLE
  At a Court held for Loudoun County October 11th 1773
This Indenture was acknowledged by JOSIAS SETTLE and ELIZABETH his Wife parties
thereto to be their acts and deeds the said ELIZABETH having been first privately examined as the Law directs and relinquished her right of Dower therein and ordered to be
recorded

pp.   THIS INDENTURE made the Fifth day of October in year of our Lord One thousand
397-   seven hundred and seventy three Between JOSIAH SUTTLE and ELIZABETH his
400   Wife of County of Loudoun of one part and STEPHEN McPHERSON in the County
        of CHESTER in Province of PENSYLVANIA of other part Witnesseth that for sum
of two hundred and forty pounds current money of Virginia to said JOSIAH SUTTLE in
hand paid by these presents doth bargain and sell unto STEPHEN McPHERSON in his
actual possession by virtue of a bargain and sale for one whole year and by force of the
statute for transferring uses into possession and his heirs a certain parcel of land containing two hundred and eighty five acres situate in County of Loudoun bounded ..
(description of land as in Lease above) .. To have and to hold the said two hundred and
eighty five acres of land unto said STEPHEN McPHERSON his heirs and assigns forever
In Witness whereof said JOSIAH and ELIZABETH have hereunto set their hands and seals
this day and year first above written

in presence of JOHN GIBSON,   JOSIAH SETTLE
    ISAAC GIBSON, MOSES GIBSON   ELIZABETH her mark ✝ SETTLE
  At a Court held for Loudoun County Octo. 11. 1773
This Indenture was acknowledged by JOSIAH SUTTLE and ELIZABETH his Wife parties
thereto to be their acts and deeds the said ELIZABETH having been first privately exa-
mined as the Law directs and relinquished her right of Dower therein and the Receipt
thereon endorsed was also acknowledged by the said JOSIAH together with the said
Indenture ordered to be recorded
(On margin: Exd. & Deliv'd to Mr. McPherson June 20th 1776)

pp.   THIS INDENTURE made the Eighth day of January in year of our Lord One thou-
400-   sand seven hundred and seventy two Between SAMUEL TALBUTT of County of
402   FAIRFAX and MARY MAGDALIN his Wife of one part and THOMAS ASKREN of the
        County of Loudoun of other part Witnesseth that SAMUEL TALBUT and MARY
MAGDALIN his Wife for the sum of five shillings current money of Virginia to them in
hand paid do bargain and sell unto THOMAS ASKREN all that tract of land lying on a
Draught of ELK LICKING RUN in County of Loudoun containing four hundred acres
more or less which said land was sold and conveyed by SAMUEL ESKRIDGE to WILLIAM
TEMPLEMAN and by said TEMPLEMAN sold and conveyed to SAMUEL TALBUT first party
to these presents by Deeds of Lease and Release bearing date the Ninth and Tenth days
of August in year One thousand seven hundred and sixty seven and recorded among records of Loudoun County beginning for the same at two white Oaks and a Hickory on a
Draught of ELK LICKING RUN Corner to land of THOMAS ASBURY thence N: 47 Wt. 79
poles to a black Oak thence No. 16. West 146 poles to three white Oaks amongst a parcel
of Stone by the side of a Glade one of the trees marked D. T.(D. S. in Release) thence So.

70. Et. 214 poles to RUSSELLs line thence along RUSSELLs line So. 40 East 87 poles to said RUSSELLs Corner red Oak thence along another of his lines N: 60. East 77 poles thence So: 19. East 134 poles to a small Hickory and white Oak and a black Oak standing Triangularly in a Glade or Draught of ELK LICKING RUN within three poles of a large marked red Oak thence So. 70 West 207 poles to the beginning And all houses Orchards and appurtenances whatsoever belonging To have and to hold the said tract of land unto THOMAS ASKREN his assigns for term of one whole year paying therefore the rent of one Peper Corn on Lady Day next to intent that by virtue of these presents and of the statute for transferring uses into possession THOMAS ASKREN may be in actual possession and be thereby enabled to accept a Release of Inheritance thereof In Witness whereof SAMUEL TALBUTT and MARY MAGDALIN his Wife have hereunto set their hands and seals the day month and year aforesaid

in presence of SIMON TRIPLETT,   SAMUEL TALBUTT
       COLEMAN BROWN, SAMUEL LOVE,   MARY M. TALBUTT
       JAMES SPENCER, JAS. LANE

At a Court continued and held for Loudoun County March 10th 1772
This Indenture was proved by the Oath of SIMON TRIPLETT and JAMES LANE Gent. two of the subscribing witnesses thereto And at another Court held for said County October the 11th 1773 the same was fully proved by the Oath of SAMUEL LOVE Gent. another of the Witnesses thereto and is ordered to be recorded

pp.   THIS INDENTURE made the Ninth day of January in year of our Lord One thou-
402-   sand seven hundred and seventy two Between SAMUEL TALBUTT of County of
407   FAIRFAX and MARY MAGDALIN his Wife of one part and JOHN ASKREN of County
         of Loudoun of other part Witnesseth that for sum of One hundred and fifty
pounds current money of Virginia to SAMUEL TALBUTT in hand paid by these presents do bargain and sell unto THOMAS ASKREN in his actual possession by virtue of a bargain and sale for one whole and by force of statute for transferring uses into possession all that tract of land lying on a Draught of ELK LICKING RUN in County of Loudoun containing Four hundred acres more or less ..(conveyances and description of land as in Lease above) .. To have and to hold the said tract of land unto said THOMAS ASKREN his heirs and assigns In Witness whereof said SAMUEL TALBUTT and MARY MAGDALIN his Wife have hereunto set their hands and seals the day and year aforesaid

in the presence of SIMON TRIPLETT,   SAMUEL TALBOTT
       SAML. LOVE, JAS. LANE,   MARY M. TALBOTT
       COLMON BROWN, JAMES SPENCER

(COMMISSION George the Third to SIMON TRIPLETT, GEORGE SUMMERS and SAMUEL LOVE Gent. for the privy examination of MARY MAGDALIN Wife of SAMUEL TALBUTT dated eighth day of January 1772; and return of execution thereof dated 9th day of January 1772 signed by SIMON TRIPLETT and SAML: LOVE)

At a Court continued and held for Loudoun County March 10th 1772
This Indenture and Receipt thereon endorsed was proved by the Oaths of SIMON TRIP-LETT and JAMES LANE Gent. two of the subscribing Witnesses thereto And at another Court held for said County October the 11th 1773 the same was fully proved by the Oath of SAMUEL LOVE another of the Witnesses. And the Commission of the Privy Examination of the feme annexed with a return of execution thereof together with said Indenture ordered to be recorded
(On margin: Del'd Febry. 22. 1777)

pp.   THIS INDENTURE made the Sixth day of October in year of our Lord One thousand
407-   seven hundred and seventy three Between THOMAS HUMPHREY of Loudoun
409   County of one part and RICHARD OSBORN of same County of other part Witnesseth that THOMAS HUMPHREY for sum of five shillings current money of Virginia to him in hand paid by these presents doth bargain and sell unto RICHARD
OSBURN a certain tract of land lying in County of Loudoun containing Seventy seven
acres be the same more or less bounded Beginning at a white Oak and running from
thence West Eighty two poles to two white Oaks the back line of the Original Patent
thence with the line of the Patent North North East one hundred and thirty six poles to
two red Oaks on a Barren Hill thence with said line North 88 East one hundred poles to a
black Oak and white Oak in the side line of the Patent extending thence South 25 d. 30"
West one hundred and fifty four poles to the beginning which is part of a tract of land
containing three hundred and thirty two acres which was purchased by THOMAS
HUMPHREY of the Honble. JOHN TAYLOE by Deeds of Lease and Release bearing date
respectively the Sixteenth and seventeenth days of December in year one thousand
seven hundred and seventy two and duly proved and recorded in the Court of County of
Loudoun And all houses orchards and appurtenances whatsoever belonging To have
and to hold the lands hereby conveyed unto RICHARD OSBURN his assigns for full term
of one whole year paying therefore the rent of one Peper Corn on Lady Day next to
intent that by virtue of these presents and of the statute for transferring uses into possession RICHARD OSBURN may be in actual possession and be thereby enabled to accept
a Release of Inheritance thereof In Witness whereof THOMAS HUMPHREY hath hereunto set his hand and seal the day and year first above written
in the presence of the five shillings being first paid
        ROBERT JAMISON, WILLIAM OSBURN,   THOMAS HUMPHREY
        JOSIAS MARKS
  At a Court continued and held for Loudoun County October 11th 1773
This Indenture was acknowledged by THOMAS HUMPHREY party thereto and is ordered
to be recorded

pp.   THIS INDENTURE made the Seventh day of October in year of our Lord One thou-
409-   sand seven hundred and seventy three Between THOMAS HUMPHREY and MARY
412   his Wife of Loudoun County of one part and RICHARD OSBORN of same County
        Witnesseth that for sum of Twenty five pounds Current money of Virginia to
THOMAS HUMPHREY in hand paid by these presents doth bargain and sell unto
RICHARD OSBORN in his actual possession now being by virtue of a Bargain and sale for
one whole year and by force of statute for transferring uses into possession and to his
heirs a certain tract of land lying in County of Loudoun containing seventy seven
acres be the same more or less and bound .. (description of land and purchase by THO-
MAS HUMPHREY as in Lease above).. To have and to hold unto RICHARD OSBORN his
heirs and assigns forever In Witness whereof THOMAS HUMPHREY and MARY his Wife
have hereunto set their hands and seals the day and year first above written
in the presence of ROBERT JAMISON,   THOMAS HUMPHREY
        WILLIAM OSBURN, JOSIAH MARKS   MARY HUMPHREY
  At a Court continued and held for Loudoun County October 11th 1773
This Indenture was acknowledged by THOMAS HUMPHREY and MARY his Wife parties
thereto to be their acts and deeds the said MARY having been first privately examined
as the Law directs and relinquished her right of Dower therein the Receipt thereon endorsed was also acknowledged by said THOMAS HUMPHREY and together with the said
Indenture ordered to be recorded

pp.   TO ALL TO WHOM these presents shall come WILLIAM HANCOCK JUNIOR of the
412-   County of Loudoun sends Greeting. Whereas SAMUEL HANCOCK of the County of
413   CHESTERFIELD deceased in his life time did give unto WILLIAM HANCOCK, his Son
         who is Father unto the said WILLIAM HANCOCK JUNR. one Negro woman Jean
alias Hannah To Have and To Hold the said Negro Jean alias Hannah and her increase
unto said WILLIAM HANCOCK the Elder for and during his natural life and after his decease to the only proper use and behoof of above named WILLIAM HANCOCK JUNR. and
his heirs forever, Whereby said WILLIAM HANCOCK the Elder is now possess'd of said
Jean alias Hannah and her increase which are Tom, Patt, George and Dennis and said
WILLIAM HANCOCK JUNR. is intitled to the reversion thereof immediately after the
death of said WILLIAM HANCOCK the Elder. Now Know ye that I WILLIAM HANCOCK
JUNIOR for sum of One hundred pounds current money to me in hand by said WILLIAM
HANCOCK the Elder of said County of Loudoun have bargained and sold unto WILLIAM
HANCOCK the Elder all that my right and title of in and to the said Jean alias Hannah and
her present and future increase either in reversion remainder or otherwise In Testimony whereof I said WILLIAM HANCOCK JUNR. have hereunto set my hand and seal this
29th day of March 1773
in presence of WM. ELZEY,   WM. HANCOCK JUNR.
          SIMON HANCOCK
  At a Court held for Loudoun County October 11. 1773
This Indenture was proved to be the act and deed of WILLIAM HANCOCK JUNIOR party
thereto by the Oaths of WILLIAM ELZEY Gent. and SIMON HANCOCK the Witnesses thereto and ordered to be recorded
(On margin: Exd. d'd Capt. J. HANCOCKS Apl. 14. 1781)

pp.   THIS INDENTURE made the Eleventh day of October in year of our Lord One thou-
413-   sand seven hundred and seventy three Between LEWIS ELZEY of FAIRFAX
415   COUNTY Gentleman of one part and JAMES WILLIAMSON of Loudoun County,
         Planter, of other part Witnesseth that LEWIS ELZEY in consideration of the
yearly rents and covenants on part of JAMES WILLIAMSON to be performed and kept by
these presents doth grant and to farm let unto said JAMES WILLIAMSON a certain tract
of land containing one hundred and fifty acres situate on both side of GOOSE CREEK
which said land is now and has been in the possession of said JAMES WILLIAMSON for
upwards of seven years To have and to hold said tract of land unto said JAMES WIL-
LIAMSON during the natural lives of said JAMES WILLIAMSON and MARY his Wife and
longest liver of them paying therefore yearly unto LEWIS ELZEY his heirs the sum of
Eight pounds current money of Virginia and plant out and maintain fifty Apple trees of
good latter fruit and at all times keep the Plantation in tenantable condition and
further not to have a Subtenant on said premises In Witness whereof said parties have
hereunto set their hands and seals the day and year first above written
in the presence of SOLOMON his mark ✗ HARDY,   LEWIS ELZEY
          HY. POTTEN   JAMES WILLIAMSON
  At a Court held for Loudoun County October the 11th 1773
This Indenture was acknowledged by LEWIS ELZEY Gent. and JAMES WILLIAMSON parties thereto to be their acts and deeds And ordered to be recorded
(On margin: Examined and d d May 8. 1784)

pp.   THIS INDENTURE made the 29th day of October in year of our Lord One thousand
415-   seven hundred and seventy three Between BRYAN FAIRFAX of County of FAIR-
418   FAX Gent. of one part and IGNATIUS BYRNS of County of Loudoun of other part
         Witnesseth that said BRYAN FAIRFAX in consideration of the rents and cove-

nants hereafter mentioned on part of IGNATIUS BYRNS doth grant and to farm let unto IGNATIUS BYRNS a certain tract of land lying in County of Loudoun in the KITTOCTON MOUNTAINS on the head Drains of SEGLAN BRANCH and bounded Beginning at a leaning white Oak corner to land JOHN HOUGH sold to WILLIAM MORLAN and extending thence with MORLANs line N: 25 West 206 poles to a red Oak saplin Corner to JOSEPH GARNERs lott thence with his line South 23 West 230 poles to a white Oak one of the Original Corners thence with One of the original lines So: 80 East 214 poles to the first station containing one hundred and fifty acres under the reservations hereafter mentioned and excepting all mines minerals and Quarries whatsoever To have and to hold said One hundred and fifty acres of land with the appurtenances unto said IGNATIUS BYRNS his heirs &c. during natural lives of him said IGNATIUS BYRNS, and his Wife MARY, and Son BENEDICK BYRNS and the longest liver of them paying BRYAN FAIRFAX every year on the twenty fifth day of December the rent of four pounds current money of Virginia Provided he or they plant at least one hundred Apple trees and keep them well pruned within a good fence and also cause to be built a Dwelling House at least twenty feet long and sixteen feet wide and other such Out houses as his way of Husbandry may require Provided also that no Subtenant shall be admitted on said Tenement In Witness whereof the parties above mentioned to these presents have interchangeably set their hands and seals the day and year first above written
in the presence of GILBT. SIMPSON,   BRYAN FAIRFAX
          PATRICK BYRN, JOSEPH PHILLIS   IGNATIUS his mark ⅂ BRYNS
At a Court held for Loudoun County Novr. 8 1773.
This Indenture was proved to be the acts and deeds of BRYAN FAIRFAX Esqr. and IGNATIUS BYRNS partys thereto by the Oaths of GILBT. SIMPSON, PATRICK BYRN, JOSEPH PHILLIS Subscribing witnesses thereto and ordered to be recorded
(On margin: D D to Mr. BRYNS Son Janry 1775)

pp. 418-421   THIS INDENTURE made the 26th day of April in year of our Lord One thousand seven hundred and seventy two Between ANN EDMONDS of County of FAUQUER of one part and JOSHUA YEATES of County of Loudoun of other part Witnesseth that said ANN EDMONDS in consideration of the rents and covenants hereafter mentioned doth grant and to farm let unto JOSHUA YEATES a certain parcel of land situate lying and being in County of Loudoun on GOOSE CREEK and bounded Beginning in BURGESSes Tract at the line which shall divide this tract from the land now held by ROBERT SCOTT running thence with the line or lines of the whole tract to GOOSE CREEK thence down the Creek to the Mouth of CROMWELLS RUN and thence up the said Run as high so as to include One hundred and fifty acres with a straight line to the beginning the same being part of a tract of land Willed to this said ANN EDMONDS by SIMON MILLAR under the reservations hereafter mentioned excepting all mines minerals and Quarries excepting what stones may be needful for building on the premises To have and to hold said One hundred and fifty acres of land with the appurtenances unto said JOSHUA YATES his heirs during the natural lives of him said JOSHUA YATES, ANN his Wife and WILLIAM YATES their Son and longest liver of them paying unto said ANN EDMONDS on the 25th day of December in year of our Lord One thousand seven hundred and seventy two and from thenceforth every year the sum of two pounds Ten shillings current money of Virginia and Quit rents Provided said JOSHUA YATES within five years do plant at least one hundred good Apple trees and keep them well pruned and under good fence and also cause to be built a Dwelling House at least sixteen feet square and other such houses as his way of Husbandry may require In Witness whereof the parties to these presents have interchangeably set their hands and seals the day and year first above written

in presence of CHAS. CHINN,   ANN EDMONDS
    JAMES MURREY, LEVEN POWELL,   JOSHUA YATES
    JAMES MURREY
   At a Court held for Loudoun County May the 28th 1772
This Indenture was proved to be the acts and deeds of ANN EDMONDS and JOSHUA YEATES
partys thereto by the Oaths of LEVEN POWELL Gent. and JAMES MURREY, two of the subscribing witnesses thereto And at another Court held for the same County November
the 8th 1773 the same was fully proved by the Oath of CHARLES CHINN another of the
witnesses and ordered to be recorded

pp.   THIS INDENTURE made the Eighteenth day of October in year of our Lord God One
421-   thousand seven hundred seventy and three and in the fourteenth year of the
424   Reign of his present Majesty George the Third King of Great Britain &c. Between
      JOSEPH ABBETT of Parish of Shelburn and Loudoun County, Carpenter, and
MARY his Wife of one part DANIEL LOSH of same Parish and County, Butcher, of other
part Witnesses that JOSEPH ABBETT for sum of Twenty five pounds current money of
Virginia to him in hand paid or well or sufficiently secured to be paid by these presents
doth bargain and sell unto DANIEL LOSH one certain lot or half acre of land situate in
TOWN of LEESBURG and County of Loudoun and numbered in a plan and survey of said
TOWN Fifty Five and bounded with and on MARKETT STREET togather with all houses
gardens and appurtenances of any kind belonging To have and to hold said lot or half
acre of land and premises with the appurtenances unto said DANIEL LOSH his heirs and
assigns which lot or half acre of land beforementioned JOSEPH ABBETT purchased of
NICHOLAS MINOR Gent. by Deed bearing date the fourteenth day of April in year of our
Lord one thousand seven hundred and sixty seven In Witness whereof said JOSEPH
ABBETT and (blank) his Wife have hereunto set their hands and seals the day month
and year first above written
in presence of STEPHEN DONALDSON,   JOSEPH ABBETT
    OLIVER PRICE, FRIED: DRIESCK   MARY her mark X ABBETT
   At a Court continued and held for Loudoun County November the 9th 1773
This Indenture was acknowledged by JOSEPH ABBETT and MARY his Wife parties there-
to to be their acts and deeds, the said MARY having been first privately examined as the
Law directs and relinquished her right of Dower therein and the Memorandum and Receipt thereon endorsed was likewise acknowledged by said JOSEPH ABBETT and togather
with the said Indenture ordered to be recorded
(On margin: Examined Deliv'd to D. Losh March 13th 1775)

pp.   LOUDOUN COUNTY VIRGINIA November 9th 1773
424-   KNOW ALL MEN by these presents that I BENJAMIN HAIT of the Province of
425   EAST NEW JERSEY and County of ESSEX, Clerk, have and by these presents ap-
      point my trusty Friend JOSIAS CLAPHAM of the Colny: aforesaid my true and
lawful Attorney with full power and authority to settle and adjust by Law or otherways
all my Business in Virginia and especially all matters of Controversy or dispute that has
or hereafter may arise between me or my said Attorney and HAMILTON ROGERS or any
other that has or now does live on a tract of land that I purchased of JOHN HOUGH, Attorney in Fact of JOHN, GEORGE and JAMES MERCERs &c. and do hereby fully impower
my said Attorney for me and in my name to prosecute at law by Ejection or otherways at
his discretion the said HAMILTON ROGERS or any other living on or in wise trespassing
on the said land. If the said JOSIAS CLAPHAM shall think proper to sell and dispose of
said tract of land or should hereafter discover that JOHN HOUGH Attorney in Fact for the
MERCERs aforesaid should have sold full right in fee simple &c. I fully impower him to

prosecute said JOHN HOUGH or ths said MERCER &c. to recover my right &c. at Law at my Attorney's discretion &c. to recover my rights &c. in any wise and from any persons whatsoever in regard to the aforesaid tract of land or to sell the same as fully and amply as I coud were I personally present in every respect In Witness whereof I have here-unto put my hand the date above &c.

BENJAMIN HAIT

At a Court continued and held for Loudoun County November the 9, 1773
This Power of Attorney was acknowledged by BENJAMIN HAIT party thereto and ordered to be recorded

pp. THIS INDENTURE made the tenth day of September in year of our Lord One thou-
425- sand seven hundred and seventy three Between JOSHUA EVANS of Cameron
428 Parish in County of Loudoun and MARTHA his Wife of one part and JOHN CARTER
of the same Parish and County Gentleman of other part WHEREAS the Vestry of
the Parish of Cameron have purchased of said JOSHUA EVANS and MARTHA his Wife a
parcel of land containing three acres for use of said Parish and for purpose of erecting
a CHURCH thereon and have nominated said JOHN CARTER as their Trustee for receiving
a Conveyance for the same, NOW THIS INDENTURE WITNESSETH that JOSHUA EVANS and
MARTHA his Wife for sum of three pounds current money of Virginia to them in hand
paid by said JOHN CARTER by these presents do bargain and sell all that parcel of land
mentioned containing three acres lying in Parish and County aforesaid near SUGAR
LAND RUN and bounded beginning at a red Oak thence N: 23 E. 5 poles to a Stake thence
S. 57 E. 7 poles to a large red Oak and a double white Oak saplin Pointers thence S. 23 W.
26 poles to a Hickory and two red Oak saplins Pointers thence N: 67 W. 23 poles to a white
Oak and Hiccory saplins thence N: 23 E: 16 poles to a white Oak and Hickory saplins on a
Hill thence So. 84 1/2 Et. 16 1/2 poles to the beginning containing three acres including
the Spring and all woods and advantages whatsoever belonging To have and to hold said
parcel of land with the appurtenances unto said JOHN CARTER and his heirs to the use
intent and purpose following and for no other intent or purpose whatsoever that is to
say To the use of the Inhabitants of said Parish of Cameron for ever for the purpose of
erecting and building thereon a CHURCH and such other conveniences as the Vestry of
said Parish or their Successors shall think fit and necessary In Witness whereof said
JOSHUA EVANS and MARTHA his Wife have hereunto set their hands and affixed their
seals the day month and year first above written
in presence of ROBERT POPKINS,   JOSHUA EVANS
     THOMAS SELF, ROBERT CAMPBELL,   MARTHA + EVANS
     EVAN DAVIS

At a Court continued and held for Loudoun County September the 9th 1773
This Indenture and the Receipt thereon endorsed was proved to be the act and deed of
JOSHUA GORE party thereto by the oaths of ROBERT POPKINS and THOMAS SELF, two of
the subscribing witnesses thereto And on the 17th day of the same Month the same was
fully proved by the Oath of EVAN DAVIS another of the witnesses. On the 9th day of
November in the year aforesaid MARTHA EVANS, Widow and Relict of said JOSHUA, personally appeared in Court and acknowledged the said Indenture (she having been first
privately examined as the Law directs and relinquished her right of Dower therein)
and together with the said Indenture ordered to be recorded
(On margin: Examined D D to HAR. LANE 1 Septr. 1774)

pp.   THIS INDENTURE made this twenty fourth day of August in the Twelth year of
428-   the Reign of our Sovereign Lord George the Third &c. Between ANTHONY RUS-
429   SELL Gentleman of Loudoun County of one part and GEORGE JOHNSTON, Attorney
       at Law, of same place of other part Witnesseth that ANTHONY RUSSELL for sum of
twenty five pounds current money of Virginia to him in hand paid by these presents
doth bargain and sell unto GEORGE JOHNSTON his heirs and assigns for ever one lott or
half acre of land lying in TOWN of LEESBURGH and County aforesaid Numbered Thirty
Four which he purchased of THOMAS PRITCHARD and Wife on seventeenth day of September in year Seventeen hundred and Sixty two To have and hold said lot with all its
appurtenances unto GEORGE JOHNSTON his heirs and assigns for ever rendering to the
Lord Proprietor of the Northern Neck of Virginia the yearly quit rents due to him In
Witness whereof ANTHONY RUSSELL hath to this Indenture affixed his seal the day and
year aforesaid
Presence of us who also saw the Receipt
  signed and Livery of Seizen made as
  herein specified STEPHEN DONALDSON,   ANTHONY RUSSELL
       HUGH NEILSON, ROBERT HAMILTON,
       ALEXR. McINTIRE
  At a Court continued and held for Loudoun County October the 1st 1772
This Indenture and Receipt under written was proved to be the act and deed of
ANTHONY RUSSELL Gent. party thereto by the Oath of STEPHEN DONALDSON Gent. one of
the subscribing witnesses, And at another Court held for the same County November
the 9th 1773 was fully proved by the Oaths of ROBERT HAMILTON & ALEXANDER McIN-
TIRE, two of the subscribing witnesses thereto, and ordered to be recorded

pp.   THIS INDENTURE made this 9th day of November in year of our Lord one thou-
430-   sand seven hundred and seventy three Between SHADRICK SAMUELS, Black-
431   smith, of County of Loudoun of one part and PHILIP NOLAND of County affore-
       said of other part Witnesseth that for sum of Five shillings current money of
Virginia in hand paid by said PHILIP NOLAND unto said SHADRICK SAMUELS by these
presents SHADRICK SAMUELS doth bargain and sell unto PHILIP NOLAND for and during
the term of one whole year all that tract of land lying in County of Loudoun containing
Fifty acres of land being part of a greater tract of land sold by PATRICK LYNCH to
RICHARD ABRELL and from said RICHARD ABRELL deceded unto JOHN ABRELL as Heir
at Law and from said JOHN ABRELL was conveyed unto said PHILLIP NOLAND by deeds of
lease and release bearing date the ninth and tenth days of October in year One thousand
seven hundred and fifty seven and is bounded beginning at a white Oak the East side of
NOLANDS FERRY ROAD it being a Corner of said large tract of land thence N. 35 1/2 W.
eighty poles to a Stake standing in a line of said great Tract thence S. 51 W. 104 poles
thence S. 35 1/2 E. 80 poles to a line of the aforesaid great Tract thence N. 51 E. 104
poles along the said line to the Beginning containing fifty acres being part of the
afforesaid tract as above mentioned And all houses orchards and appurtenances whatsoever belonging To have and to hold said land and premises unto said SHADRICK
SAMUELS his heirs and assigns for the term above mentioned paying therefore the
rent of one Peper Corn on Feast of St. Michael next to intent that by virtue of these
presents and of the statute for transferring uses into possession said PHILIP NOLAND
may be in actual possession and be enabled to accept a release of Inheritance thereof
In Witness whereof said SHADRICK SAMUELS hath hereunto set his hand and seal the
day and year first above written
in presence of us JOHN MINOR,   SHADRICK SAMUELS
       WILLIAM DOUGLASS, WM. MOLTON

At a Court continued and held for Loudoun County November 10th 1773
This Indenture was acknowledged by SHEDRICK SAMUELS party thereto to be his act and
deed and is ordered to be recorded

pp.   THIS INDENTURE made this 10th day of Novr. in year of our Lord one thousand
431-   seven hundred and seventy three Between SHEDRICK SAMUELS of Loudoun
434   County, Blacksmith,and PATTY, his Wife, of one part and PHILIP NOLAND of the
          same County of other part Witnesseth that for sum of one hundred pounds cur-
rent money of Virginia to SHEDRICK SAMUELS in hand paid by these presents doth bargain and sell unto PHILIP NOLAND in his actual possession now being by virtue of a
bargain and sale and by force of statute for transferring uses into possession and his
heirs forever all that tract of land lying in County of Loudoun containing fifty acres
., (conveyances and description of land as in Lease above).. To have and to hold the land
hereby conveyed and other premises unto said PHILIP NOLAND and his heirs and
assigns forever In Witness whereof SHADRICK SAMUELS & MARTHA his Wife hath
hereunto set their hands and seals the day and year first above written
in presents of us   SHADRICK SAMUELS
                                    PATTY (Polly crossed out) her mark ┣ SAMUELS
NB the word (PATTY) in the within Deed & above was interlined before signing six
times
          WILLIAM DOUGLASS,
          WM. MOLTON, JNO. MINOR
    At a Court continued and held for Loudoun County Novr. 10th 1773
This Indenture was acknowledged by SHEDRICK SAMUELS and (Polly crossed out) PATTY
his Wife parties thereto to be their acts and deeds (the said POLLY having been first
privately examined as the Law directs and relinquished her Dower therein) and the
Receipt thereon endorsed was also acknowledged by the said SHEDRICK and together
with the said Indenture ordered to be recorded

pp.   THIS INDENTURE made the twelfth day of November in year of our Lord One
435-   thousand seven hundred and seventy three Between JOHN HERIFORD of County
437   of Loudoun and TOWN of LEESBURG & MARGARET his Wife of one part and JOSIAH
          MOFFIT of the TOWN and County aforesaid, Merchant, of other part Witnesseth
that for sum of Twenty five pounds current money of Virginia to JOHN HERIFORD in
hand paid by these presents doth bargain and sell unto JOSIAH MOFFIT and his heirs
and assigns all that lott or half acre of land situate in TOWN of LEESBURG in County of
Loudoun lying on MARKET STREET in said TOWN and is numbered Twenty Three as by a
plan of JOHN HOUGH more fully appears it being the lott which said JOHN HERIFORD
purchased of NICHOLAS MINOR Gent. as appears by a Deed of Feofment recorded in
County Court of Loudoun bearing date the Eighth day of July in year one thousand
seven hundred and sixty five and all Houses Orchards and appurtenances whatsoever
belonging To have and to hold the lands hereby conveyed and all the premises unto
said JOSIAH MOFFIT his heirs and assigns for ever In Witness whereof said JOHN HERI-
FORD and MARGARET his Wife have hereunto set their hands and seals the day & year
above written
in the presence of   JNO. HERYFORD
                                                 PEGGY HERYFORD
    At a Court continued & held for Loudoun County November the 12th 1773
This Indenture was acknowledged by JOHN HERYFORD and PEGGY his Wife parties
thereto (the said PEGGY having been first privately examined as the Law directs and
relinquished her right of Dower therein) and the Receipt thereon endorsed was also

acknowledged by said JOHN HERYFORD and together with said Indenture ordered to be recorded

pp.   THIS INDENTURE made this Twelfth day of November in year of our Lord one
438-   thousand seven hundred & seventy three Between JOSEPH COMBS & ELIZABETH
440   his Wife of County of Loudoun of one part & THOMAS LEWIS and CRAVEN PEYTON
        CHURCH WARDENS for the Parish of Shelburne in County aforesaid of other part
Witnesseth that for sum of Four hundred pounds current money to said JOSEPH COMBS
in hand paid by these presents doth bargain and sell unto THOMAS LEWIS and CRAVEN
PEYTON Gent. CHURCH WARDENS of Parish aforesaid and their Successor CHURCH WAR-
DENS of the Parish aforesaid for ever All that tract of land lying on North West Fork of
GOOS CREEK in said County & bounded begining at a large Beach mark'd M⎣ standing
on the N. East side of said Fork, near & below the mouth of a small branch runing
thence No. 43 d. Et. 320 poles to three Wt. Oaks in a vally thence No. 43 d. Wt. 240 poles to
a black Oak thence So. 42 d. Wt. 320 poles to two small black Oaks on a stoney Hill side
thence So. 41 d. 30" Et. 234 poles to beginning containing 465 acres To have and to hold
said lands tenements & premises with the appurtenances unto said THOMAS LEWIS and
CRAVEN PEYTON Gentlemen as CHURCH WARDENS for said Parish of Shelburne in
County aforesaid and their Successor CHURCH WARDENS for the proper use and behoof
of the present Incumbent of the Parish, Minister of the CHURCH OF ENGLAND and his
successor Incumbents of said Parish for ever In Witness whereof said JOSEPH COMBS &
ELIZABETH his Wife have hereunto set their hands & seals the day & year first written
in presence of   JOSEPH COMBS
                                            ELIZA. COMBS

    At a Court continued and held for Loudoun County November 12th 1773
This Indenture was acknowledged by JOSEPH COMBS and ELIZABETH his Wife parties
thereto (the said ELIZABETH having been first privately examined as the Law directs
and relinquished her right of Dower therein) and the Receipt there under written was
also acknowledged by said JOSEPH COMBS and together with said Indenture ordered to be
recorded

pp.   THIS INDENTURE made this Eleventh day of May in year one thousand seven
440-   hundred and seventy two Between THOMAS DENT of TOWN of PIXATAWNEY in
441   PRINCE GEORGE COUNTY in Province of MARYLAND of one part and ANN HARDEY
        his Neice, Daughter of GEORGE & LUCY HARDAY, his Sister, of same place, of
other part Witnesseth that said THOMAS DENT for the natural love and affection which
he hath for and beareth to said ANN HARDEY and for sum of One shillings Sterling to
him in hand paid by these presents doth give and release unto ANN HARDEY her heirs
and assigns forever all that tract of land granted by the Honorable the LORD FAIRFAX
by his Deed bearing date the second day of July 1763 to said THOMAS DENT Begining at a
white Oak marked W H corner to the land surveyed for WILLIAM HUBEY (?) in a line of
GIDNEY CLARKE Esqr. standing on the side of the N. W. Fork of GOOSE CREEK opposite to
an old Quarter of said CLARKs extending thence So. 54 W. 200 pos. to a red Oak & white
Oak on a Hill thence N. 50 Wt. 140 pos. to a line of ISACC NICHOLDS thence with his line
No. 145 pos. to the said line of GIDNEY CLARKs thence with the said CLARKs line So. 65
Et. 360 pos. to the begining containing two hundred & twenty three acres lying in
County of Loudoun To have and to hold aforesaid tract of land unto said ANN HARDEY
her heirs & assigns for ever In Testimony whereof said THOMAS DENT hath hereunto set
his hand & seal the day & year first above written

Signed sealed and delivered before   THOM. DENT
     ROBT. H. HARRISON, GEORGE WEST,
     THOS. KIRKPATRICK, THOS. CARSON,
     ANTHY. RAMSAY
  (Space left for recording but not filled in)

pp.   THIS INDENTURE made the 22 day of October in year of our Lord one thousand
442-   seven hundred & seventy three Between ISAAC FARROW of PRINCE WILLIAM
443   COUNTY of one part and HENRY SLOAN of SOMERSET COUNTY in Province of EAST
      NEW JERSEY of other part Witnesseth that said ISAAC FARROW for sum of five
shillings to him in hand paid doth bargain & sell unto HENRY SLOAN all that tract of
land containing Four hundred & ninety five acres situate in County of Loudoun
bounded Begining at two black Oaks in a Stoney Knoll corner to WILLIAM HALLs land
then So. 65 1/2 d. Et. two hundred & sixteen poles to a Hicory in a Glade near the head of
PINEY BRANCH of BROAD RUN then No. 50 d. Et. two hundred & sixty poles to two black
Oaks and a white Oak in a line of COCKS land then No. 68 d. Wt. Two hundred and forty
poles to a white Oak corner to the said COCKS then No. 22 d. Wt. two hundred & fifteen
poles to the interesection of COCKE & CARTER then with CARTERs Course So. 45 d. Wt.
four hundred & ten poles to the Intersection of CARTER & WILLIAM HALL then with
HALLs line So. 21 d. East ninety poles to the begining the same being granted to WIL-
LIAM WEST by Deed from the Proprietors Office dated the third day of April seventeen
hundred & forty together with all houses orchards and appurtenances whatsoever belonging To have and to hold said Four hundred & ninety five acres of land more or less
above mentioned unto HENRY SLOAN his heirs & assigns for full term of one whole year
paying therefore the rent of one Pepper Corn on Lady Day next to intent that by virtue
of these presents and of the statute for transferring uses into possession HENRY SLOAN
may be in actual possession & be thereby enabled to accept a release of Inheritance
thereof In Witness whereof said ISAAC FARROW and ANN his Wife have hereunto set
their hands & seals the day month and year first above written
in presence of JOHN BRIAN,   ISAAC FARROW
     WM. BRIAN, ROBT. COFFIE   ANN her mark /\ FARROW
  At a Court held for Loudoun County December 13th 1773
This Indenture was acknowledged by ISAAC FARROW party thereto and is ordered to be
recorded

pp.   THIS INDENTURE made the 23 day of October in year of our Lord One thousand
443-   seven hundred & seventy three Between ISAAC FARROW of PRINCE WILLIAM
446   COUNTY in Colony of Virginia of one part and HENRY SLOAN of County of SOMER-
      SET in Province of EAST NEW JERSEY of other part Witnesseth that said ISAAC
FARROW for sum of Two hundred pounds current money of Virginia to him in hand
paid by these presents doth bargain and sell unto HENRY SLOAN (in his actual possession now being by virtue of a bargain & sale for one whole year & by force of the
statute for transferring uses into possession) & to his heirs all that tract of land containing four hundred & ninety five acres situate in County of Loudoun bounded ..
(description of land and conveyance as in Lease above) .. To have and to hold the said
four hundred and ninety five acres of land unto said HENRY SLOAN his heirs and
assigns In Witness whereof ISAAC FARROW & ANN FARROW his Wife have hereunto set
their hands and seals the day month & year first above written
in presence of JOHN BRIAN,   ISAAC FARROW
     WM. BRIAN, ROBT. COFFIE   ANN her mark /\ FARROW
  (COMMISSION George the Third to LEWIS RENO, JAMES SCOTT Gent. for privy examina-

tion of ANN Wife of ISAAC FARROW dated the Eighth day of December in the XIVth year of our Reign 1773. Return of execution thereof dated 11th day of December 1773 signed by LEWIS RENO and JAMES SCOTT.)

At a Court held for Loudoun County December 13th 1773

This Indenture and the Receipt there under written were acknowledged by ISAAC FARROW party thereto and the Commission annexed for the privy examination of the Feme with a return of the execution thereof together with the said Indenture ordered to be recorded

(On margin: Exam'd & Dd Mr. Sloane)

pp.   THIS INDENTURE made the sixth day of December in year of our Lord one thou-
446-   sand seven hundred and seventy three Between WILLIAM RUSSEL of County of
448   Loudoun of one part and JAMES LOVE of County aforementioned Witnesseth JOHN
         TAYLOE Esqr. of RICHMOND COUNTY by an Indenture of Lease bearing date the
eleventh day of April in year one thousand seven hundred and seventy one for the consideration therein mentioned did demise grant and to farm let unto WILLIAM RUSSEL his heirs assigns one certain lot of land containing one hundred and forty one acres in and by the recited Lease will appear. THIS INDENTURE further Witnesseth that WILLIAM RUSSEL for sum of Forty five pounds Virginia Currency to him in hand paid by these presents doth bargain sell and set over unto JAMES LOVE his heirs & assigns all that demised premises above mentioned and all Estate right, Title & term of years to come whatsoever which WILLIAM RUSSEL now hath or may or ought to have by force and virtue of said recited Lease or Indenture of Lease To have and to hold the said one hundred and forty one acres of land and recited Indenture of Lease and term of years yet to come & unexpired unto said JAMES LOVE his heirs & assigns In Witness whereof said WM. RUSSEL have hereunto set my hand and affixed my seal the day and year first above written

         December 13th 1773   WM. RUSSEL

At a Court held for Loudoun County December 13th 1773

This Indenture was acknowledged by WILLIAM RUSSEL party thereto to be his act and deed and is ordered to be recorded

pp.   THIS INDENTURE made the ninth day of December in year of our Lord One thou-
449-   sand seven hundred and seventy three Between WILLIAM WILLIAMS of County
450   of Loudoun of one part and JACOB MILLER of other part Witnesseth that WIL-
         LIAM WILLIAMS for sum of five shillings current money of Virginia to him in
hand paid by these presents doth bargain and sell unto JACOB MILLER all that tract of land lying in County of Loudoun between the SHORT HILL and BLUE RIDGE on the head Dreans of PAINEY RUN and bounded Begining at a black Oak by a swampy Mash Corner to HOWARD HAVEN extending then South fifty seven degrees thirty minutes West one hundred and thirty four poles to a red Oak saplin then North twenty two degrees West one hundred & fifty four poles to three white Oaks in a fork of a small branch marked C C 1745 then North fifty six degrees East one hundred & twenty poles to a Chesnut by a swamp or Drain corner to said HAVEN thence with his line South twenty three degrees East one hundred and fifty eight poles to the first station containing one hundred acres being part of a tract of land of one thousand seven hundred and twenty six acres granted to CATESBY COCK Gent. by Patten from the Proprietors Office & by said COCKE transferred to JOSHUA GORE by his Attorney in Fact, AENEAS CAMPBELL, & by said GORE transferred to ANDREW and ADAM HATFIELD and from said HATFIELDs to FRANCIS SCHOOLING to go herewith and all Houses orchards and appurtenances whatsoever belonging To have and to hold the land hereby conveyed unto said JACOB MILLER and

assigns paying therefore the rent of one pepper corn on Lady Day next to intent that by virtue of these presents and of the statute for transferring uses into possession said JACOB MILLER may be in actual possession and be thereby enabled to accept a release of the Inheritance thereof In Witness whereof said WILLIAM WILLIAMS hath hereunto set his hand and seal the day and year first above written
In presence of   WILLIAM WILLIAMS
   At a Court held for Loudoun County December 13th 1773
This Indenture was acknowledged by WILLIAM WILLIAMS party thereto to be his act and deed and ordered to be recorded

pp.   THIS INDENTURE made the 10th day of December in year of our Lord one thou-
450-   sand seven hundred & seventy three Between WILLIAM WILLIAMS of County of
453   Loudoun & Parish of Shelburn of one part and JACOB MILLER of other part Wit-
         nesseth that for sum of one hundred and forty five pounds current money of
Virginia to said (blank) in hand paid by these presents doth bargain and sell unto
JACOB MILLER (in his actual possession now being by virtue of a bargain and sale for
one whole year and by force of statute for transferring uses into possession) and his
heirs forever all that tract of land lying in County of Loudoun between the SHORT HILL
and BLUE RIDGE on the head Dreans of PINNY RUN and bounded .. (description of land
and conveyances as in Lease above) .. To have and to hold the lands hereby conveyed
and all and singular other the premises hereby granted unto JACOB MILLER his heirs
and assigns for ever In Witness whereof WILLIAM WILLIAMS hath hereunto set his
hand and seal the day & year first above written
in the presence of   WILLIAM WILLIAMS
   At a Court held for Loudoun County December 13th 1773
This Indenture and the Receipt thereon endorsed were acknowledged by WILLIAM
WILLIAMS party thereto to be his acts and deeds and ordered to be recorded

pp.   GEORGE the Third by Grace of God of Great Britain France & Ireland King Defen-
453-   der of the Faith &c. To CHARLES BROADWATER, WILLIAM PAYNE & BRYAN
454   FAIRFAX Gentlemen Greeting. Whereas FLEMING PATTERSON Gent. and ELIZA-
         BETH his Wife have by their several Deeds of Feoffment bearing date respective-
ly the Twenty sixth day of February last past sold and conveyed unto HENRY McCABE
the Fee Simple Estate of three lots or half acres of land situate in TOWN of LEESBURG in
County of Loudoun and Number Sixteen, Eighteen and Thirty Two And Whereas said
ELIZABETH cannot conveniently travel to our said County to make acknowledgment of
said Conveyance, Therefore we do give unto you or any two of you power to receive the
acknowledgment which said ELIZABETH shall be willing to make before you and when
you have received her acknowledgment that you distinctly and openly certifie us
thereof in our said Court under your hands & seals CHARLES BINNS Clerk of our said
Court at the Court House the fourteenth day of July in the Thirteenth year of our Reign
1773
   FAIRFAX Ss.
   This is to certify that we the subscribers agreeable to the within mentioned dedimus
have taken the privy examination of said ELIZABETH PATTERSON touching her free
consent to said Conveyances of three lots of land in TOWN of LEESBURGH to HENRY
McCABE & have taken her acknowledgment thereof and that she doth the same freely &
without the threats of her husband and is willing the same should be recorded
Dated this 15th day of October 1773   CHAS. BROADWATER
                                                        BRYAN FAIRFAX

At a Court continued and held for Loudoun County December 14th 1773
This Commission and the Execution thereon endorsed were returned into our Court and
ordered to be recorded

Test   CHAS. BINNS Cl Cur

Finished Saturday the 11th
April 1774 JNO. CHAMBERLAIN

ABBETT. Ann 56; James 56;
  Joseph (Carpenter-95); Mary 95.
ABRELL. John 97; Richard 97.
ACT of ASSEMBLY:
  Assess Titheable persons for clearing & re-
pairing the GREAT ROAD leading from VESTALS
and WILLIAMS GAPS to Towns of COLCHESTER &
ALEXANDRIA 34;
  More Effectual Transportation of Convicted
felons to his Majesty's Plantations in America
34, 35.
ADAM. James 56; John 46, 48, 49, 50, 56;
  Robert 13.
ADDINGTON. Henry 66.
ADDLEMAN. Daniel 1, 2; Elizabeth 1, 2.
ALEXANDER. John 29; Robert 69.
ALLEN. Isaac 22; Joseph 89; Sarah 21, 22;
  William (of Amwel in Co. Hunterdon-21), 22.
ALLISON. William (Mercht-47).
ANDERSON. John (of Fauquier Co.-84), 85.
ASBURY. Thomas 90.
ASKREN. Elizabeth 89; John 89;
  Thomas 89, 90, 91; Thos. Jr. 89.
AUTON. William 56.
AWBREY. Francis 51, 87; George 21.

BAIRD. James & Co. (Merchts. of Glasgow-19).
BAKER. Phillip 1, 2; Ulionah 2;
  William 37, 38.
BALL. Farling 25, 26; John 87; Mary 25, 26.
BALLENDINE. John (Mercht-5), 6; Richard
  Henry 6; Thomas William 6.
BANNER. Peter 37.
BARKER. John 17.
BAYLY. Samuel 65.
BEAKES. Nathan (of Trenton-21), 22.
BEALL. Josa: 35.
BEANS. William 61.
BEATY. David 23, 24.
BERKLEY. Barbara 21; John 2.
BEST. James 26, 27; Thomas 26, 27.
BICKMAN (BUCKMAN). George 58; James 58.
BINNS. Charles (Clerk of Court-102), 103.
BISHOP. John 2, 42.
BLACKBURN. Thomas (of Prince William Co.-10),
  53, 56.
BLAIR. David (Mercht. of Town of Fredericks-
  burg, County of Spotsylvania-19).
BLINCOE. Thomas 63, 64.
BOGGESS. Henry Junr. 86; Nancy 13;
  Robert 13; Vincent 13.

BONHAM. Samuel 88.
BOONE. Hezekiah 31, 32.
BRANCH: Beaver Dam of Goose Creek 10, 13;
  Beaver Dam of Kittockton 61; Cabbin 63;
  Licking 63; Muddy Lick 45; Piney Branch of
  Broad Run 100; Seglan 94; Stallion 43.
BRENHOR. Phillip 66.
BREWER. Henry 67.
BROADWATER. Charles 83, 102.
BRONAUGH 4; William 73.
BROWN. Coleman 91; Dawson 10; James 50, 51;
  Mildred 77, 78; Richard 82;
  William (of Prince William Co.-77), 78.
BRUESTER 86.
BRYAN (BRIAN). John 100; Thomas 42;
  William 100.
BRYANT. Morgan 83, 85.
BUCHAN Robert (of Province of Maryland-42).
BUCKINGHAM. Bezail 45.
BUCKNER. Anthony (of Prince William Co.-76),
  77, 78; Mildred 77, 78; Payton 76.
BURGESS. Charles (late of Lancaster Co.-15);
  Tract of 94.
BURWELL. Robert 76, 77.
BUTCHER. Samuel 6, 7.
BUTLER. Joseph 38, 39.
BYRN(S). Benedick 94; Ignatius 93, 94;
  Patrick 94; Mary 94.

CADWALLEDER. James 61.
CALDWELL. Joseph 14, 15.
CAMPBELL. Aeneas 18, (of Province of Maryland
  -20), 72, 101; Alex. 52; Robert (Taylor-71),
  72, 96.
CANBY. Samuel (Mercht-21), 39, 40.
CARLYLE. John 27, 62, 70.
CARR. Thos. 62.
CARRINGTON. Timothy 44, 45.
CARROLL. Daniel (Son of Dempsey-11);
  Dempsey 11, 21; Dempsey Jr. 11, 12;
  William Porter (Son of Dempsey-11), 12.
CARSON. Thos. 100.
CARTER. John 96; Landon 20; Robert 38.
CAVENS. John 27.
CHAMBERLAIN. John 37, 61, 103; John Jr. 72.
CHAPMAN. Thomas 52.
CHATTAM. Jno. 86.
CHESSIRE. Joel 6; Samuel (of Stafford Co.-6).
CHINN 24; Charles (of Fauquier Co.-15), 16, 17,
  95; Charles Jr. 16, 17; Christopher 17;
  Elijah 16, 17; Rawleigh 15, 16, 17; Thomas 25.

FEARSNER. Christopher 30, 55, 56; Sarah 55.
FEAZEL. Philip Senr. (Farmer-12).
FEGAN. Daniel 58.
FIELD. Nathaniel 31, 32.
FITZHUGH. John 63, 64; William 67.
FORSTER. Thomas 16.
FOSTER. Mary 20.
FOUCH. Isaac 62, 63.
FOX. William 67.
FRANCE. Agnes 55; John 55.
FRENCH. Alexander 36.
FRYREAR. John Peter 24.
FULLERTON. Humphry 48.
FURR. Edwin 73.

GARDNER. Eloner 6; Joseph 6, 29;
  Joseph (Son-6); William (of Fairfax Co.,
  Planter-6).
GARLAND. Griffin 44, 45.
GARNER. Joseph 94.
GARRETT (JARED). John 82, 88.
GIBSON. Alice 8; Isaac 90; James 8;
  John 8, 90; Joseph 8; Moses 90; Widow 8.
GLASSFORD & HENDERSON 76, 77.
GOING. Joseph (Labourer-21).
GOLDING. James 76, 77.
GOODIN. Amos 22.
GORE. Joshua 18, 57, 83, 85, 86, 101;
  Joshua Jr. 77; Thomas 14, 67, 77.
GRAHAM. Duncan (of Caroline Co.-15), 16, 25;
  John 16, (of Prince William Co.-24), 25;
  Mary 15, 16; Richard (of Dumfries in Prince
  William Co.-86).
GRANT. John 16, 25, 83, 85; Mr. Jr. 10.
GRAY. Willm. 77.
GRAYSON. Benjamin 19, 53, 70; Elizabeth 70;
  Spence (Revd.-19), 65, 66; William 19, 52, 54.
GREEN. Charles (late of Fairfax Co., Clerk-73),
  89; Thomas 46, 47.
GREGG. George 25, 26, 69, 74; Samuel 61;
  Thomas 10, 51, 58, 68, (Joyner-82);
  William 26.
GREIG. Amos 57.
GRIFFITH. Charles 38, 39; John 5, 47.
GRIMES. Charles 55.
GROVES. John 75.
GUNNELL. Henry 70; John 26, 77, 86;
  Wm. 13, 54.
GUY. George 16.

HAGUE. Francis 14, (Yeoman-39), 40, 72, 80;
  John 12, 20, 80; Samuel 68; Thomas 39, 40.
HAIR. Thomas 37.
HAIT. Benjamin (of Province of East New Jesey,
  County of Essex-95), 96.
HALL. William 100.
HAMILTON. Archibald 74; James 13, 14, 32,
  33, 45, 72, 77, 79; Robert (of Leesburg, Inn-
  holder-7), 9, 72, 97; William 65, 66.
HANBY. John 26, 74, 84.
HANCOCK. Samuel (of Chesterfield Co.-93);
  Simon 72, 73, 93; William (Son of Samuel,
  Father of William Jr.-93); William Junior 93.
HARDING (HARDEN). Edward (of Fairfax Co.-69),
  70; Mary 69, 70.
HARDY. Ann (Niece of Thomas Dent, Daughter of
  George & Lucy Hardy, his Sister-99); George 99;
  Lucy 99; Solomon 65, 93.
HARFORD. John 42.
HARLE. John 5; William 5.
HARRIS. Henry 18, 72; John 58; Samuel 83, 84.
HARRISON 5; J. 75; Mr. 53; Robert H. 10, 100;
  Valentine 75.
HART. Robt. 16.
HATFIELD. Adam 18, 101; Andrew 18, 101.
HATTLY. Samuel 44.
HAVEN. Howard 18, 101.
HEALE. George 17.
HENDERSON. Alexander 65, 66, 76; Ann 15;
  James 14, 15.
HENDREN. Elizabeth 8, 9; John (of Fauquier
  Co.-8), 9.
HERYFORD. James 38, 39, 54; John 18, 38, 39,
  70, 98; Margaret (Peggy) 70, 98.
HICKSON. Matthew 25; William 74.
HISKETT. Benjamin 28, 88.
HOCKLEY. Richard (of Philadelphia-10), 11.
HODGE. Thomas 35.
HOGE. Joseph 56, 57; Solomon 10.
HOPEWELL. Samuel 75.
HOPKINS. John (of Salsbury Co. of Lancaster
  Pennsylvania, Inn Keeper-58).
HOUGH. Amos 39, 40; John 6, 7, 11, 13, 28, 33,
  34, 54, 60, 69, 70, 72, 74, 75, 79, 80, 81, 94, 95,
  96, 98; John Jr. 39, 40, 47; Joseph 79, 80;
  William 10, 57.
HOWELL. Abner 24; Hezekiah 28; John 58.
HUGHS. Edwd. 24.
HUGUELY. Jacob 3, 4.

MATTHEW. Jesse 80, 81; John 80, 81.

MEAD . John 40, 85; William Jr. (Farmer-12).

MEEKS. Richard (of Richmond Co.-71); (Will mentd-71).

MERCER. George (late of Old England-78), 79, 80, 95; James (of Spotsylvania Co.-78), 79, 80, 95; John 32, 75, 79, 95.

MICHEL. Phillip 62.

MIFFLIN. Thomas (of Philadelphia, Mercht.-25), 26.

MILLAR. Simon 94.

MILLASON. Jonathan 88.

MILLER. Jacob 101, 102.

MINOR. John 16, 97, 98; Nicholas 7, 24, 36, 70, 71, 72, 95, 98.

MIRKILL. William 17.

MITINGER. Benhard 57.

MOFFETT. Josiah 18; (Mercht.-98).

MOLTON. Wm. 97, 98.

MONK (MUNK). Jonathan 32.

MOORE. Cleon 65.

MORGERT. Phillip 17, 62.

MORLAN. Jason (Quaker-32), 33; William 94.

MOSS. John 64, 67.

MOUNTAIN. Blue Ridge 18, 19, 46, 49, 51, 59, 60, 101, 102; Great 4; Hogg Back 14; Kittockton 26, 27, 69, 79, 94; Round Hill 42; Short Hill 18, 19, 30, 59, 101, 102.

MURRAY. James 95; Mr. R. 9.

MYRES. Jonathan 86, 87.

NAWLES. Sarah 4, 5; William (Blacksmith-4), 5.

NEILSON. H. 26; Hugh 42, 43, 54, 97; William 36, 42, 43, 48.

NEW. Anthony 16.

NEW JERSEY. Amwel, Co. of Hunterdon 21, 22; Essex Co. East New Jersey 95; Proclamation Money of 21; Somerset Co. in East New Jersey 100; Trenton 21.

NEWTON. John (of Westmoreland Co.-53); Willoughby (of Westmoreland Co.-11).

NICHOLDS. Isaac 99.

NIXON (NICKSON). George 57, 58; George Junr. 58; James 57; Jonah 58.

NODING. John 86.

NOLAND. Ferry Road of 97; Philip 63, 65, 97, 98; Philip Sr. 24.

OLDACRE. Henry 75.

OMHUNDRO. (Ann (Mother of William Remey-11).

ONEAL. Ferdinando 47.

ORSEBORNE. John 46, 49, 50; John Jr. 49; Morris 49; Richard 46, 49, 50; Samuel 49; Thomas 46.

OSBORN (OSBURN). John 60, 61; John Jr. 59; John Sr. 59, 60, 61; Richard 59, 60, 61, 92; Sarah 59, 60, 61; William 92.

OTT. Elizabeth 30; Margaret 30; Nicholas 30.

OWSLEY. Thomas (Planter-1), 4, 5, 13, 35, 45, 47, 73, 77.

OXLEY. Clare 31, 32, 54; Everitt 31, 32, 54; Henry 31, 32, 54, 69; Henry Jr. 31, 32; Jessee 54; Johanna 31, 32; John 31, 54; Rachel 54.

PADGET. Francis 41.

PALMER. John 88.

PARISH. Robert (of Frederick Co., Mercht-10), 11.

PARKER. Henry 84, 85; Joseh 73.

PATENT: Catesby Cocke 40; John Graham/John Grant 16, 25; John Hough 33; Amos Janney 15; William Lane 5; Charles Lewis 64; Lee Massey 65; Richard Meeks 71; William West 100.

PATTEN (POTTEN). Hy. 5, 73, 93; James 36; John (of Kent Co. on Delaware River in Pennsylvania-35), 36.

PATTERSON. Elizabeth 47, 48, 49, 102; Fleming (late of Leesburg, now of Fairfax Co.-47) 48, 49, 102; Hugh 42, 43; John 47, 48; Thomas 48, 49.

PAYNE. W. 63; William 64, 70, 83, 102.

PEACHY. Samuel Jr. 65.

PEARSALL (PIERCEALL). Jacob 40.

PELL. Richard 63, 64.

PENNSYLVANIA. Bucks Co. 22; Chester Co. 89, 90; Currency of 9, 10, 24, 26, 64, 66, 69, 72, 85; Frediffrin in Cheshire Co.-88; Kent Co. on Delaware River 35; Philadelphia 10, 11, 25, 26; Province of 10, 72; Salsbury in Co. of Lancaster 58, 59.

PEPTERCOE. Francis 29.

PERVICE. Colo. 84.

PEW. Samuel 42, 43.

PEYTON. Ann 4, 36, 37; Craven 4, 10, 30, 31, (Sheriff-33), 34, (of Leesburg-36), 37, 40, 45, 46, 49, 50, 56, 58, 67, 77, 81, 82, (Church-warden-99); Frances 4, 11; Francis 4, 5, 11, 33, 34, 45, 76, 77, 78, 84, 85.

PHILLIPS. Benja. 50, 51.

PHILLIS. Joseph 94.

PLACES. Amapole on Bull Run 77; Brays Quarter 44; Erwins Folly 80; (contd)

PLACES (contd). Glade called Captain Hickory
  3; Mountain Chapple 45; Neabscoe Furnace
  50, 51, 57; New Quarter 43; Old Quarter 43;
  Towlston Mansion House of Bryan Fairsax 6.
POOL. Benjamin 2.
POPKINS. John 9; Robert 9, 65, 74, 96.
PORTER. Mary 21.
POSEY. John Price 52.
POTTS. Ann (Widow-1); Nathan 46;
  Samuel 1; Stacy 22.
POULTNEY. John 65.
POWELL. L. 4; Leven 11, 24, 25, 33, 34, 36,
  37, 45, 52, 53, 75, 77, 78, 95.
PRICE. Oliver 30, 31, 95.
PRITCHARD. Thomas 18, 40, 97.
PURCEL. Thomas 50, 59.
PYLES (PILES). Jemima 61, 62; John 61, 62, 64.

RAINEY. Jacob 43.
RAMSAY. Anthy. 8, 65, 66, 100.
RATEKIN. James 27.
RATTRAY. Jas. 77.
RAWLS. John 4.
RAYNES. Anthony 41; John 41;
  John (Father of John-41).
REDMOND. John 61.
REED. Jonothan 22.
REEDER. William the Younger (Farmer-53)
REES. John 3.
REGAN. Michael 29.
REMEY. William (of Fairfax Co., Planter-11), 12.
RENO. Lewis 100, 101.
RICE. Evan 9.
RICH. Samuel 1, 2, 50, 51.
RICHARDSON. Joseph 59, 60, 61.
RIGER. John Bartholomew 18.
RINGO. Cornelius 41; Philip 41.
RIVER. Great Falls of Potomack 86;
  Potomack 58, 86.
ROACH. Richard 26.
ROAD. Church 62; Great 42, 45, 77; Main 9,
  32, 77; Mountain 5, 74; New 43, 44; Nolands
  Ferry 97; Old Main 20; Paynes 55; Trammells
  Rolling 5; Vestalls Gap 34; Williams Gap 34.
ROBERTS. Richard 46.
ROGERS. Hamilton 95.
ROPER. Tho: 54.
ROSS. David (of Town of Bladensburgh, Prince
  George Co., Maryland-36), 37; Hector 65, 66;
  James 27, 28.
ROSZEL. Sarah 45; Stephen 45, 46.

RUMSEY. James 64, 67.
RUN: Bull 77; Cromwells 94; Cub 6; Difficult 3,
  5, 55; Dutchman 30, 55; Elk Licking 41, 71,
  90, 91; Horsepen 43, 63; Limestone 80;
  Painey 101, 102; Pantherskin 8; Piney 18, 19;
  Sugarland 64, 67, 74, 96.
RUSSELL 91; Andrew 6; Anthony 97; John 50;
  Ruth 50; Samuel 50, 51; William 50, 51, 101.
RUST. Benjamin 70, 71; Benjamin (of Richmond
  Co.-71); William 52, 53.

SAMUELS. Patty 98; Shadrick (Blacksmith-97),
  98.
SANDERS. Thos. 54.
SANDS. Edmond 2, 26.
SANFORD. Daniel 44.
SAVAGE. Margaret (Widow of Charles Green-73);
  William (of Prince William Co., Surgeon-73).
SCHOOLING (SCHOOLEY). Elizabeth 19;
  Francis 18, 19, 101; William 80.
SCOTT. James 100, 101; Robert 94;
  Samuel 64, 67; Susanna 67.
SEALE. Anthony (of Prince William Co.-76).
SELF. Thomas 96.
SEMPLE. John 86.
SHAFFER. George 58.
SHIP. Scarsdale 35.
SHIPPEN. Edward (Clerk of General Quarter Ses-
  sion of Peace in Lancaster in Province of Penn-
  sylvania-58), 59.
SHORE(S). Thomas 45, 77.
SIGLER. Jno. 18.
SIMPSON. Gilbert 94.
SINCLAIR (SINKLER). John 23, (Trustee of Dutch
  Settlement-61), 62.
SISSON. Ann 71; Henry 71.
SKINNER. Cornelius 76, 77, 78; Nathaniel 76,
  78; Richd. 78.
SLOAN. Henry (of Someset Co. in Province of East
  New Jersey-100); Mr. 101.
SMITH. Elizabeth 38; Henry 57, 62; John 17;
  Nathaniel 69; Samuel 10, 30, 56, 57, 73, 83;
  Thomas (Farmer-53); William 11, 35, (Farmer-
  37, 38, 45, 57, 72, 73, 77.
SNIGERS. Edward 22.
SNYDER. Christian Charles 66, 67.
SPENCER. James 91.
SPRIGG. Edward Jr. 65.
STANHOPE. William 40.
STAPLETON. John 80, 81.
STEER Joseph 47.

STEPHENS. Richard 44.
STODDARD. Henry 6.
STONE. Francis 44, 45.
STOTT. Bryan 17.
SYRETCHBERRY. Robert 14.
SUDON. Thomas 60.
SUMMERS. Francis 12; Geo: 12, 42, 91.
SUTTLE. Elizabeth 89, 90; Josias 89, 90.

TALBUTT. Magdalin 90, 91; Samuel (of Fairfax
 Co.-90), 91.
TASSY. James 38; William 38.
TAYLOE. John (of Richmond Co.-50), 51, 57,
 60, 72, 85, 92, 101; John (Father of John-51).
TAYLOR. George 29; Henry 42; John 42;
 Joshua 42; Mahlon 14, 86, 87; Susanna 42.
TEMPLEMAN. William 90.
THOMAS. Enoch 66; Ephraim (of Bucks Co.
 Pennsylvania-22); Evan (Son of Elizabeth
 Askren-89); James 67; Joseph 65.
THOMPSON. Isaac 61; Israel 7, 34,
 (Quaker-37), 58, 61, 72; Jonah 61; W. 65, 66.
THORNTON. John 10, 18, 54, (Attorney at Law-
 56), 65, 69, 70.
THRIFT. Jeremiah 35.
TODHUNTER. John 23.
TOWNS (Also see Leesburg). Alexandria 34,
 37, 69; Colchester 34; Dumfries 19;
 Williamsburg 33; Winchester 10, 36.
TRACTS. Arcadia 46, 49; Burgesses 94;
 Frying Pan 63; Mc. McCarty's Sugarland 5;
 Newgate 53; Piedmont 30, 55;
 Shannandale 46, 49.
TRAMMELL. Gerrard Jr. 35; Rolling Road 5.
TREBLE. John 72.
TRIPLETT. Martha 47; Simon 11, 37, 38, 47,
 53, 54, 78, 91.
TYLER. Charles 19; John 19.

USSELMAN. Michael 55.

VAN OVER. Henry 28, 88.
VERTZ. Catherine 30; Conrad 30;
 Peter 31; William (Farmer-30), 31.
VESTRYMEN. of Shelburn Parish: William Smith, Stephen Donaldson, Thos. Lewis, James
 Hamilton, Thomson Mason, Francis Peyton, Craven Peyton, Josias Clapham, Leven Powell,
 John Lewis, Thomas Owsley, Thomas Shore (as of 23 April 1773); 45, 77.

WARDER. Jeremiah (Mercht. of Philadelphia-10)
 11.
WALKER. Elizabeth 71; John 84, 85;
 Thomas 71.
WARMAN. Thomas 47.
WARNER. John 5, 29.
WASHINGTON. Hannah (Fairfax) who married
 Warner Washington-83), 84, 85; Warner (of
 Frederick Co.-83), 84, 85, 86.
WEST. Charles 4, 28, 33, 34, 36, 37, 81;
 Elizabeth 70; George 3, 55, 62, 64, 69, 70, 100;
 Hugh 70; Jane 7, 8; John Jr. 70; Joseph
 (Farmer-7), 8; Thomas 81, 82;
 William 36, 81, 100; William Jr. 89.
WHITACRE. John 83, 84, 85, 88.
WHITE. Alexander (Attorney at Law of Winches-
 ter-36); Matthew (Farmer-2), 3, 4; Robert 3.
WHITELY. William 42.
WHITLOCK. James 5.
WILDMAN. Wm. 62, 63; Wm. Jr. 62, 63.
WILLIAMS. Benjamin 79; Evan 25; Jenkin 47;
 Thomas 4, 11; William 18, 19, 59, 101, 102.
WILLIAMSON. James 93; Mary 93.
WINN. Minor 7.
WOOD. Lashley 40, 41.

YATES (YEATS). Ann 94; Joseph 28;
 Joshua 94, 95; William 94.
YOUNG. Barnard 59.

Heritage Books by Ruth and Sam Sparacio

Westmoreland County, Virginia Deed and Will Abstracts, 1745–1747
Westmoreland County, Virginia Deed and Will Abstracts, 1747–1748
Westmoreland County, Virginia Deed and Will Abstracts, 1749–1751
Westmoreland County, Virginia Deed and Will Abstracts, 1751–1754
Westmoreland County, Virginia Deed and Will Abstracts, 1754–1756
Westmoreland County, Virginia Order Book, 1705–1707
Westmoreland County, Virginia Order Book, 1707–1709
Westmoreland County, Virginia Order Book, 1709–1712
Westmoreland County, Virginia Order Book, 1712–1714
Westmoreland County, Virginia Order Book, 1714–1716
Westmoreland County, Virginia Order Book, 1716–1718
Westmoreland County, Virginia Order Book, 1718–1721